MW00584532

UP CLOSE
AND
PERSONAL

UP CLOSE AND PERSONAL

THE INSIDE STORY OF NETWORK TELEVISION SPORTS

JIM SPENCE

WITH DAVE DILES

ATHENEUM PUBLISHERS

NEW YORK 1988

Atheneum Publishers
Macmillan Publishing Company
866 Third Avenue, New York, N.Y. 10022
Collier Macmillan Canada, Inc.

Library of Congress Cataloging-in-Publication Data
Spence, Jim.
  Up close and personal.
  1. Television broadcasting of sports—United States.
I. Diles, David L. II. Title.
GV742.3.S64 1988   070.4'49796'0973   88-3449
ISBN 0-689-11943-7

10 9 8 7 6 5 4 3 2 1

Printed in the United States of America

To my wife, Lynn, who has been with me
from the beginning

AND

To the talented and dedicated people who
over the years have worked in television sports
at the three major networks, with special recognition
to my friends and associates at ABC Sports.

CONTENTS

CONTENTS

PREFACE

The opportunity to write a book is one that reaches a very limited number of people. I am most grateful, then, to my editor, Ken Bowden, who conceived the project, and to Atheneum Publishers. I feel honored to be able to present *Up Close and Personal: The Inside Story of Network Television Sports*.

I spent over twenty-five years at ABC Sports, initially as a production assistant, a gofer—you know, go for the coffee, run errands, etc.—then as assistant to the executive producer of "ABC's Wide World of Sports," and as coordinating producer of that series and vice president of program planning. In 1978 I became senior vice president, and for eight years had responsibility on a day-to-day basis for the supervision and coordination of all areas of what became the most significant television sports organization in history.

Those twenty-five-plus years were a wonderful experience, including the opportunity to meet many outstanding people, to travel to a lot of exciting places, to witness memorable events, and to be involved in a challenging, exciting, and meaningful enterprise. I am grateful to have been a part of an industry and a company that provided so many hours of special sports entertainment to the American public.

My intention in this book is to inform and entertain you with some insights into the personalities and events and inner workings of network television sports from the perspective of my tenure at ABC. In choosing

to write it, I felt an obligation to be candid but balanced in my choice
and treatment of subjects—so the book would be both credible and
meaningful.

Up Close and Personal: The Inside Story of Network Television Sports is,
then, a sometimes strong, sometimes humorous, sometimes controversial, sometimes straightforward—but I trust always a fair and honest—
look at network television sports, an industry deeply imbedded in the
consciousness of a large segment of the American public, but until now
as remote and inaccessible as the heroic figures that give it life. I hope
you enjoy this drawing back of the curtain.

UP CLOSE
AND
PERSONAL

1

TELLING IT LIKE IT
REALLY IS

*Howard Cosell:
the Metamorphosis of
a Superstar*

In a quarter century at ABC Sports, the question I was asked most was: What is Howard Cosell really like? He is a complex man, but I think I can provide some insights that will answer that question once and for all.

I've said often, both about him and directly to him, that, except for my wife, Lynn, Howard Cosell has been the most important person in my life. In the very beginning, in the learning stages of my career, Howard Cosell taught me the importance of integrity and honesty in life.

I had come to ABC in 1960 as a production assistant—the lowest man on the television totem pole, popularly known as a "gofer"—but by early 1966 had risen to the level of coordinating producer of "ABC's Wide World of Sports." My climb up the network ladder from then on paralleled that of Cosell. We worked closely on the telecast of the famous Cassius Clay/Sonny Liston "phantom punch" fight, and countless times on a variety of programs throughout the succeeding years.

Frequently, in those days, we'd have Cosell and Ali, and perhaps one of the fighters Ali had conquered, in the studio to do commentary as we replayed one of his fights. Sometimes it was quite a task trying to build a decent program out of a short fight, but Cosell inevitably made the shows work. He had marvelous suggestions on what would and wouldn't play, and he took direction well. He had a strong sense of show business, plus a superb journalistic ability to ferret out facts, and he always came to the studio well prepared. He also had the knack of threading a storyline through our live telecasts, which made the shows much more interesting and meaningful to viewers. His tremendous recall—perhaps even a photographic memory—has been widely trumpeted, but that was only a part of it. He also brought to sports television a tremendous perspective on life, along with an outstanding historical background on just about any subject we'd cover. Because of these factors, plus his courage, Howard Cosell must be considered the pioneer of true journalism in network television sports.

In the early days, if Howard had a concept for a show or an idea how a subject should be handled, he'd telephone me and we'd discuss the matter and exchange ideas. Many times I'd seek him out for his opinion. Because of his radio commitments, Howard has always been a very early riser, so it was not uncommon for him to call me in what I considered the wee-small hours. Over time, we grew quite close. We'd have dinner together with our wives, and in all our dealings there was a genuine concern for each other and for each other's families. We confided in each other, and I grew to cherish our relationship.

Howard Cosell came along at precisely the right time. Someone once said that show business is a lot like sex in that timing is everything. Cosell arrived when the nation was in a state of unrest, when there was a lot of discontent. The post–World War II baby-boom kids were going to college, and they felt disenchanted and disenfranchised. Our heroes—the Kennedys, Dr. Martin Luther King—were being murdered all around us. Young Americans were being slain in Vietnam for reasons that still are not clear. Young people were burning draft cards and ROTC buildings. We had flower children and love-ins and protest marches and sit-ins and picket lines. It was a time when it seemed the nation was in danger of losing its conscience and its character.

It was a perfect time for the appearance of an interesting, intelligent, articulate, and provocative man with an entirely different dimension on sports issues, including the championing of the constitutional rights of a black fighter. It was time for people to quit looking upon sports as merely an amusement: there were social and economic and legal issues involved, and, by God, Howard Cosell would not only explain them, but also tell you exactly what he thought of them in very blunt and arresting language. He was not just part of the momentum of the times; he *gave* momentum to the times. Instead of merely being along for the ride, he was creating his own ride, and it would last for more than thirty years.

For so many years, sportscasters had spent most of their time fawning over athletes, coaches, and managers and being intimidated by front-office personnel. It was as though these people were gods, and most media people seemed to be downright afraid of them. Not Cosell. He made up his mind early that he would do *his* thing, *his* way. And it worked for him. He could be exasperating to the point of creating some very difficult problems, but, through it all, you had to respect his mind. It was so quick and broad and facile.

The late Jimmy Cannon, the New York sportswriter, is credited with the line: "Can a man who changes his name and wears a wig *really* tell it like it is?" Howard Cohen did change his name to Cosell, and he does wear a hairpiece. As for his pet phrase, "Telling it like it is," I always thought it worked for him, yet at the same time that there was a distinct touch of arrogance to it. It was as if Howard was really saying, "I'm the only source of truth in this business." We all know he really believed that. And, as a matter of hard fact, he was for a long time the *best* source of honesty and integrity in sports broadcasting, and sometimes the only source of it.

No one could have handled the Muhammad Ali situation like Cosell did, because no one was as qualified or as courageous. Part of all that, I'm sure, was that Ali recognized quickly that Cosell could command air time, and thus become a route to even greater fame for Ali. At the same time, I know that Ali honestly respected both Howard's intelligence and his willingness to take a stand. Obviously, it helped enormously that Cosell stood *with* Ali. The two developed a great chemistry, so that Howard was able to ask the hard, direct questions and evoke answers no one else could have produced. The two had been close from the very beginning, but Cosell's stand on Ali's refusal to go into the U.S. Army—"I ain't got nuthin' against them Viet Congs"—was the major solidifying factor in their long relationship. It did no harm, either, that Howard knew boxing and the people in it, and made it a point to do his homework. Ali respected that.

His relationship with Ali helped Howard enormously in achieving major celebrity status. And it is difficult to exaggerate the level of celebrity Cosell by then enjoyed. Here's an example.

An ABC sports group had gone to New Orleans for the Sugar Bowl classic between Notre Dame and Alabama, and all of us were to attend an official dinner at Antoine's. We gathered in the cocktail lounge of the Royal Sonesta Hotel. Wives and girlfriends flocked to Howard, woman after woman having her picture taken on his lap. More Cosell enthusiasts began to fill the lobby just outside the cocktail lounge. Howard and I decided that, since the restaurant was just a short walk from our hotel in the French Quarter, we and our wives would walk there. People in the lobby followed us.

No sooner had we gone through the hotel doors than Howard began a running dialogue with tourists in the street. They immediately recognized him and began yelling at him, happily and festively, in keeping with the occasion. He loved every minute of it. I don't know that I ever saw Howard happier than he was that night. People were showing affection for him, kidding with him. It was the Pied Piper all over again, and by the time we got to the restaurant, there were hundreds of people following him, happy that the great man was paying attention to them. By then, he was beside himself with laughter, wallowing in the recognition he was receiving.

And, yes, he *was* getting affection from the crowd. Every so often, a "How's your buddy Ali?" would punctuate the boister-ousness, but that night it was not a question laced with bitterness or racial overtones, but rather a good-natured inquiry made in friendship. The people were walking down the famous Bourbon Street with a man who had attained stardom practically in spite of himself, and you didn't have to be an expert in behavioral science to comprehend that they were not only accepting Howard Cosell, they were embracing him. He was tickled beyond belief, almost giggling with pleasure. Every so often, he'd look at me and throw back his head in laughter, and say, "Isn't this something? Do you believe this? Aren't these people beautiful?" It was an experience to warm the coldest heart, and one I'll never forget.

It was the best of times, and nothing could have spoiled Howard Cosell's mood that night. And, of course, it prompted him to do his standard routine, selecting an attractive couple walking near us and telling the woman: "I hope you realize, my dear, that you married well beneath yourself. You're a beautiful woman, a wondrous creature, and you deserve much better than this man with you. There's still time for you, you know. You're still young and supple enough to get out. As for him, well, after our chance meeting tonight in the streets of this magnificent city, your relationship with him will never be the same. For as long as you live, every time you are in his embrace, you will think of me."

Again, he threw back his head and laughed that familiar laugh, the one that sounds curiously sinister and forced. The woman and her husband laughed right along with the rest of us. It was a routine he knew like the back of his hand and one we who were close to him had heard many times before. Later, as he became so vicious and so bitter, watching him perform this public exhibition became a chore and an embarrassment because by then the meanness in him had taken over and the humor was mostly gone.

For as long as I've known him, Cosell would flirt like this with women, and, as in New Orleans, he'd do it right in front of their husbands or boyfriends and his wife, Emmy. In the middle of a crowded cocktail party, he'd boldly step up to a couple and launch a mock assault on the man. He'd poke fun at the fellow for the way he was dressed, or the way he combed his hair, or make some snide remark about the guy's supposedly poor performance in bed. Everybody would be giggling nervously, but Howard would barge right on, boasting to the woman, "You know, Sally, you really married beneath yourself, my dear. If you spent just thirty minutes with me, you'd throw this bum out of the house this very night."

At this point, the ritual called for everybody to laugh. This was all part of Howard's shtick and everybody was supposed to know it and accept it. As far as I know, no one ever punched him in the nose because of it. Also, as far as I know—and I'd stake my life on it—Howard Cosell has never been unfaithful to his wife.

It was common practice whenever Howard came to the main floor of ABC Sports for him to make some remark about one of the secretaries. He'd comment about how she filled out her blouse, or the amount of leg she showed below her hemline, and he'd talk a great game about how wonderfully well they'd perform together in bed. To be sure, it was tasteless, but I'm certain it never went beyond that. The secretaries were shocked at first, but eventually they all came to understand that it was merely Howard doing his thing.

One afternoon, Howard was on the elevator at ABC headquarters at Fifty-fourth Street and the Avenue of the Americas in Manhattan, and had in tow a well-known sports figure he was taking upstairs. My secretary joined them for the ride up to the sports department on the twenty-eighth floor. She was a generously proportioned woman, but also a streetwise New Yorker who had seen Howard do his shtick countless times. She knew, as all of us did, that he was all talk.

"I'll have you right now in this elevator, my dear," Howard promised her, to the shock and possible amusement of his guest. "Take your clothes off this very minute. You realize, my dear, it is destiny that has brought the two of us to this moment in our lives. It's a moment the two of us will share and an ecstasy we shall treasure for as long as we both shall live."

She had my lunch in her hand, and flipped him a casual remark: "Sure, Howard, just like always."

Getting the brush-off like that persuaded Howard that, in order to impress his guest, he would have to do more than talk, so he proceeded to attack the buttons on the young lady's blouse. She decided to go along with the act, for she knew Howard was harmless. Nervously, he unbuttoned the top button, then fumbled around until he had undone two more. By then, her brassiere was exposed and fairly bursting with its occupants, but she made no protest. Instead, she looked Cosell squarely in the eye and challenged him, "Well, go on Howard." He tittered like a nervous teenager on his first sexual exploration, chewed more vigorously on his omnipresent cigar, salivated on his chin, but uttered not another word. He was really out of control. He had created a situation to try and embarrass someone and wound up being himself humiliated.

Howard Cosell had begun to change in the mid-seventies, and eventually he actually became a different person from the one I had known originally. The bigger his celebrity, the greater his insecurity. I can say this without hesitation: In the later years of our relationship, Howard Cosell turned into one of the most insecure human beings I have ever met. And, for the life of me, I don't know why. Here was a man, a very moral man, a solid family man who had a deep and secure and loving relationship with Emmy. He had two daughters and four grandchildren whom he cherished. He was bright, articulate, successful, and recognized beyond his wildest imaginings. He deserved tremendous credit for contributing enormous amounts of time to many charitable causes, for which he received deep appreciation. He had made millions of dollars, traveled the world, been applauded and honored time and time again. Yet, today, I think he is one of the unhappiest human beings on this planet.

In the early years, whether at a bar, a cocktail party, an office get-together, or another kind of public situation, Howard would do his predictable routine and get by with it without leaving a sour taste. People laughed with, or at, the stooped figure with the caustic wit, the biting humor. That was just Howard. But in the later years, the stuff became increasingly vicious, bitter, even at times downright venomous. Howard was no longer funny. He was vitriolic. He didn't trust anyone. You had to ask yourself, "Is there a solitary soul in this world that Howard Cosell likes?" He changed loyalties so fast it was impossible to keep track of him. He was arrogant, and mean behind people's backs. He was blasting everyone indiscriminately. When stories like that make the rounds, you can lie for a while and insist you didn't say it, or insist you were misquoted. With Cosell, they happened so frequently that all of us knew we were dealing with a man whose problems and insecurities had overwhelmed him. Instead of enjoying his success, he let it devour him. It was awful to see.

I remember one night—it was in the sixties—Howard and I took our wives to a charming little restaurant, Le Boeuf à la Mode, near our apartment on the Upper East Side of Manhattan. We'd no sooner gotten comfortable at our table than Howard began whispering: "Look! Those people are staring at me. They recognize me, they really do. Can you see them watching our table and whispering to each other? Look at that couple over there. You can tell they're talking about me. They know who I am."

He was excited and genuinely pleased at the attention. He was as fascinated by their fascination as they were curious about him. Then, in one of the great put-downs of all time, Emmy Cosell said, "Just take off that hairpiece of yours and they'll never recognize you."

The poet Robert William Service wrote scores of verses about the gold rush days in the Klondike, one of which addressed the matter of finding gold. The lure, Service said, was not so much in the gold itself as in the *finding* of the gold. In a sense, I think that's the way it always was with Howard Cosell. Continuing to be successful, continuing to be accepted, continuing to be famous was an obsession with him. When he appeared on the scene, Curt Gowdy, Chris Schenkel, and Ray Scott, all pretty much middle-of-the-road WASP types, were much better known. Cosell did not creep onto the scene; rather he burst onto it—and, to some people, not as a great journalist but as "that obnoxious Jew from New York."

However, as well as Howard had established himself as a major performer, no one at ABC was prepared for the flak we got when Roone Arledge, president of ABC Sports, decided to put him on our "NFL Monday Night Football" package in 1970.

Cosell had brought to sports broadcasting a dimension of journalistic responsibility it had not seen before, and one that is impossible to measure even now. For that reason alone, Arledge was solidly in favor of putting Howard in the booth on "Monday Night Football," and I concurred because of the journalistic quality he would add to the broadcast. My sole concern was whether three men in the booth might be one too many. Most of the time, as it turned out, that wasn't the case, even though the egos in sports broadcasing are sometimes so fragile that announcers have been known to actually count the number of minutes they are on camera. When Roone made the Cosell call, NFL Commissioner Pete Rozelle was also all for it.

Right out of the starting blocks, we received a tremendous amount of criticism, not just from sportswriters and television critics, but from fans. The telephone calls ran solidly against Cosell. Howard was affected by the criticism and considered quitting the series after five telecasts. Rozelle was instrumental in Howard's continuance, visiting him in his apartment to ask him to remain with the series. There was so much pressure to take him off the air that, at one stage early on, then ABC President Leonard Goldenson almost caved in to it. Howard has always felt well disposed to Goldenson, and he believed that sentiment was reciprocated. But Goldenson was ready to dump Cosell, feeling the negative response of the public would adversely affect the sale of commercial time. Had Arledge not stood up so firmly for Howard, he would have been long gone. During one meeting Goldenson called to discuss the possible departure of Cosell, Arledge made a particularly strong pitch, telling the president, "I think the mix in the booth is good, I think Howard is getting to be good, and, in the long run, when people get used to it, it will be very successful. Let's ride it out and see what happens."

What happened was that "Monday Night Football" became one of the most dynamic and successful television sports packages in the history of the industry, with Howard becoming the catalyst of the production. He made Don Meredith blossom, and he helped Frank Gifford become a more significant part of the mix. But Howard and I will always disagree on why "Monday Night Football" worked. He took all the credit for himself, to the point of stating: "I *am* 'Monday Night Football.' " The reality is that the package, not his persona, was the most important element. Shakespeare said it all when he said, "The play's the thing."

It's my opinion that the criticism of Howard Cosell, when "Monday Night Football" first went on the air, had as much to do with his support of Muhammad Ali as anything else. To be brutally frank, a lot of Americans looked at him, not a handsome man, and listened to that gratingly irritating voice, and perceived in both demeanor and tone a haughty manner, and decided he was first and foremost a Jewish guy from New York who supported blacks.

Over the years, some viewers have asked me if Cosell took on a different character and assumed a different style once he went on the air. The answer is no. What you see is what you get, but over the years his personality changed and the essence of the man underwent a metamorphosis. I can't pin down the exact time these changes took place, but I know for certain that, the more successful he became, the more widespread his fame and the larger his bank account, the more disagreeable he became, the more difficult he was to deal with.

In a one-on-one situation, he'd be okay. But the moment there was the hint of a crowd, it became an audience. It was as if a camera light went on, and Howard felt compelled to perform. He became a caricature of himself. Unwittingly, perhaps, he was *doing* Howard Cosell. And in the process becoming less and less likable.

As his behavior became more irrational—both on and off the air—the more criticism he generated, which in turn would send him into ever more towering rages. He became almost feral, salivating as his voice rose to somewhere between a bellow and a glass-shattering roar. He'd stalk the halls at ABC in search of allies who would join him in his detestation of his detractors. The severest of these always had been the late Dick Young, the syndicated New York sports columnist. I can't tell you the number of times Cosell stormed into my office holding a copy of Young's column.

"Did you see this trash?" he'd demand. "Have you seen this piece of shit? Do you know what this son of a bitch wrote about me today? Do you *know? Do you?* These attacks on me simply have to stop. My network must do something about this man. He's a *madman!*"

There was no point in trying to calm him down. You had to let him go until he ran down. He'd make the rounds, bitching to me; to Chuck Howard, then the vice president in charge of program production; to director Chet Forte, his frequent gin-rummy adversary; to Irv Brodsky, who was in charge of sports publicity; even, when he could find him, to Roone Arledge.

"This is the most despicable man in America," he'd rant. "I'm telling you, this man has to be stopped. You know it's all jealousy, don't you? He's never forgiven me for having him taken off the Jets' radio broadcasts on WABC Radio. The man was an embarrassment, and after we removed him from the broadcasts, he dedicated his life to destroying me."

Other writers infuriated him, but none ever got as deeply under his skin as did Dick Young.

We never needed a clipping service when it came to Cosell. He unearthed every word written or spoken about him, and he'd bring them all to the twenty-eighth floor like a puppy carrying in the morning newspaper. When the reviews were favorable, he'd tell you how bright and articulate that particular writer was, and what respect he had among his fellow journalists, and what a marvelous perspective he had on life. A bad review, though, would prompt another tirade against "those two-hundred-dollar-a-week clerks."

With Howard, it was always simple to divide the teams. The good guys were those who liked him. Those who did not like him were the guys in the black hats.

A vignette of Howard at the Montreal Olympic Games in 1976 will give you a great deal of insight into the persona of the man, beginning with his endless bitching and moaning about having no private time, no more of those quiet moments to himself. "I simply must give all this up," he'd say to me, or to whomever happened to be around. "Look at this—people following me everywhere, demanding my time. It's wearing me out and I can no longer tolerate it. I'm quitting. I'll never sign another contract. I've had it."

The truth is, he could not live without the very celebrity he pretended to hate. And he had plenty of it in Montreal. By then, the Ali association and "Monday Night Football" had brought him to the zenith of his fame. Also, even though his "Saturday Night Live with Howard Cosell" variety show had folded after twenty-two weeks on the air, it had given him entrée to many celebrities outside the realm of sports.

ABC Sports and the sales department held lavish parties for clients—sponsors and advertising agency personnel—not just at the Montreal Games but at nearly all of our big live events. Most of our on-air "talent" hated them and tried to duck them, but not Howard. No one on the staff was more faithful about attending, nor more helpful in dealings with sponsors and agencies. Even though he'd complain loudly about being asked to show up and stroke the clients and sometimes say a few words—"You people must, simply *must*, let me get my rest. I cannot continue at this pace. It's *impossible*. The demands that you make on me are totally unreasonable. Don't you *understand* that?"—he would have been terribly upset had he been ignored. He was never contractually required to make one single appearance, but the invitation to mingle for an hour or so with these people was a command performance to him. He loved it. He wanted it. He *needed* it.

One afternoon in Montreal, Howard went to the Olympic Village, where the athletes from the various nations were housed, and where the security made the place look like an armed camp. This was the first summer Olympiad after the tragic killing of the Israeli team members in Munich, and the Montreal Organizing Committee rightfully pulled out all the stops to guard against any recurrence of terrorist activities. The place was wild with rumors. The watch was tripled at airports and train and bus terminals. Everywhere you looked there were people in uniform—the Canadian Army, the Canadian equivalent of our National Guard, the Royal Canadian Mounted Police, the Montreal police, and the Quebec Provincial Police. The Olympic Village was circled by a chain-link fence with barbed wire strung across the top. Getting into the village was a major undertaking.

First, there was intense screening of media people seeking credentials. Then, even after you got your credentials, you could not simply stroll into the village, but had to have previously made an appointment with an athlete or coach, the exact time and subject of which had to have been approved. Finally, it was required that all those involved in the interview—in this case a producer, a cameraman, a sound-recordist, and other technicians, as well as Cosell—go through an additional screening process. In order to proceed through the gates into the village, it was necessary to pass through a building just outside the gates. There, you had to submit to further questioning before obtaining another credential, of a different color from the first and including your picture on the front, whereupon you deposited your original credential in the building. Once finished with business in the village, you had to reenter the building, surrender the special credential, and receive back your original credential. It might have been a pain-in-the-neck procedure, and I'm certain lots of people griped about it, but it was an understandable precaution in light of the mayhem in Munich.

When Cosell and his crew arrived that day, everyone but Howard made the required right turn to go through the building in order to exchange credentials. Cosell instead barged straight for the gate, despite cautions from his crew members that he, too, would have to endure the five-minute procedure. Imperiously, he waved them off and continued straight for the main gate. Of course, he was stopped and politely informed he needed another credential in order to gain admittance to the Olympic Village.

Howard came to an abrupt stop and faced the person who had spoken to him. She was very young, probably a teenager, and very attractive in her bright red uniform, and the meager pay she was almost certainly getting did not call for her to take the abuse that would follow. At first, Howard gave her only a sort of pitying smile as he began to speak in low and measured tones.

"My dear," he began, "you don't seem to understand. I have an appointment to do a very important interview in the village. I am perilously close to being late and I cannot abide tardiness. Now, if you will excuse me."

He started to walk past her toward the huge, almost prisonlike gates. Quickly, she called after him:

"Sir, please. If you will take just a moment and go to that building over there, I'm sure they will issue you the proper credentials that you must have to enter the village. It'll take just a moment. Sir?"

In a flash, Cosell wheeled and turned on her, and this time there was only venom in his voice. No more Mr. Nice Guy. This was it. She had her chance to bow and scrape and she had blown it.

"My dear, I'll have you fired. I'm the single most recognizable figure in television today, and I will not tolerate this kind of infantile behavior. Do you understand? This is a ridiculous exercise and I simply do not have time for it."

Now he was trembling. He had his forefinger almost in the girl's chest. She was befuddled. About all she was able to offer was, "But, sir . . ." There was no stopping him now. He was boiling.

"Get me someone in authority! The American Broadcasting Company will not be treated this way. You people are treating these young men [the Olympic athletes] as though they are prisoners. Let me remind you, this is not Auschwitz!"

While Howard was bellowing, he got more authority than he bargained for. Several uniformed and armed men quickly made their presence plain. Assuming the role of spokesman, one man with a beret cocked jauntily to one side looked Howard Cosell straight in the eye, and in a very calm voice said: "Sir, it doesn't matter who you are. Right now you will stop talking to this young lady in that tone of voice. She is merely following orders. She is doing her job. We have very strict regulations and they *will* be followed. If you have an appointment to see someone in the village, then you must go through the same procedures that apply to everyone else. There are no exceptions. And do it now, sir, if you expect to get into the village. Otherwise, you may leave. Do you understand, sir?''

Howard understood all too well, but at that moment his ego was so bruised that if he could have gotten the young woman fired and the officer demoted to buck private, he'd have done it, in a heartbeat. The incident had drawn a crowd and Howard had been humiliated. Incidents like that recurred over the years and they surely took their toll, but at the time he'd shake them off with a shrug and quickly turn his attention to someone easier to impress, or, if necessary, steamroller.

The change in Howard Cosell was most dramatic in the decade of the seventies. He was the media's foremost authority on boxing (and in my opinion no one before or since has done boxing commentary as well as Howard Cosell). His radio shows were classics of the genre, even though most of them were done without benefit of scripts: he thought about what he was going to say, then said it. He had become a fixture on ''Monday Night Football.'' He'd had his flirtation with a live variety show. ABC acquired ''Monday Night Baseball'' in 1976, and that fall Howard took on additional responsibilities by doing commentary on the playoffs. The next season, he became a fixture on baseball.

This was perhaps the strangest occurrence in his career, and it took some accomplishing because anyone within earshot of Howard would at some time or other have heard him denigrate baseball, calling it most probably ''an activity whose time has passed.'' According to Cosell, the owners were money-grabbing carpetbaggers who neither knew nor cared one whit about the game. Managers were dummies who thought the game involved more strategy than smart people knew it ever did. The people who covered baseball were freeloading sycophants who were either too lazy or too terrorized by the lords of the game to report facts in a responsible manner. ''A medieval pastime,'' was another Cosell description of baseball. ''It is a laborious and tedious game played by dull people who take a painfully long time to perform this awful function.''

15

When ABC Sports decided to place Howard in the baseball booth, we knew there would be bloodletting. Baseball people are traditionalists; Howard Cosell is anything but. The establishment made its objections known at the outset, and Arledge made it just as clear we would not budge. The conversations became very heated. At one point, Roone told the then commissioner, Bowie Kuhn, and his director of broadcasting, John Lazarus, that if baseball would not budge, there would be no deal. Arledge showed tremendous strength, and correctly so because it was a matter of principle whether we would allow the people who run the sport to dictate the choice of announcers. The odd thing is that, after these fireworks had died down, Howard and Kuhn developed a warm friendship.

Was it mere "hype" to put Cosell on baseball? You could argue that, but you'd be wrong. He was there for the journalistic qualities he brought to the telecasts: the raising of serious issues and the offering of strong commentary. No one had the kind of journalistic impact he did, and this was as true with baseball as with any other sport.

For as long as I can remember, Howard boasted about his strong bond with ABC Chairman Leonard Goldenson, sometimes referring to him much as another man might talk about his own father. I never thought the relationship was as strong as Howard tried to have people believe. Leonard understood Cosell, and, like the rest of us, had much respect for his abilities and the contributions he made, not just to the ABC network but to television in general. But when Cosell got out of control, Goldenson not only was aware of it but unhappy about it.

A perfect example is the brouhaha that accompanied the Larry Holmes/Randall (Tex) Cobb fight we televised in November 1982, Howard's last professional boxing telecast. On the face of it, based on Cobb's record, this looked like it could be a decent scrap. It turned out to be an awful mismatch and a terrible spectacle, and Howard had every right—in fact, an obligation—to call it that way. The referee should have stopped the fight early on.

To the best of my knowledge, Howard had not raised a single objection, nor even a question about the match, before it took place. However, once it began to develop as a gross mismatch, he grabbed hold of it like his life was at stake and he absolutely beat his point to death. I mean, he was like a bulldog chewing on a burglar's pants leg. He would *not* let up. I can't recall in all my years of television anyone hammering and hammering and *hammering* a point like Cosell did that night. He had met his journalistic obligation many times over. It got to the point where you just wanted to scream, not about the fight but about Howard's behavior over it.

A few days later, I flew to Acapulco for a board meeting of our affiliated television stations. One of my great vices is my love of golf, so, as quickly as I could check into the hotel, I headed for the golf course. Leonard Goldenson was on the putting green, and naturally I walked over to him to say hello. Once we'd exchanged pleasantries, he said, "What was wrong with Howard during our boxing telecast the other night?"

I explained that I thought Howard had a right, even a duty, to call it a terrible fight that should have been stopped, but that he'd gone way too far.

"That's exactly the way I feel, Jim. He just ruined the whole telecast for the viewers at home. Why does he do that? Why does he *feel* he has to do that?"

We chatted a while about Howard's insecurities, but neither Leonard nor I had any real answers about why he found it necessary to dominate every telecast on which he appeared. We agreed that he had gone well past the point where the play was the thing.

Howard would later claim to have received a message from Goldenson, thanking him for what he described as preserving the integrity of the network on the Holmes-Cobb telecast. That's a far cry from the story the chairman of the board told me. And, when I returned to New York, I made it a point to talk with Howard about his performance. I told him I thought he belabored the issue to the point of getting out of control. I was still trying to make my case when he flew into a rage: "What do you mean, I dominated the event? I saved your ass is what I did. I'm not the one responsible for putting that mismatch on the air. You people, you geniuses on the twenty-eighth floor, *you* put it on the air and *I* saved your ass. It's my reputation on the line, and I tell it like it is. *My* credibility is at stake. You'll not strip me of my integrity because you want to put a terrible mismatch like that before the American public. The people know me, Mr. Spence. They rely on me to tell it like it is.''

That was Howard Cosell's way of dismissing, almost with a flick of his hand, the professional opinion on an important broadcasting issue of the senior vice president of ABC Sports. It didn't matter then, and it won't matter now, that two years before the Holmes-Cobb fiasco I had staunchly defended Cosell at our board of governors' meeting with the affiliate stations. We were in Los Angeles, and Kent Replogle, the chairman of the sports committee for the affiliates, was very upset about Howard. The essence of what he said was that quite a large number of stations believed that Howard Cosell was more of a liability than an asset, not just to our cause but theirs. The stations applauded our other announcers, but were dead set against Cosell.

Roone Arledge was in that meeting, and could have come to Howard's defense, but, for whatever reason, he chose to remain silent. I wasn't scheduled to speak but I asked for a chance to, and I made it clear from the outset that my talk would be in defense of the man they had maligned.

"We think Howard Cosell is a positive force," I began, assuming that I was speaking not just for myself but for everyone charged with the responsibility of operating the sports department. "Sometimes he is excessive, for sure, but I think it is unfair to call him a liability. If we let him go, CBS or NBC would pick him up in a minute. I just want the record to show that I think Howard Cosell is very valuable to all of us. Everyone who has ever dealt with him has had some difficulty, some pushing and pulling battles along the way, me included. But he's important to us; he's been an integral part of ABC Sports for many years, and he gives us credibility we would not otherwise have."

I wouldn't suggest for a minute that I got a standing ovation when I completed my remarks, but at least I had made my point.

Despite our differences in the later years, Howard knew how I felt about him.

More than once, he threatened to quit, and I always did everything I could to calm him down. Each time he made his threat, he'd launch a tirade against Arledge, with much of his criticism aimed at Arledge's "absentee management," as Howard called it (those who have been devoted to President Reagan might prefer to term it "detached" management). Eventually, though, Howard's need to be stroked and pampered became a major irritant. When he began his campaign against "jockocracy" (he didn't invent that term, but I'm sympathetic to some of his views on it), he'd come whining to me about the difficulty he had working with Frank Gifford and Don Meredith on "Monday Night Football." They were his main targets, but few members of the announcing staff were spared. He kept saying it all was beneath him, that he was wasting his time. Indeed, down deep, I think he feels he wasted his life in sports.

A number of years ago some leading members of the Democratic Party of New York State came to Howard and asked him to run for the United States Senate. He said his family talked him out of running for the seat presently held by Senator Daniel Patrick Moynihan. I'm convinced Howard Cosell would never run for office because he simply could not bear the thought of losing. That would be rejection that he could not accept. Any possibility of not winning, of not dominating, was abhorrent to him. He was never prepared for the second half of the "Wide World of Sports" opening, the part about "the agony of defeat."

It really boiled down to this: Here was a man without a single athletic skill, but with a brilliant mind trained in law, who was attempting to establish himself with a legal career when suddenly he was somehow thrust into sports broadcasting. Instead of getting out in the early days—for instance, when the criticism first got heavy—he stayed with broadcasting because it had clearly become a sure road to fame and fortune. It was he who made the choices.

The games people play, the "silly little contests" he claimed to resent, were feeding not just his family but his insatiable ego.

ABC Sports never intended for him to be its totem, its image-maker, as he liked to suggest. We never sat down and said, "Hey, look what's happening, we are Howard Cosell and he is us." But there can be no question that Howard became so big, so powerful, so well known, that he had great impact on the image of ABC Sports. Eventually, he became so major a player in so many of our programs that, when people thought of ABC Sports, a lot of them thought mainly or even entirely of Howard Cosell. Jim McKay, Keith Jackson, Frank Gifford, and others won't like reading that very much, but that's the way it happened. We would have been very successful without Howard Cosell; we were a whole lot more successful because of him.

Howard's persona helped us in areas where he was not even directly involved. He had access to everybody, and people responded to him—perhaps, to some extent, because of a fear factor. He had a lot of important air time, he had lots of viewers and listeners, so people paid attention to what he said and did. Some writers were unfair to Howard—and to ABC Sports—in suggesting that he actually controlled the sports department at the network. That is simply untrue. Howard contributed ideas for segments of "Wide World of Sports" and, as senior producer of "SportsBeat," certainly exhibited strong influence over that program. He also had input on other shows over the years, as did his colleagues, but he did not have control over any program, including "SportsBeat."

That is not to say he didn't try to *achieve* control, which he did with every ounce of energy he could muster. He'd question your credentials, your education, your ancestry, and anything else that came to mind, if he thought he could win a point. Many producers and directors have felt the lash of the Cosell tongue, have suffered the insults and the humiliation, often in public, and some of them ultimately rolled over and played dead rather than endure further hassles with the man. Howard always became stressful during such arguments, and, the lower your rung on the management ladder, the louder and more vituperative his attack. The tactic was always intimidation, sheer bullying, and much of the time it worked for him. "I'm surrounded by incompetents," was his favorite cry in times like that.

He could not stand for even one of his ideas to be rejected. If you were producing or directing an event and he suggested doing something in a particular way that did not fit in with your plans—say, for example, he wanted the camera to pick up a particular shot and the idea either didn't make sense or couldn't be squeezed into your time schedule—well, with Howard it was not possible to merely shrug it off and proceed. A blowup was inevitable. A minor point lost would always become a major problem. His ego was such that he thought he knew more about every facet of television than anyone else, and, in that regard, he became terribly burdensome both on the air and around the office.

In the spring of 1984, I sent Howard Cosell the following telegram:

> DEAR HOWARD: CONGRATULATIONS ON YOUR 25TH ANNIVERSARY AT ABC. YOU HAVE BEEN A TRUE BROADCAST PIONEER AND HAVE MADE A TREMENDOUS CONTRIBUTION TO BOTH OUR INDUSTRY AND THE AMERICAN PUBLIC. WE ARE PROUD TO HAVE YOU AS A MEMBER OF THE ABC SPORTS TEAM. BEST WISHES FROM ALL OF US AT ABC SPORTS.

He never acknowledged having received it. By that time, he was too wrapped up in his own bitterness to hear or see what anyone else was saying or doing. I hadn't expected a dozen roses or lunch at Lutèce in return, but a telephone call would have been nice.

The man who had turned a sportscasting career into top-billing appearances with Johnny and Merv, Sonny and Cher, Dean and Mike and Flip, David Frost and Bob Hope and Danny Thomas, who had made guest appearances on "The Odd Couple" and been featured in Woody Allen movies, was himself playing a role. Difficult as it is for me to say, the role was somewhat that of a clown. And, remember, it has been said that most clowns, out of costume and out of the spotlight, are unhappy people.

In the broadcast booth, he would get carried away with his own commentary to such an extent that it sometimes would

detract from the game itself. Once, during a baseball telecast, the producer, Dennis Lewin, asked Howard through his headset to ease back and do a little less talking. Howard immediately ripped off his own headset, slammed it on the announce table, and stalked out of the booth.

Bob Goodrich is a bright and talented producer who worked his way up through the ranks after an outstanding football career as "the other end" at SMU when Jerry Levias was getting all the headlines. Bob has worked countless shows with Howard—in fact, he was the producer of "Monday Night Football" during Cosell's sunset years. A psychology major at SMU, and possessor of anything but a jock mentality, Goodrich knew he had to handle Howard delicately. Most of the time it worked, but there were several occasions when Howard had a knee-jerk reaction when Goodrich suggested he back off and not talk quite so much.

"He'd go five or ten minutes without saying a word," said Goodrich, "and I'd ask the stage manager in the booth if Howard had left. I've had enormous respect for the man, and generally we got along very well. But he blew up at me two or three times and once was so furious in a bar after one Monday night telecast that he accused me of ruining 'Monday Night Football.' I just walked away from it. I attributed it to him perhaps having been over-served. On another occasion when he blasted me, I simply told him he was full of shit."

It is a sad commentary that, in all the years he worked at ABC Sports, and for all the fine contributions he made, Howard Cosell never concerned himself with what made the business tick. Worse, it was clear to everyone that he never gave a damn. If there is one industry that demands a total team effort it is television, but Cosell had very little respect for any of the behind-the-scenes people who made it possible for him to appear on the air.

Once I became senior vice president in 1978, and was actually handling the day-to-day operation of the sports department, with Arledge concentrating almost solely on news, I determined to try and do something about this and wrote the following letter to Howard:

Dear Howard:

I have said many times to many people over the years that the two most important people in my life have been my wife and Howard Cosell. I have said this based on my sincere and earnest respect and appreciation as a business colleague and friend. Specifically, I will always be indebted to you for helping me to learn the importance of honesty and integrity in life.

I, therefore, am, and have been, disturbed at how our relationship has evolved. I would like for us to discuss this relationship—which is most significant, in my opinion, in light of our respective positions within the ABC Sports framework—and attempt to reestablish our earlier status.

I have examined carefully the reasons I attribute to the current status and have reduced a very complex situation to one basic point—lack of respect. Not everyone in life can always agree. People have their own opinions and feelings. I don't ask you to agree with me or anyone else when you, in your heart and mind, don't agree. But I do ask you, in the strongest possible terms, to respect the right of a person to have his own point of view. I fully respect your right to your points of view.

I would like to reestablish our personal relationship—and importantly—to reinvolve Howard Cosell in the mainstream of our operation. If you are in accord with what I propose, I would like to meet with you at first opportunity. If not, then the basis of our relationship will be clear.

I look forward to hearing from you.

Regards,

Jim

The letter struck a nerve. Cosell called me immediately and suggested we meet for a drink at the nearby Dorset Hotel bar right after work, which we did.

"Hey, I got your letter," he said. "You know, Jimmy, you and I don't have any problems."

And that was the end of it. To diffuse the issue, he quickly moved on to another subject. He wanted no part of a confrontation, nor even to put our differences on the table for discussion, so we could come to a settlement or an understanding of some kind. He was obviously concerned about my letter, but he could not bring himself to tackle an issue of such substance, even though he was a man who placed so much emphasis on telling it like it is. It was clear from our meeting that Howard was not going to change his thinking. Nor was I.

In September of 1984, Stan Isaacs reviewed "Monday Night Football" without Howard Cosell. In his article in *Newsday* he led off by saying that if Milton Berle, the hula-hoop, and Spiro Agnew could come and go, so, then, could Cosell. "And the republic still stands," he remarked.

Here are excerpts from Isaacs' column:

"Frank Gifford, Don Meredith and O. J. Simpson, who had worked together before, carried on ably enough. Nothing fancy, nothing memorable, but at a level that we have come to think of as competence on the tube. . . . The quality of the games themselves is the line that ABC and people in football have been highlighting for some time. They agree that Cosell had tremendous impact in the early days of the 15 years of the serial, but they have been saying for some years that the ratings are dependent not so much on the high jinks inspired by Cosell in the booth, but on the games themselves. Some even suggest that of late Cosell hurt the ratings, which fell to an all-time low last season.

"What nobody is saying aloud, because they are all gentlemen about these things, is that they are happy to be rid of Cosell. An NFL official said, 'In the early years he made a significant contribution. People who were not your regular football fans would tune in to see what the sucker would do. But the last few years, he became a tired act. He had always been negative, but in the past few years it was not an entertaining negative.' "

Then Isaacs quoted an ABC "insider" that "we recognize what he did, but nobody is sorry to see him leave. We are all tired of the aggravation, the abuse of people, his temper tantrums."

Isaacs wrote that ABC had handled Howard's departure from the Monday night scene with dignity and class, and added that both Gifford and Meredith had said nice things about him on the telecast.

Needless to say, I was not at all pleased when I read the next paragraph in the column: "Jim Spence, senior vice-president of ABC, whom Cosell has referred to as an errand boy, noted weeks ago that Cosell would not be back on Monday Night Football."

That column appeared September 5, 1984, but I didn't get wind of it for a couple of weeks. When I did, I went after the facts. I called Isaacs to find out if Howard had actually called me an errand boy. Stan said Howard not only had called me that, but said other, even less flattering things that Isaacs, in the interests of good taste, declined to put into his column. I told Isaacs I planned to confront Cosell about the column and asked him if he'd stand behind not only what he wrote, but his conversation with Cosell that preceded it. His answer was "Absolutely."

I then took the matter to Cosell, making a copy of Isaacs' column and stapling it to a handwritten memo that said:

> Howard—I find your reference to me in the attached to be both unintelligent and somewhat pitiful. Jim.

I received the following replay, handwritten at the bottom and on the back of my original memo:

> Jim—I despise Isaacs and told him so. He wrote falsely to get back at me. How do you feel about the way he wrote about *me* in contrast to all the columns from all over the country. He writes this way to produce the exact effect he did with you.
> H.C.

The other columns Howard alluded to made him feel good, since some writers and critics had said more favorable things about him after his departure than they did while he was on "Monday Night Football."

Had the writers and broadcasters ever learned how much drinking Howard Cosell was doing before—and, yes, during—the games he covered, their earlier criticisms would have seemed like a handful of confetti compared with the artillery they would have aimed at him. I've debated whether to bring this out, and it has caused consternation within me, but I cannot write a book like this without telling it like it *really* is. The facts are these:

Howard Cosell was a regular drinker before, during, and after telecasts, and some of the time it became a major problem.

Everyone knows about the infamous Philadelphia incident on the "Monday Night Football" telecast in 1970, when Howard got so drunk he couldn't pronounce the name of the city he was in without slurring. It was obvious this was a case of a man getting more than just a little tipsy. Howard had consumed too many of his "silver bullets," and it became apparent to all who saw or heard him. It was particularly clear to Dandy Don Meredith, because Howard threw up all over Don's new cowboy boots.

Finally, Howard had to leave the broadcast booth, and, after that, he disappeared. The game was over, people were asking questions, the ABC switchboard was lit up, and no one could locate Cosell. Eventually, in desperation, someone called his New York apartment, from where a sleepy Emmy Cosell assured the caller that Howard was snug in his own bed, sleeping it off. He had taken a cab from Philadelphia to Manhattan.

I had worked late that night and my wife and I were having a bite to eat when the game came on the air. Even half-listening, I knew something was wrong. The telecast wasn't very old when Emmy called me at home:

"Jim, are you watching the game?"

I told her I was.

"Well, then, can you tell me what in the world is wrong with Howard?"

I told her I didn't know, but that I'd try to find out and call her back.

As soon as I hung up, I called the production facility (ABC's production truck) at Franklin Field in Philadelphia. It was no mystery what was wrong. When I called Emmy back, I told her the problem was one of "alcoholic consumption." Those were my exact words to her, because I wanted to say it as gently as I could. She thanked me and hung up.

At Roone Arledge's request, our public relations man, Irv Brodsky stated that Howard had indeed taken one drink at our pregame hospitality headquarters, where he was always so gracious with advertisers and agency people. Then he had had a "reaction" to that one drink because, at the same time, he was taking antibiotics for a case of influenza. And, as we all know, one must not mix liquor and medication.

Howard's drinking wasn't necessarily noticeable on the air. But vodka, his favorite drink, was available for him in the booth on both football and baseball telecasts, and he nipped at it during the course of the games. I learned this from both producers and also from his fellow announcers for the first time in late 1984.

Why did none of them come to Roone Arledge or to me, or to someone in authority at ABC Sports, and report this behavior? The assumption was, and probably still is in most quarters, that, like so many of us, Howard enjoys a few pops now and again, and that, with all the stress and tension connected with his work, a tiny touch before and/or during a big game just might relax him a bit. Certainly, I did not condone drinking on the air, and neither did Roone.

Another factor is that people were dealing here with a major personality, a superstar. Despite his hunched posture, weak handshake, and wig, Howard Cosell, broadcaster, was an imposing figure to producers and directors, and an even more threatening one to lower-level operatives like unit managers and production assistants. Was a guy making, say, one-twentieth of Cosell's salary, with no visibility but total vulnerability, going to turn him in?

Arledge's secretary was swamped with calls and letters after that incident. She gave each caller the official company line, that Howard had consumed one drink, which, together with the flu pills, gave him such a reaction that his speech became slurred.

One caller wouldn't buy it. "That's bullshit," he screamed. "Just plain bullshit. The bastard drinks in my place. I'm a *bartender*, you hear? I serve the man regularly. I know very well what Cosell sounds like when he's drunk. And he was *drunk!*"

When Arledge returned to his office, his secretary told him about that particular call. Roone's reply was succinct: "The fact is, my dear, Howard was very, very drunk."

Okay, it was a network cover-up, but that was no reason to call out the National Guard. The man had made a mistake, and one that an awful lot of high-powered and "respectable" people make regularly but can get away with solely because they're not in the public eye. The trick was to put it behind us. I'm sure Howard was embarrassed by it all, although, knowing him, he may have talked himself into believing that he really *had* taken some pills, then had just this one teeny little drink.

We all assumed he had learned his lesson and that it would not happen again. Wrong!

During the 1984 American League Championship Series between Detroit and Kansas City, Howard again got out of control. And, again, it showed on the tube. Worse yet, he and Al Michaels got into an argument on the air in Kansas City. Howard kept interrupting Al, and there they were, the two announcers, battling back and forth during the course of the baseball game. I was watching and I quickly realized something was terribly wrong.

The following morning, I got a telephone call from Barry Frank, Michaels' agent. He was extremely upset about what had taken place the night before. Barry said Al had told him Cosell was drinking heavily and was impossibly argumentative, and that Al could no longer tolerate it. Al said it was undermining the professionalism of, and was a hindrance to, the broadcast.

I immediately called Michaels to verify what had happened, and Al left no doubt about the size of the problem. As a viewer, I knew it was bad, but after Al and I finished talking, I realized it was worse even than I had surmised. We could no longer escape the fact that a lot of people had been covering up for Cosell.

My next call was to Chuck Howard, who was producing the Detroit-Kansas City series. I told him to confront Cosell about the drinking. Chuck was very defensive and made it clear he wanted no part of a confrontation with Howard Cosell.

Finally, I told him: "Listen, Chuck, you must immediately speak with Howard. It's your responsibility as the producer."

Again, Chuck resisted, and soon we were yelling at each other. Finally, I ended it: "Chuck, I want you to go immediately to Howard and inform him—and you may quote me if you like—that we never again will stand for him consuming alcohol during an ABC Sports broadcast. Tell him it is absolutely forbidden and will not be tolerated."

Whether Chuck Howard actually had such a talk with Howard Cosell is a matter of speculation. The subject simply was not brought up again. Clearly, our production people had known of the problem for a long time and had merely tolerated it.

More clearly, it was just as well that Cosell's time as a major performer at ABC Sports was drawing to a close. Just as the pretty woman in the streets of New Orleans had married beneath herself, according to the Law of Cosell, he, too, was now performing at a level beneath his earlier standards. From the time he had his first taste of stardom, he had threatened to quit. Soon, he would do so.

With all of Cosell's bitching about print journalists, both sportswriters and television critics, they somehow were unbelievably easy on him about the drinking issue. It wasn't that they did not know; countless times they saw him holding court in hotel bars and at gatherings around the world, and many times he had far too much to drink. Then he'd take off on his favorite targets—about "jockocracy," or about Pete Rozelle and the National Football League, or about the antitrust laws, or about the writers themselves. They had to hear him that one time at the NFL winter meetings in the Arizona Biltmore bar in Phoenix, because only the very heavy sleepers could have missed it:

"Roone Arledge, the great Roone Arledge," he bellowed, a half-filled glass of vodka in one hand and a cigar in the other, "here's a man who has his name on more shows he has never seen than any man in the history of American television. I thought I was a genius. I'm not a genius. He's a genius. Do you hear me? An absolute genius. I'm telling you, Roone Arledge is a genius, to have gotten away with all he has. And he has my network so totally in his control, its executives so firmly in his grasp, why, Roone Arledge controls Fred Pierce. If Roone Arledge asked Fred Pierce to lie down and let Roone piss on him, little Freddie Pierce would do it. And that's telling it like it is." (Pierce was president of ABC Television at the time.)

That's the way it happened. My wife and I were eyewitnesses. And that was not an isolated incident. His ego forced him to find some way to try to impress and dominate every room he occupied.

The celebrated author David Halberstam once wrote, "Howard dominated because he HAD to dominate; it seemed to mean so much to him . . . it was exhausting to be with him; more than anyone I know, he sucks the oxygen out of a room."

Ever since Halberstam wrote that in 1982, Cosell has hated him, too.

Even when the network cancelled Howard's award-winning weekly "SportsBeat" show, he refused—or was unable—to look at things in an objective light. He had begun the show in the late summer of 1981, and the fact that it ran some five years is a tribute not only to Howard and his considerable skills, but to the network as well. The show never made a dime—indeed, it lost as much as $1 million a year, until finally it could no longer be sustained no matter how great or worthwhile the content.

It was a dandy show, and Cosell did some of his finest work on that program. He dug out some great stories, created some moving portraits, did many poignant pieces that tugged at the viewer's heart. Nevertheless, the financial drain was such that the network wanted to cancel the show as early as 1983, and would certainly have done so had I not fought for its survival and won a temporary victory. When all of us agreed that the time to cancel could no longer be postponed, I made the call to Cosell because, over my twenty-five years with ABC, Roone Arledge had never been prepared to make that kind of call. When I reached Howard, I prefaced the bad news by telling him how many good things the program had accomplished. I knew it would not be an easy call, because that kind never is, and in this particular case you were dealing with an extraordinarily sensitive man who had publicly said that "SportsBeat" would be his television legacy. After telling him of the respect we had for him, and for his show, I informed him that the decision to cancel had been made.

He was short.

"Thank you. I knew about the decision."

And we hung up.

He could not have known, because the decision had just been made. He could have anticipated it, and obviously had. The cancellation of television shows that do not achieve acceptable rating levels and which lose money can rarely be a surprise.

By then, Howard Cosell was a man practically adrift at the network with which he had carried on a tempestuous love affair dating from the mid-1950s. He had left "Monday Night Football" after the 1983 season, cutting himself loose from it, then sniping nastily at his old broadcast partners—not to mention the NFL and the game itself. He had then talked himself off the 1985 World Series telecasts, even though he had worked on baseball during the regular season. Finally, he had lost his beloved "SportsBeat," the show he called his signature program, the one for which he wanted to be remembered. Fittingly, "SportsBeat" was the last telecast Howard ever did for ABC Sports.

There's no telling how long he could have stayed on football had he chosen to remain with our Monday Night series, and he was still an important contributor to our baseball telecasts. But then in his book *I Never Played the Game*, which came out in 1985, he took off on almost everyone at ABC. We were all sick and tired of his bad-mouthing of everybody and everything.

The issue was much greater than ABC Sports publicly stated. For the record, we simply said that it would have been awkward for Howard Cosell to be assigned to a telecast and be compelled to work with Al Michaels, an announcer he had so roundly criticized. Therefore, we said, Howard Cosell would not be assigned to the 1985 World Series.

In our private meetings, Roone Arledge and I had had Cosell up to here. Frankly, he had dug such a huge hole and buried himself so deep in it that there was no way out—except for him to leave, that is. Every few days, we'd see a blurb somewhere about how his book told everyone what was wrong with ABC Sports. It was like sitting in a foxhole and waiting for the next round of mortar shells to land on you.

Someone remarked that Howard must be an advocate of Dylan Thomas and was following the Welsh writer's advice: "Do not go gentle into that good night/Old age should burn and rave at close of day;/Rage, rage against the dying of the light."

Howard surely was not going gentle, and his rage had been at the intolerable level for too long. He wanted out and we wanted him out. He had a contract that obligated us to use him on several events in 1986—the Kentucky Derby, the Preakness, and the Tournament of Champions Tennis at Forest Hills—and we negotiated a settlement, relieving him of his obligation for those assignments. He was bitter and frustrated. He insisted the network had squandered his talents, that his intellect had been wasted. He once wanted to be an anchorperson for ABC News; another time he urged Roone Arledge to make him a roving news correspondent. He felt the world had never really been fully exposed to his true brilliance.

Soon after it was determined that Howard Cosell would no longer be associated with ABC Sports, I suggested at a staff meeting that we honor him, and all of us agreed that he richly deserved such recognition. We discussed a farewell dinner or reception. The plan was to bring together the top people in sports and broadcasting, along with others who were special to Howard and to ABC Sports, and to give him a tremendous send-off. He was sixty-seven and certainly wealthy enough to retire, and he had said for quite some time that it was what he wanted to do. So I called him and began to tell him what we had in mind.

"We'd like to honor you," I said, and those were the only words I could get out.

"I don't want to be honored," he broke in sharply. "I don't want to attend any social affairs. If you want to talk about my departure, talk to my lawyer, Bob Schulman."

End of conversation. End of ABC Sports career. Sad, indeed!

2

$309,000,000!

*Calgary and Seoul:
the Astonishing Deals for
the 1988 Olympic Games*

Three hundred and nine million dollars!

That is the most money ever paid for a single event in the history of television anywhere in the world, sports or otherwise. The event is the most prized in all of television sports, perhaps in all of television: the Olympic Games.

In January 1984, bidding for the rights to these games—the 1988 Winter Olympics in Calgary, Alberta, Canada—was scheduled to take place in Lausanne, Switzerland. When our ABC Sports negotiating team left New York for those sessions with the International Olympic Committee and the Calgary Olympic Organizing Committee, we had a wide assortment of feelings, but mostly feelings of concern, uncertainty, anxiety, and uneasiness—indeed, almost a sense of impending doom about what lay ahead in that lovely city on the shores of beautiful Lake Geneva. But none of us contemplated what was to occur, which was the most demanding, frustrating, infuriating, nonsensical, and historic negotiations in the saga of American television sports.

The 1988 Calgary negotiations marked the end of an era in the business of television sports. When ABC Sports at long last was awarded the rights to the games for $309 million, it represented an increase of $217.5 million, or 337 percent, over the cost of the rights to the 1984 Winter Olympics in Sarajevo, Yugoslavia, which themselves had gone for the then unheard of price of $91.5 million.

It would be the last of the quantum leaps in television-rights fees for sports packages in this country.

My first involvement in negotiating for telecasts of Olympic Games concerned the 1976 Summer Games at Montreal. We acquired the rights to those games for $25 million, and got the Winter Games in Innsbruck, Austria, that same year for $10 million. We paid $15.5 million for the 1980 Winter Games in Lake Placid, and provided worldwide coverage. The Summer Games in Moscow that year cost NBC $87 million, an understandable increase in light of the mystique surrounding their location. But those games never got on United States television, because of the boycott inspired by President Jimmy Carter. In addition to the $91.5 million we paid for the 1984 Winter Games in Sarajevo, we doled out another $225 million for the Los Angeles Summer Games that year.

Its prior Olympic involvements had produced healthy profits for ABC, but for the network to take the 1988 Winter Games for $309 million was outrageous despite our objective. Our Olympic priority for 1988 clearly was Calgary vis-à-vis the Summer Olympic Games in Seoul, South Korea, since the Winter Olympics were to be staged in North America and we would be able to televise live most of the key events. If the rules conveyed to us in person by the consultant to the Calgary Committee had been followed, we would never have paid $309 million.

There had been a lot of behind-the-scenes maneuvering at ABC before our party took off for Lausanne. In meetings involving the highest officials of the network, it was determined that, at the very outside, we could take our offer for the 1988 Winter Games to $275 million. That wasn't some figure pulled out of a hat, but rather one based on very careful and considered estimates of costs and potential revenues. We'd been around the block a time or two in this business of presenting the Olympic Games telecasts and making them good, sound financial packages. I don't think anyone—even at CBS or NBC—would dispute that ABC had done a superior job, not only of televising the Olympic Games, but in making those telecasts strong contributors to the profit column. The International Olympic Committee and the organizing committees from the various host nations recognized that, too.

Before the bidding began in Lausanne, Barry Frank was the key to the deal. Frank is senior vice president of International Management Group (IMG), the Mark McCormack outfit that is the parent company of Trans World International (TWI), which had been hired as television consultant to both the Calgary and Seoul organizing committees.

Barry Frank had begun his television career at the network level under Roone Arledge at ABC, and had worked at ABC from 1965 to 1970, becoming, in effect, second in command to Arledge in running the sports department. Although he later had a fling as the head man at CBS Sports, Barry's best memories, if not his loyalties, were at ABC. We had a number of meetings with him prior to the big one in Lausanne, with the result that he knew well ahead of time that we were prepared to go as high as $275 million. At one point, he assured me, "That'll get it." He said he could say that with assurance, since he had discussed our position with Dick Pound, chairman of the IOC/Calgary Television Negotiating Committee. I would later learn, shortly before the meeting in Lausanne, that Dick Pound really was not on board as far as Barry's conviction was concerned. Later still, despite Frank's previous assurances that ABC's suggested outside bid of $275 million would be sufficient, he told me that this figure would not necessarily get the job done.

We held numerous meetings in New York to determine our strategy and sales potential. We knew what the market was telling us; we knew how many hours of programming we could sustain; we knew how many commercial minutes we could realistically figure on selling, and for how much money. There was a lot of crystal-balling involved, and at the end of it all the $275 million figure was a realistic one, based on the market at that time and what our financial experts and sales people estimated it would be in 1988.

Additionally, Barry and I had carefully gone over every angle and detail during our private meetings. We ascertained that CBS would not be a major player for the rights and, as it turned out, that was correct. We figured NBC would enter the fray just like ABC Sports would—balls out—and that's what happened.

Despite our protests, the International Olympic Committee decided to utilize a sealed-bidding procedure for disposition of the Calgary television rights. We were opposed to bidding—the simultaneous submitting of their financial proposals in sealed envelopes by all contenders—as a matter of principle.

We felt strongly that such a process allowed the IOC to consider only the money being offered, while ignoring the vital, nonfinancial aspects of a network relationship. We agreed to be part of the Calgary process on the basis that, although sealed bids would be tendered, the ground rules also would provide for negotiations that would allow for consideration of production experience and expertise, promotional capability, technical competence, and other factors critical to the artistic as well as the commercial success of the enterprise.

Right up to and including the morning of bidding day, January 24, Barry Frank promised us that everyone understood and would abide by all the preagreed conditions. The heart of these was that, if during the bidding it became apparent that one network was well ahead of the others—in other words, if one network's bid was significantly higher—then the bidding would be halted and the negotiations I alluded to earlier would commence between the leading network and the IOC/Calgary Television Negotiating Committee. We had Barry's repeated assertions that it was no one's intention to let matters get out of control.

The IOC was determined that there would be no favoritism partly because of the committee's sensitivity over developments during the competition for U.S. television rights to the Sarajevo Games. In 1980, we had gotten a leak from the Sarajevo people that the bid we had to beat by CBS was $90 million. That enabled ABC to come in at $91.5 million and conclude the deal.

We had our own "Deep Throat" when we entered the negotiations for Calgary, just as we had for Sarajevo, and the knowledge that we again would have inside information on what the other networks were bidding served to lessen our concerns. Still, we kept reminding Barry that we wanted to be on guard against the session disintegrating into a flat-out money fight.

"Believe me, it won't come to that," promised the man who was the paid consultant to the Calgary Committee. "Everyone understands that at any time along the way the committee can call a halt to the whole thing. The minute it appears one network is clearly superior financially, why, the committee will then opt to negotiate unilaterally with just one of the parties. It's *not* going to get out of hand. You have my word on that."

Mark that down in your little black book as one of the most misleading statements, deliberate or otherwise, in the history of television sports.

The sealed bidding began at 2 P.M. In the first round, CBS bid $182 million, NBC, $200 million, and ABC $208 million. Then CBS went to $195 million, NBC to $250 million, and ABC to $261 million. That's when CBS dropped out.

(I subsequently learned certain members of the negotiating committee were concerned that CBS' withdrawal meant the bidding had already escalated to unreasonable levels, but Barry Frank told the committee it was not its obligation to worry about the U.S. networks and that the committee should continue to keep the pressure on ABC and NBC.

Frank was motivated solely by money since the TWI commission was determined by how much the winning American network bid. Specifically, TWI's arrangement with the Calgary Organizing Committee called for a payment of $125,000 if the bidding reached $200 million, then 1 percent of the next $25 million, 1 1/2 percent of the subsequent $25 million, 2 percent of the next $50 million, and 2 1/2 percent of anything over $300 million.)

It was high-stakes poker that, once there were only two players left, became showdown poker. In the third round, ABC went to $280 million, which put us $12.5 million ahead of NBC. We thought the bidding should have stopped then, since we had exceeded the $275 million figure discussed prior to our coming to Lausanne. Besides. $12.5 million dollars has to be "a substantial lead" in anyone's language.

Still, Barry and the committee let it rage on. In round four, we bid $300 million, which put us $19.5 million in front of NBC. (At that juncture, I discovered later, there was sentiment in the committee room to stop the bidding and attempt to negotiate an agreement with ABC, but Frank urged that the bidding process be continued.) What we had been told would never happen was, indeed, occurring—a wild, out-of-control, money-is-all bidding session.

We would come down to Salon 2, just off the lobby of the sumptuous Lausanne Palace Hotel, with our latest sealed bid. Then, after each round, we would be given a sheet of paper with a new set of instructions, along with a notation telling us how much time we would have to prepare our next bid. Throughout the process, Roone Arledge and I had been upstairs in his suite, speaking on the telephone with Fred Pierce, then the president of ABC, in New York. We were furious when we got yet another set of instructions for round five. I had already had one strong exchange over the phone with Barry Frank, shouting at him at one juncture, "This is crazy. It has to stop!"

All he said was, "Jim, I know. I'm trying."

Here we were, less than one month away from televising the 1984 Winter Games in Sarajevo that we'd bought for $91.5 million, and we had put in a bid of more than three times that amount and had not even acquired the rights for the Calgary Games. It was sheer insanity.

After the third round, ABC and NBC got instructions for the next round, while CBS got a look-alike envelope containing a polite thank-you note. CBS had not submitted a bid for the third round and was consequently asked to withdraw. Naturally, our people—and I'm sure the NBC people as well—thought we still had a three-handed game. We subsequently discovered that CBS had, in fact, removed themselves from consideration. Later, I learned that CBS was asked to submit empty envelopes in subsequent bidding rounds, to give the appearance of continued three-network competition! CBS properly rejected that request, but did post themselves near the meeting room in order to give an appearance of still being active participants. While I question such conduct, CBS's action really had no effect on ABC or NBC.

$309,000,000!

Before the fifth-round bidding, the networks received the following instructions from the negotiating committee:

"The Committee recognizes and appreciates the interest and responsiveness demonstrated by the networks, and has decided that it will not on its own initiative eliminate any network. Should any network elect not to meet the minimum bid set forth below, the committee would appreciate being so advised in writing at any time prior to the deadline set forth below."

ABC and NBC each bid $300 million in round five. We simply repeated our bid from the previous round, but NBC had increased its bid from $280.5 million. We were deadlocked! By not asking for a proposal in excess of $300 million in round five, the committee was, in essence, demonstrating its concern that the numbers were perilously high.

Roone Arledge and I were doing the talking for ABC. Arthur Watson, the president of NBC Sports and a very decent man, represented his network along with Bob Mulholland, than president of NBC. We were summoned to Salon 2 with the committee and told that our bids were identical and that we, not the committee, must break the tie. We seriously considered withdrawing at this time, then quickly decided against it. By then, we felt like we were trying to swim the English Channel from England to France, and a mile or so from Calais had encountered a school of hungry sharks. It was dangerous to continue, but we were so close to shore that it would have been tragic to quit. It was both an emotional and an intellectual decision, but, even in retrospect, I'm not sure I could have gone along with any other move at that point.

Said the IOC spokesman: "We are going to toss a coin and one network is going to make the call. Then, whichever of you wins the coin toss can decide whether to bid first or second. Whoever goes first can make a bid, then the other network will have fifteen minutes to make its bid. And that bid, gentlemen, must exceed the other bid by at least one million dollars."

I could not believe that this august and historic body had turned the process into nothing short of a carnival. No one could deny that Roone Arledge deserved more credit than anyone else for the impact of the modern Olympiad on the American public, and thereby for the gigantic television-rights fees the Games had been able to command. Now that success was being used as a bludgeon against him and his network in a degrading process rooted, in part, in greed.

After issuing the instructions, Dick Pound asked which of us would make the call of the coin flip. Art Watson said he would. Now picture this: Here we were, five bids behind us, the last ones of $300 million, and we were about to engage in a coin flip! Pound made the flip but Watson never made a call either way. I suppose Arthur was so nervous he couldn't bring himself to say either heads or tails, and I can understand that. He was very embarrassed.

"I'm sorry, I'm sorry," he repeated. "I'll call it this time."

Pound flipped the coin in the air a second time, and it bounced off my shoulder and onto the carpeted floor. They picked it up and determined that Watson had won, and NBC said it would go first. We had already decided, should we win, to let NBC go first, then react to their bid. And, at my suggestion, the committee agreed to a thirty-minute time period for submitting the initial bid, and then for a fifteen-minute interval thereafter.

About thirty minutes later, NBC's bid was opened. We were told it was for $304 million. The committee reminded us that we had fifteen minutes to respond, or get out of the game.

The new rules stated that we had to bid at least $305 million. Roone quickly got on the telephone again with Fred Pierce in New York, while I remained in the lobby with Charlie Lavery, then vice president of program planning for ABC Sports. I had told Roone I thought we should go at least to $307 million. He and Pierce finally decided on a bid of $309 million. That way, we would send NBC a clear message that we were not about to be bluffed out of this high-stakes game. Charlie wrote the $309 million figure on a piece of paper and sealed it in an envelope, then I submitted it in front of the NBC representatives. When our figure was announced, the faces of the NBC delegation dropped like an elevator with a broken cable. NBC now had fifteen minutes to respond.

Charlie and I hurried back to Roone's suite to caucus and discuss strategy, and then we left to return to Salon 2. Minutes later, Roone's telephone rang. It was NBC, asking us to join them in the committee room. Roone was so livid he refused to accompany Charlie and me. As soon as we got to the committee room, Arthur Watson announced that NBC was withdrawing. The NBC people all congratulated us, and quickly left the room. They were thorough gentlemen all the way, but you could tell how upset they were. They had busted their guts, given their all, and it really was a sad situation for them.

I did not know exactly how I felt at that moment. The committee was congratulating us on our acquisition of the rights. I knew I had to say something. I made it brief:

"We at ABC Sports are extremely pleased to acquire the rights to the 1988 Winter Olympics in Calgary, and we look forward with great anticipation to working with the Calgary Organizing Committee."

I left it at that. On one hand, we had battled so hard and worked so diligently that I was glad we won. On the other hand, I felt as much a loser as a winner. I surely didn't feel like celebrating. It was the first time I fully understood the meaning of the word "bittersweet." We shook hands all around, then went to Arledge's suite. We had exceeded the network's guidelines by $34 million, and I think, in our heart of hearts, each of us knew that we were wrong—and, on top of that, that we'd been had. I know I did. It just wasn't fair to dismiss the whole thing by saying, "Well, I'm only the senior vice president of ABC Sports, so it wasn't my call. It was Fred Pierce's decision." The whole deal was crazy, it was vulgar, and all of us knew it, even though right then we weren't eager to openly admit it.

After ABC had acquired the rights, Dick Pound expressed his concern about ABC's level of financial commitment; that it was potentially unhealthy for the IOC as well as for the network. After all, if ABC were to lose serious money on Calgary, that could negatively affect future Olympic deals.

We had been back in Arledge's suite only a few minutes when Barry Frank called, asking for a private meeting with Roone and me. The three of us gathered in my suite, next door to Roone's. Barry quickly started to explain how sorry he was that things got "out of hand." He insisted he could not control the process.

He could not hide his embarrassment. He said Juan Antonio Samaranch, president of the International Olympic Committee, would not go for the deal that Barry had proposed and promised to us. (Samaranch lives in the Lausanne Palace Hotel, where all of this was taking place, but had not been present during any of the proceedings.)

We must have been in that room for about forty-five minutes, and Roone could not bring himself to be more than barely cordial to Frank. To this day, Arledge believes that Barry deliberately screwed ABC. Me? I can't exonerate Barry, but my jury is still out as to whether he was solely to blame. What is very clear is that the American Broadcasting Company in general, and ABC Sports in particular, were grossly misled.

Long after the debacle was over, Barry Frank's boss, Mark McCormack, admitted to me during a meeting in New York that "We (TWI) wanted to show people what we could do. It was vital to get every dollar we could."

For the record, the dollars Barry Frank generated for his company amounted to almost 2 million. I'm confident that when he took it to the bank, the teller didn't ask Barry any embarrassing questions about how he got it; nevertheless, he certainly pleased the Calgary Organizing Committee.

After the hollow victory, half a dozen of us sat around Arledge's suite—Charlie Lavery; Georges Croses, then vice president, European relations; Charlie Stanford, then vice president, legal and business affairs; and Donna de Varona, Roone's special assistant, in addition to Roone and me. We tried to assess the damage over drinks and late snacks.

It was beyond amazing; it was shocking. In 1960, CBS had paid $50,000 for the rights to the Winter Games in Squaw Valley, California, which, incidentally, were hosted by Walter Cronkite. Four years later, ABC had paid somewhat over $500,000 for its first Winter Games at Innsbruck. Now, for precisely the same package, ABC had to cough up *309 million clams.* Not one soul in that room felt like raising a clenched fist in celebration, nor giving the *V*-for-victory sign. The battle had taken too great a toll on all of us. The victory, if indeed you could call it that, was specious at best.

The next day, following the actual signing ceremony, we had to endure a news conference. The whole process was gnawing at me and all I wanted to do was go home, but we had planned to stop in Paris on the way back to New York. As we traveled, and through dinner that night in Paris, we kept trying to pump ourselves up, saying things like, "Well, the important thing is that we got the rights." But this was one of those times when all the rah-rah stuff went for naught. We all were, one might say, umpumpable.

It was clear to me then and there that this was the end of an era. This had been the last of the quantum leaps, and in that regard it was a landmark negotiation. It signaled the end of the huge "easy money" times in American sports television and, in that regard, it was long overdue. It was even clearer that ABC had not been dealt with fairly. Barry Frank can't have it both ways: He had told us in the morning on the day bidding opened that it would not get out of control, that negotiations were to be permissible under the ground rules; then, after the smoke had cleared that night, he told us that Samaranch would not go along with the original arrangements, and would permit only sealed bidding.

The Lausanne episode is a classic example of what can happen in any business when the whole world knows you are "balls out." One thing it taught us was to be much more careful a little later, when the IOC and the Seoul Organizing Committee opened discussions with the three networks about the 1988 Summer Games. I knew then and there that ABC would not be a major contender. But Barry Frank was also the television consultant to the Seoul Organizing Committee, and he was still playing that good old all-out, every-last-dollar IMG game.

In fact, Barry floated some talk on the street about Seoul getting $1 billion. He didn't fool anyone in the United States, but he deluded the poor Koreans about the supposedly unlimited supply of cash available from American television. Roone and I met several times to discuss the Seoul Games, and finally decided we should not even get involved unless and until there was some sensible and ironclad procedure set up for the disposition of the rights. I was stronger on that point than Roone. ABC Sports had become the prime source of revenue for the entire Olympic movement; in both television exposure and money terms, we had been almost single-handedly responsible for the success of the Games. We had made them a very attractive package, and I bristled at the thought of ABC being pushed around ever again.

There was a meeting in Seoul to discuss technical matters, but, as a way of making a stand, we decided not to send a delegation. It wasn't that I expected the IOC to suddenly come out in favor of ABC Sports; rather there had to be some consideration given to factors such as production expertise and promotional abilities, instead of just dollars. That's the real reason Barry Frank was personally in favor of ABC having the Olympic Games all along; he knew we could present and promote them better than anyone else.

The intelligent way to dispose of the rights would be to have an understanding between the IOC and a host city's organizing committee whereby broadcasters are assured up front that all of the pertinent factors will be weighed. In this manner, the IOC would be able to control its own destiny and not be beholden to numbers placed in envelopes by the American networks. I suggested that the bid procedure be thrown out in favor of preliminary negotiations with each network, followed by the selection of one network for continuing negotiation. If the negotiations succeeded, fine: A deal would be consummated. If the discussions bogged down, the committee then would move on to talk with the other networks. I put this concept to the IOC and the Seoul Organizing Committee in April 1984, was asked to define it in writing, and did so, and my letter did have an effect. There were no sealed bids, and, in essence, they followed our suggestions. We originally planned to avoid that April meeting, too, but had second thoughts and I went to Seoul as head of an ABC delegation. The Seoul Organizing Committee was then led by Roh Tae Woo, who was elected president of South Korea in December of 1987.

At that time, ABC had not made a determination whether we were going to take part in any negotiations for the Seoul Games. But we ended up agreeing to participate, after being categorically assured that the committee would not utilize the sealed-bid procedure it had used for Calgary. So, once again, in September 1985, all three networks packed up and headed for the Lausanne Palace Hotel.

The ABC delegation left New York with very specific guidelines, but not much stomach for what would take place. If I were asked, straight out, if we really wanted to televise the Seoul Games, I'd say yes, although I was far and away ABC's staunchest advocate. ABC had a number of reservations, which made our trip to Lausanne as much a courtesy to the IOC as anything else. Our top bid, on orders from our top brass, was going to be $225 million, plus $50 million nonguaranteed for cable telecasting rights—period. We knew there would be no way to get the rights for that kind of money, so, had it not been for slighting the IOC, we likely would not have gone at all. We believed CBS would not be much of a contender either, so that, if we had pulled a no-show, the IOC would have lost most of its leverage and conceivably would hold that against us in the future.

Our $225 million figure was in line with the rights fee for the 1984 Los Angeles Games, even though the coverage from Seoul could not possibly be as attractive for viewers or advertisers. The Los Angeles coverage was mainly live, as Calgary would be. Seoul's major events would be mainly tape-delayed or live in off-peak hours, which just isn't the same in the minds of either viewers or the advertising community. There was the additional factor that South Korea is not the most politically stable sector of the world, as we have seen in recent times, which could create problems that might be difficult or even impossible to surmount. Then, although an interesting choice for the Summer Olympics, Seoul was far from what you might call a romantic location.

All those factors brought us to the negotiations with a plan to play things very close to the vest, but another situation back home needed careful consideration as well. By then, the deal had been struck for Capital Cities Communications' friendly takeover of ABC. With a $3.5 billion merger staring us in the face, there was a natural uncertainty over Capital Cities' reaction to our programming commitments, and also about individual careers. We knew all about Cap Cities' reputation for being "lean and mean," and it was obviously no time to be dealing in excesses.

Fred Pierce, who had taken some tough and courageous stands during his presidency, made no bones about where we stood. He'd discussed the Seoul situation with the new Capital Cities people, because he thought he owed it to them. After all, it would be their burden or their joy come 1988. Pierce was quoted on this matter in the *Wall Street Journal,* and what he had to say made Barry Frank hit the ceiling. Barry beefed about Pierce doing a "prenegotiation mind-set thing" in public. After bitching to me about Pierce's comments over the telephone, Frank also put his complaints in a formal letter. Naturally, I sent the letter on to Pierce, and all it did was make him assume a tougher stance. There was no possible way he would let ABC go beyond the $225 million figure. Like Roone, he felt we had taken a royal screwing on Calgary. As the old saying goes, "Screw me once, shame on you; screw me twice, shame on me."

Each of the networks met with the IOC and the Seoul representatives, and our $225 million figure left us exactly where we thought it would—third and noncompetitive. That evening, as Roone and I chatted with some CBS officials in the bar near the lobby, all of us felt NBC was in the process of hammering out a deal. As it turned out, NBC was alienating the committee.

It was Barry Frank's street talk about a possible billion-dollar deal that had fouled the proceedings, by raising the Koreans' expectations way beyond what was feasible in the real world. The disappointed Koreans finally said they would settle for $750 million, but they might as well have demanded the moon. Eventually, they lowered their demands to $600 million, then came down another notch to $500 million, before at last proposing a guaranteed figure of $300 million with an "upside potential" of $600 million based on possible commercial revenues generated.

This was nothing more than a face-saving gesture on the part of the Koreans. That sort of thing is an absolute essential to the

Oriental mind, and the Seoul Committee needed a face-saver to take back to the people in Seoul and to the president of South Korea. This way, they could go back and say, "Well, the billion-dollar figure was merely pie-in-the-sky, but we wound up with the chance to make $600 million."

In my opinion, NBC made a huge mistake in not agreeing to that deal. Hell, the key figure was the $300 million guarantee. Beyond that, you could agree on any number you wanted so long as it was based strictly on revenue; the actual figure became a moot issue. In my judgment, NBC should have locked in a deal in Lausanne. But nothing was consummated, the Koreans and the IOC were upset, and, as it turned out, NBC nearly blew the whole package. It was decided there would be still another round of negotiations with each network back in New York.

I knew Roone Arledge would never attend that negotiating session, set for early October. He loves the thrill of victory but he cannot abide the agony of defeat. He basked in the glow of his own victories but, when we had to take our lumps at ABC, he absented himself. I am reminded of George C. Scott's sensitive portrayal of General George Patton in the film *Patton*. There was that stirring scene where Patton, addressing his troops before a momentous battle, told them—among other things—that Americans love a fight and love a winner, but will not tolerate a loser. That's Roone Arledge, in spades. You go ahead, if you want, and take the tired, poor, huddled masses. That'll be Roone you see riding off into the sunset. He's the guy in the white hat, the cowboy who gets the girl.

In any event, Arledge came up with one of what I've always called his "convenient priorities," we had our meeting without him, and we reaffirmed the financial proposal we had made in Lausanne. It was not enough then; it would not be enough now. But we surprised the committee with this unique new proposal: Why not consider a network pool, letting two or even three networks get involved with the televising of the Seoul Olympic Games? I think the committee was concerned about the possible negative impact of such an approach on its long-term rights fees. It was also a bit late in the game for the pool concept. In any event, we received no reply to our suggestion.

The Seoul Committee was so hung up on locking in the "upside potential" deal—those monies in excess of the $300 million guarantee—that it could not come up with an agreement with NBC. Finally, Barry Frank and Dick Pound called me and said the committee wanted still another meeting with ABC. We ended up with a telephone conversation rather than a face-to-face session. The upshot of it was that if ABC would go to the $300 million figure the deal would be plopped in our corporate lap. (Actually, Frank kept pleading with us to go to $310 million, obviously so he could show a $1 million increase over the Calgary deal.)

It was after nine o'clock when I got home that night. I had intended to call Fred Pierce at his home to discuss the committee's latest proposal. It was late, and I knew Pierce's mind-set on the matter, so I decided to catch him the next morning when he was fresh. At about 11:30 P.M., I had another idea and called Barry at home.

My counterproposal was this: Let's structure a deal with not only an upside potential, but one with a downside potential as well. If things go swimmingly, you'll get a whole lot more than the $300 million guarantee; if we have trouble selling the commercial time, your guarantee would slide down to, say, $275 million. Barry agreed that such a proposal might work. I told him I'd put it to Fred Pierce first thing the next morning.

The ABC president said, "Let me noodle this around a little bit, Jim. That's interesting. I'll get back to you." About half an hour later, Pierce called me back:

"It's no deal," he said. "I've thought about it, and we simply can't go for it. I have pledged to the Capital Cities people that we will not go beyond the $225 million figure for the network rights. The cable thing is a bit iffy, and under any circumstances we'd have to bump the network side and I just can't justify that. I appreciate what you are trying to do, but we're going to pass."

Immediately, I called Barry Frank and gave him the news. Later, I learned Barry went to CBS and tried to get them to go to $300 million, and got the same response. Neal Pilson, who was responsible for CBS Sports, couldn't reach then CBS chairman Tom Wyman, or CBS might have acquired the Seoul Games.

All the while, NBC was putting pressure on the committee to come up with a firm answer. With no other options left, the committee finally accepted the NBC deal for a guarantee of $300 million with an upside potential of $500 million, depending on the advertising revenues the telecasts generate.

The Koreans have about as much chance of seeing $500 million as you and I do of winning the Olympic decathlon. It just ain't gonna happen. Thus, for the first time in Olympic history, the money paid for United States television rights to the Summer Olympics will be less than that paid for the Winter Games in the same year.

Fred Pierce had some regrets about the Calgary business, mainly that he would not be at ABC to oversee matters:

"Our bid was based on intelligence, not happenstance. This was to be a good Olympiad from a lot of standpoints: It's on this continent, thus much of the coverage would be live; there would be expanded coverage in the right time zones; and we thought at the time the price escalation was justified if we went to $260 million or even to $270 million. Leonard Goldenson (then chairman of the board for ABC) happened by my office right at the critical time, and we discussed the $309 million bid. But I'm the one who triggered it.

"I knew, also, that we would not want to be seriously involved in the Seoul Olympic Games bidding. There could be no guarantee that this would be an Olympiad devoid of politics. Our track record in televising the Olympics was excellent. We had made money on all of them, and our owned and operated stations had made a lot of money, too, because of the commercial spots we made available to them. Sure, the economy has changed, but if you set a low watermark, that's likely to be just about where you will wind up.

"The new management [Capital Cities] seemed predisposed to losing a considerable amount of money on the Calgary games. [ABC Sports lost over $50 million.] They have that right, to write it off as a loss if they so choose. But you can't make money on something if you have already made up your mind that you are going to lose. I'm convinced that if our management were still there, we would not lose."

The earliest records of the Olympic Games tell the story of Pherenice, who wanted to see her son, Peisidoros, compete as an Olympic pugilist. But in those days, women were not permitted even to watch the competition. So the mother dressed in men's clothing, pretended to be her son's trainer, and was near his side when he won. She was so excited that she embraced and kissed him after his victory, and her disguise was made known. Pherenice was brought to trial, but she made such a strong and impassioned plea about motherhood and love that the judges ordered her released. However, at the same time, to guard against any further such intrusion, the judges ruled that all trainers would have to appear naked at the Games.

The ABC Sports team that did the negotiating for the Calgary Olympic Games centuries later could understand that feeling of nakedness, of being stripped bare, as it were.

Historians are not certain of the exact origins of the Olympic Games, but the first recorded Olympic Games took place in Greece in 776 B.C. It is known that the Games existed for more than a millennium, and that in the early days the winners were saluted by orators, poets, and musicians, received lavish gifts, were exempt from taxation, and were permitted to build monuments to themselves in their home cities. And we know that the ancient Greeks and Romans fought terribly over the Olympic Games. The Greeks accused the Romans of allowing their champions to capitalize financially on their fame. The Romans retaliated by setting fire to the buildings used to house the Olympic athletes, and by destroying everything they could in the vicinity of the Olympic stadium.

The squabbling got so far out of hand that Emperor Theodosius of Rome declared the Games a public nuisance and barred them after 394 A.D.

The Games would not be revived for more than fifteen hundred years.

Sometimes—not often, but once in a while—I know just how old Theodosius must have felt.

3

SURVIVAL FIRST, LEADERSHIP LATER

The Seat-of-the-Pants School of Broadcasting

ABC Sports stands today as a monument to Roone Arledge.

I have only one quarrel with that: Some other names should be on the monument, and the name at the top of it should be that of Ed Scherick.

Ed Scherick founded Sports Programs, Inc., the predecessor organization to ABC Sports, in the late 1950s. He remembers precisely how it evolved and, in turn, created ABC's "Wide World of Sports":

"I had been with an advertising agency and I had saved a little money. I was involved with Falstaff beer and had helped put together the first 'Game of the Week' in baseball, and it just seemed the time was right for me to step out on my own. In those days, CBS Sports was run like a country club under the auspices of the news department. ABC had no sports at all. NBC pretty much had it all—the Rose Bowl, the World Series, and Gillette in their hip pocket as a sponsor. The first guy I brought into the organization was Jack Lubell. He'd been at CBS but was looking to get out. A little later on, I met Chet Simmons and brought him into the organization. We had an office on Forty-second Street in New York and we were all crammed in there together, throwing ideas around, arguing and shouting—my God, Jack Lubell and I had some awful shouting matches—but we kept coming up with shows for the networks. Then we did Big Ten basketball on a sort of Midwest network. That's when we hired Jack, to produce and direct the basketball package.

"Roone Arledge came over to us in 1960. I went over to the NBC television station in New York to check out a show called 'For Men Only.' While I was there, a friend introduced me to Arledge. He was producing local shows, mainly kids' stuff. He had a puppet show, as I recall. We struck up a conversation and he seemed bright enough. Not long after that, we obtained the rights to the Saturday night fights and were going after NCAA football.

"How we got that is an amazing story. I knew Tom Gallery, who ran NBC Sports, like the back of my hand. I knew he'd go into the NCAA meeting prepared for anything. He'd be carrying two separate bids in two separate envelopes. If he was pretty certain no one would be bidding against him, he'd pull out the smaller bid. So I sent an innocuous-looking guy named Stan Frankle over with our bid. I told him to hang around in the room and sort of look inconspicuous, which was easy for Stan. If anyone asked who he was, he was instructed not to lie, but he also was told not to volunteer anything. Stan was carrying two envelopes, too. He was under orders to present the smaller bid in the event CBS didn't enter the bidding, the larger one if CBS got into the game. As it turned out, CBS didn't bid, Gallery went in with his lower bid, and we beat him and stole college football right out from under NBC. Somehow, I knew our low envelope would be higher than NBC's low bid.

"That meant we needed more manpower, and that's when I hired Arledge. We paid him ten thousand that first year.

"We also had a bowling show and Jim Spence worked on that one. We needed an accordion show—you know, one with some elasticity in it—to go on following our Saturday night boxing. Johnny Johnston was a pretty good entertainer, a singer and a sort of half-assed movie star. He had an interest in bowling since his mother had been a professional bowler, so we figured he'd be a good announcer for a show called 'Make That Spare.' We did it right across the river from New York City in Paramus, New Jersey, and it was a pretty damned good little show. It set the stage for the 'Pro Bowlers Tour,' which, except for 'Wide World of Sports,' is the longest continuing sports show on ABC.

"As for 'Wide World of Sports,' it began in the spring of 1961. We were doing a game of the week, but, back then, baseball was confined to the area that you might call the North and the Midwest. There was no baseball in many parts of the country, and we had to black out the cities that had big-league ball. I thought we should come up with some programming for the other half of the country. My idea was to replay some sporting event that wasn't so dominant that it had been in every newspaper headline. First items I thought of were the Drake Relays and the Penn Relays. Back then, no one gave much of a damn about track and field, and I thought there'd be enough interest to justify a show. It wasn't some brilliant stroke of insight that caused me to come up with the idea for the show, but more a matter of economic necessity. Sports Programs had a contract to produce and negotiate all of ABC's sports shows, and, while Arledge and Lubell and the others were my employees, they were in effect functioning as the ABC network sports department. I told ABC we needed a show that could go everywhere on the weekends, and that's how 'Wide World of Sports' was born. Chet Simmons is the man who came up with the title, although I think he might have lifted a little bit of it from NBC, which had something called 'Wide Wide World' at that time.

"The first place we went to negotiate was with the Amateur Athletic Union. The AAU had all the power in amateur sports back then, and I figured we could get in on the ground floor on televising some of their events, and that's exactly what happened. But I'm a Jew, and, since there was still a great deal of prejudice at that time and since Arledge is a Gentile, I sent him in to do the negotiating. I remember early meetings with Tug Wilson, who was commissioner of the Big Ten back then. You couldn't find a Jew anywhere in the Big Ten, so I'd wait outside and send Roone inside to make the deal. That's how we came up with the Russian-American track meet, all because we got our foot in the door first with the AAU.

"When we did an event, we'd take just a handful of people with us—the announcers, the producer, the director, and maybe one or two others—and we'd hire a control truck from the local station in the area and use their cameramen and their technical director. One time, we were doing a basketball game at Michigan State and the truck had to come from Lansing to East Lansing, no more than a couple of miles. A station called WJIM was supplying the truck and the cameras, and we probably paid them a thousand dollars or fifteen hundred. Well, it was getting late and still there was no truck in sight, and I was getting panicky. Jack Lubell was directing, so I sent him up the road toward Lansing and told him to call me back at the motel the minute he spotted the truck. Finally, the truck showed up, two hours late.

"That was just the start of our troubles. We had to beam the game to the roof of the telephone company, which was using that as a pickup point to put our feed onto the phone line. All of a sudden, the generator on the roof of the phone company went out, and we lost the picture. I literally helped carry another generator to the roof of that building. Looking back, I suppose they were the good old days, but most of the time I think of them as mostly very hairy days.

"Back then, there were only forty-five million television homes in the whole country. Now there are about ninety million. Just think of it."

Ed Scherick was amazing for exploring, conceiving, creating, producing, acquiring rights, and doing all of it lots of times on sheer guts. Then he just walked away from it a few years after he had started Sports Programs, Inc., selling the company to ABC for a reported $1 million in ABC stock. (Later he would become a successful movie and television producer.)

"I just walked out," he said, "and never walked back through those doors again."

Why?

"Because I was moving on to something else. It was a part of my life that was finished. I never regretted it. I never looked back. The only thing I regret is Roone Arledge's attitude toward the history of this business, and you can quote me on that. Roone has never once given credit to anyone else, in any way, shape, or form. And this is something I've told him many times. He takes all the credit for himself. He just shrugs and claims it's not his fault. He says people just keep writing those things."

Chet Simmons would carve out an outstanding career for himself. As a young man, he was in advertising, then joined Scherick and Lubell for seventy-five dollars a week. He moved to NBC in 1964, went from there to head up the all-sports cable network, ESPN, then became the first commissioner of the United States Football League. He has vivid memories of the early days at Sports Programs/ABC:

"At the beginning, there were just the three of us—Scherick, Lubell, and myself—and I was low man on the totem pole. Then the late Jim Colligan came aboard, and Barney Nagler helped out on our boxing shows. We worked in conjunction with a real legend in the business, Dick Bailey. He had been at ABC and went out on his own, leasing facilities to anyone wanting to do programming. He and Scherick were a dandy pair, Scherick getting the rights and producing shows, and Bailey's company providing the mobile units and doing all the networking to set up the regional outlets. We flew by the seats of our pants lots of time. Lubell did the producing and directing and I did whatever else needed to be done. I was just a kid. I'd spent three years in the service and one year in an advertising agency, I had a young wife, and I was in seventh heaven just to be working in television.

"Scherick was one of the most brilliant people I have ever known. Lubell was technically very creative. It was wild just being around them; they were the original 'odd couple.' They constantly fought, and here I was, this young kid, sort of refereeing their battles. But through it all they had enormous respect for each other, even though I remember one time when Lubell literally lifted Scherick off the floor with his hands around Ed's neck. I thought Jack was going to kill him, because all the while Scherick was making these gurgling noises with his tongue hanging out. Finally, Jack let him go and said, 'Don't worry about it. But we *will* take care of this later.' I don't even recall what they were battling about because they were always scrapping, but it wouldn't have shocked me if murder had been committed. It was an incredible time in the history of television sports. It really was the beginning of it all.

"As I look back, they were fighting to survive. NBC was comfortable with baseball and bowl games, CBS was just like a country club with the Masters and the NFL, and ABC had nothing. Perhaps the smartest move Ed Scherick made was to forge a relationship with Tom Moore, who became president of the ABC Television Network. Tom was one hell of a sports fan. Another guy Scherick worked with was Oliver Treyz, who was president before Moore. Ed also deserves a lot of credit for seeing the opportunity ABC had.

"I remember the time we were all gathered in Tom Moore's office waiting to see if Stan Frankle got NCAA football. It seemed like we'd waited forever and we thought the telephone call from Stan Frankle would never come. When it did, and he told us we got the package, we just went nuts. Here we were, this little company, and suddenly we had two major pieces of business, since 'Wide World of Sports' was about to start.

"Those early days were the most exciting times of my life. One time, I had to leave the office early because my wife was about to have a baby, and Scherick began screaming at me, 'You can't possibly leave now. You just cannot leave here.' I left anyway, and my wife gave birth to our first child, a little girl, and Scherick sent over a blue bunny. Later, I told him that blue was for boys and pink was for girls. Some years later, when we had our second child, a boy, that silly-assed Scherick sent us a pink bunny. He was a madman.

"Jim McKay was at CBS doing a show called 'The Verdict Is Yours,' and we brought him over—which turned out to be a pretty good move, wouldn't you say? Roone Arledge deserves a lot of credit for all he did in those days; he played a very specific part, a big role. But Ed Scherick was the guy who got all those early things accomplished, and he did it by hard work and sheer brilliance. He just wouldn't take no for an answer. He was a bulldog. He'd work all day, every day, and then he'd work far into the night. I went to bed each night with a pad of paper and a pencil next to me, because you never knew when he was going to call you. He was crazy but he was wildly brilliant."

Chet Simmons is a nice, talented man who has never been given proper credit, either, for his pioneering contributions to sports broadcasting. Had he been more of a street-fighter, he would still be at ABC Sports. Although as far as I know, Simmons never publicly complained about it or discussed it, he allowed Roone Arledge to steamroller him. Roone quickly moved in and became the darling of Tom Moore, and everybody knew it. Tom Moore deserves a tremendous amount of credit for his unyielding support during the formative years of ABC Sports. The foundation that he made possible led to ABC Sports becoming the industry leader.

The empire Arledge helped build is a far cry from the early days, when everyone was flying by the seat of his pants much of the time and the ability to see humor in troublesome situations was critical to survival. Some of the craziest moments occurred during the early days of the old American Football League. For instance, there was the game from the Cotton Bowl in Dallas involving the old Dallas Texans. Jack Lubell was producing the telecast and Jack Buck was doing the play-by-play. They started the telecast, Buck set the scene for the game, then led to a commercial. During the commercial, Lubell looked up at the bank of television monitors in the control truck and noticed that the kicker was approaching the ball and the game was about to start. Lubell slammed down his headset and raced from the truck all the way onto the field. Meanwhile, Abner Haynes had fielded the kickoff and was being tackled. Lubell charged up to Haynes, grabbed the football out of his hands, and ran it over to the referee where he shouted:

"You cocksucker, never again kick off until I tell you you can kick off! Do you understand? Now go and do it again!"

Meantime, the commercial break had ended and we were back on the air, where the cameras were showing the confusion on the field. Buck handled it beautifully. He said, "Ladies and gentlemen, we are back live at the Cotton Bowl in Dallas and, unfortunately, we have an irate fan who has run out onto the field and is creating a disturbance." And, of course, the AFL, ever cooperative, kicked off a second time as if nothing had happened.

We did those AFL telecasts for five years until Sonny Werblin, who later would run the New York Jets, got involved in the negotiations and talked NBC into putting up $36 million. At the time, that was a little rich for our blood, so we passed. Joe Foss, who was AFL commissioner at the time, made a confidential call to us, offering one last shot, but we again passed.

Jack Lubell, now retired, remembered a less-than-smooth Big Ten basketball telecast at Bloomington, Indiana, in the very early days:

"We had gone to bed at the end of an absolutely beautiful day, and woke up to find a foot of snow on the ground. The storm prevented the regular Big Ten officials from getting to the game, so we rounded up a couple of high-school officials and explained how we did things, how we had certain signals for commercials, and so forth. We told them we'd have a guy with a flashlight in the broadcast booth and he'd signal them when we wanted a time out, in order to get in our commercials. Well, either they didn't pay attention or they just ignored us, because the whole deal went haywire. I don't know, maybe they just panicked. Anyway, I was yelling my lungs out in the truck, and the referees were out on the court apparently not giving a damn about our commercials. So I sent one of our assistants onto the court with orders to 'just grab 'em and tell those sons of bitches to wait until they see the light.' Hell, one of the officials threw my guy right off the floor. We finally got things straightened around, but it was murder for a while around there."

Well, back in 1964 it was hell for a while during the telecast of the USA-USSR Track and Field Meet from Los Angeles. Roone Arledge was in charge of the telecast, I was the field events producer, and a very competent professional, Lou Frederick, was my associate director. At a critical moment during the telecast, Roone called for us to roll some prerecorded coverage of the shot put. It didn't roll. Roone called for it a second time, in a voice a bit more stern. I was passing along the instructions to Lou. Again, no tape of the shot put. Finally, Roone yelled:

"Where's the goddamned tape?"

I was screaming at Lou, asking him why the tape wasn't rolling.

At last, Lou responded in calm, measured tones, "It is not rolling because the tape machine is *on fire.*"

Our early college football experiences were at times equally confusing. We hired a couple of announcers who became one of the greatest football broadcast teams in history. Curt Gowdy and Paul Christman were the perfect pair, Gowdy with his strong play-by-play performance, and Christman with terrific analysis and a great sense of humor.

The first game we did—in 1960—was between Alabama and Georgia with Fran Tarkenton, who later would work for ABC Sports, quarterbacking for Georgia. The madcap Scherick just about drove Gowdy, Christman, Arledge and everyone else crazy with his antics. Never quiet, he'd race back and forth between the mobile unit where Roone, who was producing the telecast, and the others were trying to call the shots, and the booth where Gowdy and Christman were trying to call the game. It was so bad that, before our third telecast, Gowdy and Christman met with Roone and threatened to quit if Scherick didn't stay out of their hair. Roone didn't want Ed in the mobile unit, either, and told him how critical it was for him not to interfere. Still, Scherick showed up at Lawrence, Kansas, for the next game. Unwelcome in the booth, an intrusion in the truck, he became frantic as he tried to find a place where he could watch the telecast. Finally, he wandered into a nearby building on campus, saw an open office with a television set, and promptly made himself at home. He turned on the set, propped his feet on the desk, and was fretting about the coverage of the game when another man appeared at the door and said, "Excuse me, sir?"

Ed said, "Be quiet."

"Excuse me, sir."

"Be quiet," Scherick sharply told him. "Can't you see I'm trying to watch this telecast?"

The other guy stood his ground. "Excuse me!" he replied, "but I'm Dutch Lonborg, and I'm the athletic director here at Kansas, and *you,* sir, are sitting in *my* office!"

My first meeting with Scherick occurred in late summer of 1960. I had graduated from Dartmouth, having majored in Spanish with a dream of becoming a foreign correspondent or a sportswriter, but had made a two-year detour as an infantry lieutenant at Fort Benning, Georgia. The first year in uniform I was a public information officer, and they put me in charge of the Battle Group basketball team. I'd played freshman ball at Dartmouth under Coach Al McGuire, and maybe they figured some of his genius might have rubbed off on me. It hadn't, but I had the chance to play on an Army team with Hal Greer, who had been a star at Marshall University and later had an outstanding career in the NBA with Philadelphia. It was while I was in the Army that I met Lynn Chapman, who was to become my wife.

When my Army tour was up in July 1960, I headed for New York to seek a job. I had grown up in Eastchester and Armonk, New York, and my home state was the natural place to look for work. I had interviews with The Associated Press, *Sports Illustrated*, and the *New York Times*, and when they all agreed I wasn't quite ready to set the world on fire as a writer, my uncle, A. W. (Budd) Spence, Jr., who was a senior executive at a New York advertising agency, phoned one of his pals at CBS, Tom Dawson, on my behalf. Dawson set me up with Bill MacPhail, then the head of CBS Sports. I didn't hook on there right away, but they offered me a job for the fall when they'd be getting back into their NFL coverage. But that same day, they thought it would be good for me to meet a young production assistant who was already working there. As soon as I entered his little office, he pulled me aside and half-whispered, "Jim, if you want to get into sports, CBS isn't the place for you. You ought to try and hook up with ABC. They're the people who are going to be putting a lot of emphasis on sports. That's the place to be." Even before he told me his name, I recognized him as a former All-American basketball player at Columbia, Chet Forte. It was arranged for me to meet with Bill Mullen, who was in charge of sales at ABC, and he, in turn, directed me to Ed Scherick at Sports Programs, Inc.

When the time came for my appointment two days later, Scherick let me sit in the outer office for forty-five minutes before he yelled for me to join him. I walked into his office in a condition somewhere between nervousness and terror, with the edge going to terror. I carried with me clippings from my days as sports editor of the campus newspaper at Dartmouth, and work I had done as a stringer for AP and the *Times*. After a few minutes, he noticed the packet.

"What's all that stuff?"

"Well, those are some clippings I brought . . ."

"I don't give a damn about those clippings. Put 'em away."

I put them away.

We chatted for a time, but kept getting interrupted by telephone calls. He had two phones on his desk and sometimes he'd be on both of them at once. Finally, he looked hard at me and asked, "Are you sure you want to work here?"

I told him I did, and he then explained that he needed a production assistant to work on postgame shows for college football and pro football under producer Jim Colligan. I was so excited I didn't even ask him what a production assistant did.

"Now, this isn't a permanent job," Scherick warned. "We're hiring you for the football season, and we're gonna pay you sixty-five dollars a week. Understand?"

I understood. But I had a job nonetheless. I was then instructed to meet with Scherick's assistant, Chet Simmons, who asked me when I wanted to start. I told him I was ready right then. He suggested I get a bite to eat, then come back after lunch. I did, and stayed more than twenty-five years.

So what did I do as a production assistant? All I knew about television was that if you turned on the set, most of the time you got a picture, and at first my work at Sports Programs was commensurate with that knowledge. I changed the water in the old copying machines of the era. I made reservations for our crews, arranged tickets for sponsors and agencies, on weekends helped set up the postgame shows for our football telecasts, and worked as a gofer on "Make That Spare." I also toted Scherick's luggage from the office to his apartment when he'd come in from a road trip. Television sports was an industry in its infancy, I sensed we were embarking on exciting times, and through all the menial tasks I remained thrilled to be a part of it (as I still am). I was less than adroit at making reservations, since I hadn't really traveled much at that point in my life. The long and short of it is that I booked Gowdy and Christman into some god-awful hotels. Indeed, if Gowdy walked through my door right now he'd call me Fleabag, which is the name he and the late Christman hung on me—Fleabag Spence—because of the terrible dives I booked for them.

The ABC network was in a heap of trouble back then. Those were difficult times in the areas of both entertainment and news, and on top of that ABC was dwarfed by both CBS and NBC in its number of affiliated stations. Until Scherick came along, no one had much faith in anything, but Ed gave ABC something to crow about. Tom Moore and Leonard Goldenson, who was president then and later became chairman of the board, deserve a lot of credit for having confidence enough to take the kind of chance they did with Sports Programs. Or maybe it was just plain guts born of desperation.

Chuck Howard came along at the same time I did. He had been in a management-training program for a career in banking, but from the beginning was production-oriented. He's a bright man with a wealth of knowledge about sports and with good journalistic instincts. We competed with each other for acceptance, for attention, and, yes, for Roone's favor. Through the years, Chuck and I did battle many times, and occasionally in very loud voices, but through it all we maintained a healthy respect for each other that holds firm to this day. Early on, Chuck got promoted more rapidly than I did and acquired a lot of power in production, wielding great influence particularly over the assignment of producers and directors and announcers—always with Roone's authorization—and eventually becoming vice president.

As much admiration as I have for Chuck as a producer—and I never met anyone more in command during a live telecast—I had strong concerns about the way he dealt with people. Howard has a tendency to be insensitive, and it made him some definite enemies along the way, along with damaging his career at ABC Sports. He was hurt when he was not appointed senior vice president of production (which role went to Dennis Lewin), and left after Dennis Swanson took over from Arledge as president of ABC Sports in 1986. Chuck's style as a producer was to shout and intimidate people, but in the main he was able to put it all behind him once the show was over. Chuck was a mighty important figure in the growth and development of ABC Sports, and no one in sports television has produced more major-event telecasts than he has.

Chet Forte was to become a major figure at ABC Sports. It took him three years to heed his own advice to me and "go to ABC." Chet, a 5'8½" guard, was a first team All-American alongside Kansas's Wilt Chamberlain. Chet is unsurpassed as a director, with a keen sense of timing and excellent sports knowledge, and Roone Arledge allowed him to "march to his own drummer" in terms of the assignments and compensation he received. In both cases, Chet was given favorable treatment beyond what was good for the department or Chet himself, causing jealousy and resentment among his peers.

The two acquisitions of talent that most influenced the early success of ABC Sports were Jim McKay and Chris Schenkel. While McKay has become a major star, the fact remains that Schenkel is the man who gave ABC instant credibility in the marketplace. Chris was a major broadcasting figure in New York in those days. He was the voice of the New York Giants; he was doing television, including the Masters golf tournament and horse racing, for CBS; he was doing Monitor Radio for NBC; local sports shows for the ABC station in New York, and bowling for ABC Television on a free-lance basis. Chris was everywhere, and when ABC landed him, it landed a man and a voice who was not only well known to, but very popular with, sponsors and advertising agencies in New York.

Here are a few Chris Schenkel memories of those early days:

"I had gone to New York in 1952 and a lot of good things had happened to me by the time I hooked up with ABC. I'd done the Monday night fights, the Giants on television, and in all I guess I did eight NFL title games and it seemed the Giants were in just about all of them. The most memorable, of course, was the 1958 title game between the Giants and the Baltimore Colts. I think somehow that ushered in a new awareness and a new importance in sports. Tex Maule wrote in *Sports Illustrated* that that game was the greatest one ever played. It caught everybody's fancy, and right away you could sense a new attitude. There's no question that this game was the beginning of a new level of acceptance for pro football. To my recollection, this was the first time earplugs were used to open a communications link between the producer or director and the announcer. Thereafter, some producers and directors overused that system; I think they must have been frustrated announcers because they'd yammer away constantly at you.

"My coming to ABC was a combination of Roone Arledge wanting me and the CBS brass being out of town. Roone was a big New York Giants fan, and I'd met him casually when he was at the old Dumont network and I was doing the Monday night fights over there. He called and offered me a hundred twenty-five thousand dollars a year to come to ABC. I was making seventy-five thousand dollars at CBS and I tried to get CBS to match his offer. Jim Aubrey was CBS president then, but he was out of town and no one else would make the decision. I thought about all the things I'd be giving up, and then I thought about how much more I could do for my family with all that money. I went for the dollars. Besides, Roone had guaranteed me I'd be back doing football within a year. That's the one promise he kept.

"I was, well, I guess you could say I was Roone's fair-haired boy for quite a while, maybe until the early seventies when he started chipping away at my assignments, taking me off college football and golf. No one remembers, but I was the anchorman at the Munich Olympics in 1972, and that's when Roone started gushing all over Jim McKay. For a long time then, he had a crush on McKay. I don't mean that in a nasty way, but Roone always played favorites and McKay became his boy. That lasted for a while until Frank Gifford gained his favor. I've never spoken out about it, but the truth is that Roone downgraded me every time he got a chance. I'm the guy who took him to the Masters, who took him to his first Indianapolis 500 and helped him get the television rights from my good friend, the late Tony Hulman. I took him to the Kentucky Derby and introduced him to the late Wathen Knebelkamp, and I know that paved the way for ABC to later get in solidly there. And I'm the guy who introduced him to

Pete Rozelle over lunch at '21.' Roone Arledge is a man with a damned short memory."

Chris Schenkel is one of the best friends I've ever made in this business. He took me under his wing when I was a young production assistant and could not have been nicer to me. He showed me a lot of the ropes I needed to learn and has never been anything but a gentleman to all who encounter him. Few people know how much he did for ABC Sports in its struggle to do battle with the other networks on an equal footing.

4

THE THRILL OF VICTORY . . . THE AGONY OF DEFEAT

The Incredible Story of "ABC's Wide World of Sports"

"Spanning the globe to bring you the constant variety of sport. . . . The thrill of victory and the agony of defeat. . . . The human drama of athletic competition. . . . This is 'ABC's Wide World of Sports.'"

It isn't quite up there with the one that begins, "Four score and seven years ago . . ." And it is not to be confused with that other one: "In the beginning, etc."

But it has held up remarkably well, this description that signals the beginning of the longest-running and most successful sports anthology series in the history of television. It's closing in now on three decades—which isn't bad for a series launched as a stop-gap summer fill-in show on Saturday, April 29, 1961, and one whose very debut was up in the air until a teetering sponsor gave it a thumbs-up sign just twenty-eight days before it was due to air. (Roone Arledge and host Jim McKay collaborated in changing the original "Wide World of Sports" billboard to those familiar words spoken at the beginning and end of each "Wide World" program since 1962.)

ABC's "Wide World of Sports" has changed the face of television, and brought more meaning and depth and awareness and knowledge of sports to the average viewer than anyone could have imagined. It is one of the main reasons ABC has garnered more than twice as many Emmy awards as CBS and NBC combined. And yet, not even the most optimistic soul at the network would have bet a dime that the series would survive its original twenty-week plan, and saliva tests would have been ordered for anyone bold enough to predict that it would celebrate its silver anniversary with ample ratings and solid sponsor support.

Had a tobacco company's answer been no instead of yes, none of this would have come about. ABC founder Leonard Goldenson had given us his blessing to proceed back in 1961. We had set a deadline for selling the program, and literally only hours before the deadline did the R. J. Reynolds Tobacco Company call in the order for the commercial time that made it happen.

The embryo of the program was the brainchild of Ed Scherick. It was his idea to present to the American public a series of lesser-known, or little-known, sports events. Not everything had to be football, baseball, basketball, or hockey, he reasoned. There was a category right below that, and he felt that by introducing people to the myriad of events within it, taking place all around the world, we could give a unique flavor to the show. Scherick, then, was responsible for the concept; Arledge deserves credit for executing it.

Chuck Howard was then a production assistant, and Roone instructed him to come up with a list that included whatever sporting events were scheduled on a week-to-week basis. Chuck made an exhaustive study of the *New York Times* and ended up with a huge list. With this in hand, Sports Programs, Inc., went about the business of acquiring rights.

A word of explanation may be in order here about how the sports television business works. The first step is to acquire "rights." Today the acquisition process is normally accomplished through negotiations, or bidding, through the organization that holds the rights. Back then, as has been the case over the years, there was no bidding for the unique events seen on "Wide World of Sports." Not too many people were interested in competing for the rights to televise, for instance, the Japanese League All-Star Baseball Game, or the Masters Waterskiing Championships in Georgia.

One time, we were asked to bid on the U.S. National Open Table Tennis Championships and were given a *firm* deadline by which we were to submit our proposal. Neither we, nor CBS or NBC, responded to the organizers; we then got a second letter informing us that the original deadline had been extended. So much for bidding!

Network television sports is financed, like all other network programming, by the sale of commercial time to the advertising community. (Increasingly, the financial burden is being shifted from the networks to organizing groups in order to insure the viability of the programming. Organizers are either required to guarantee sponsor support or are purchasing time periods from the networks.) The rights having been obtained and a date/time period established for the telecast, the network sets a commercial unit price and begins attempting to sell the event, or the show. Generally, there are ten minutes of network commercial time per hour allocated for national sale during weekend daytime programs (additional time is set aside for sale by the local stations affiliated with the network). Each of the major networks today has over two hundred affiliated stations, and these "affiliates" are asked to carry, or "clear," all the network shows; although, except for the affiliates that are owned and operated by the networks, this isn't mandatory. Affiliates are paid by the networks for carrying network programming, and also can sell their own commercials in "station breaks."

With the networks, and local stations as well, ratings translate into money. Generally speaking, the ability to sell a show depends almost entirely on its potential ratings, which means the number of people likely to watch it across the nation. A rating is the percentage of the total number of television homes in the United States. For example, there are presently approximately 89 million television homes in the country, thus a 10.0 rating means that about 8.9 million homes were tuned in to that particular program. When you hear or read about the "share" of audience being a 25, it means that 25 percent of those watching television at that particular time were watching the show. The higher a projected rating, the more a network can charge for a commercial. If a projected rating level isn't attained, advertisers receive something known as "make goods," either in the form of free commercial units or, in some cases, cash rebates.

Commercial sales, after deduction for the advertising agency's commission, provide the revenue stream to cover overhead, acquire rights, produce the programs, pay the affiliated stations, and make a dollar. Television is no different from any other businesses in that the intent is for revenue to handsomely exceed costs. That's called "profit."

When "Wide World of Sports" got off to a faltering start, Tom Moore, then vice president of programming for ABC, bravely predicted the anthology series would offer viewers coverage of the widest variety of sports events ever presented on television. There was a time, early on, when Moore and Arledge were meeting with an advertising agency and a potential sponsor and Moore was pitching a sale.

"It's a fantastic event," he enthused. "I mean, it's really unbelievable. It's over in Paris, and these cars race right around and through the Arc de Triomphe. It's terrific."

He made just the slightest bobble. He was pitching an automobile race when, in fact, the event was a horse race of great tradition in France, the Prix de l'Arc de Triomphe.

But most of those early pitches worked. And ABC came up with off-beat events like cliff-diving and rugby, surfing, sky-diving and figure-eight stock-car racing, barrel-jumping and baton-twirling. We even covered a rattlesnake hunt in Oklahoma. Hurling is the national game of Ireland, but Americans didn't know that until we put it on "Wide World of Sports." That part about the "constant variety of sport" led us to include competition on skates and skateboards, trampolines and dog-sleds. The mixture included kick-boxers, rock-climbers, cowboys and chess players, cricketeers and Sumo wrestlers, firemen and Little Leaguers. American audiences learned that the behavior of the English who play cricket is not always cricket, and that Australian Rules football is about as close to street brawling as one can get without ending up in jail. The ground rules were simple: If something is visually exciting, let's try it.

Events like these were never the principal focus of "Wide World," but they added a distinctive flavor to the program: They were fun, people enjoyed them, and they were good for the network's bottom line. The backbone of "Wide World of Sports" was, and continues to be, major events in significant international sports. For example, we televised world championships in figure skating, gymnastics, skiing, and boxing, in addition to covering major auto races, world-title fights, the Harlem Globetrotters, and in recent years leading endurance events—the Ironman Triathlon in Hawaii and the Bicycle Race Across America. Our intent was to air these competitions live or as soon as possible after they occurred. And, of course, as "Wide World" became more and more successful, the other networks tried harder and harder to copy the show.

We could have obtained for nothing the rights to many of the "minor" events we aired, but we almost always paid something, even though it was often as little in the early days as five hundred dollars. We insisted on paying, even when the rights were offered free, in order to attempt to maintain cooperation on the part of the organizers. We got a lot of events because of the autonomy we enjoyed at ABC Sports. We could make decisions and move quickly. NBC Sports was under the control of the news department, and CBS Sports in those days had recently become a separate entity, having been under the aegis of CBS News. We had no red tape back then. Technically, we were the training ground for many of the developments we now take for granted. We used underwater cameras for swimming and diving; we buried a camera in the ground to get better shots in covering the Cheyenne Frontier Days Rodeo; we put cameras in airplanes and helicopters to get better pictures of the National Air Races.

We even filmed in a flowerpot. Robert Riger, who was a producer-director, having achieved great prominence as a sports photographer and artist, was an expert on fires. During the filming of the twenty-four hours of Le Mans automobile race, in France, there was a major accident on a long straightaway portion of the course, the Mulsanne straight, but Riger had none of his cameras stationed in the vicinity. When he screened the film back in New York, Bob sensed that missing that crash robbed the story of some of its drama and excitement. So, working in his apartment in New York, he decided to recreate the accident, using miniature cars in a flowerpot! He put a match to the cars and filmed the blaze, then edited the footage right into the "Wide World of Sports" segment—where, to be truthful, it looked pretty good.

Riger is the guy who was known around our office as the only man to produce a show in which a tobogganer rode his socks off. Bob showed a competitor at the top of the run, but when the supposed same rider zoomed across the finish line, his socks were of a different color—a dead giveaway that Riger had used two different contestants.

It was on "Wide World" that we first saw Roone Arledge's emphasis on the personalities involved in the events and his increased use of people-oriented commentary; it was the beginning of ABC's way of doing things, "Up close and personal."

There was innovation on the very first show. We went live from two different events, the Penn Relays at Franklin Field in Philadelphia, and the Drake Relays in Des Moines, Iowa. Only weeks before the premiere, Tom Moore christened the show "ABC's World of Sports." The "Wide" part was added six days before the show aired. Jim McKay hosted that first telecast as he covered the Penn Relays, where there had been so much rain that half the cameras couldn't operate because of wet cables. The Drake Relays marked the first of over 600 "Wide World" assignments for Bill Flemming, a significant contributor to the success of ABC Sports for many years. Bill worked the Drake relays with Jim Simpson. I was part of that first telecast, and screwed up my first assignment.

I was a production assistant for the Drake Relays part of the show, which was being produced by Jack Lubell. He had gone to Iowa several days early to set things up, but before leaving he had dictated the format for the show to his secretary, and I was under orders to bring it with me when I came.

71

The airlines back then were about as efficient as they are now. I put the format in my luggage; the luggage got lost; I arrived in Des Moines without luggage and, of course, without format. I also left Des Moines with a part of my ass missing—chewed out by Jack Lubell.

"Check luggage only if you absolutely have to," Lubell screamed at me, "and make certain never to put anything important in it. Always carry with you the things that are important."

I needed just one more hard lesson before I got it down pat.

We planned to cover the British Open on "Wide World of Sports" in July of 1961. The tournament was scheduled to conclude on Friday, but there had been heavy rains at Royal Birkdale in Southport, on the northwestern coast of England, and play was postponed. Jim Simpson, our announcer, did a report on the rain and interviewed Arnold Palmer about it standing alongside the eighteenth green. My job was to pick up the videotape at the BBC studios in London where the interview had been recorded, race to the airport, and get the tape back to New York for showing on "Wide World of Sports" the following day. The flight was to take us from London to Shannon in Ireland, then to Boston, and finally on to New York.

When the plane stopped in Shannon, everyone else raced into the duty-free shop. Suddenly, I remembered my Des Moines fiasco and Jack Lubell's screamed advice. Yep, I'd done it again: checked the goodies with my luggage. When I explained my concerns to an airline official, he was good enough to let me go into the baggage section and retrieve the videotape, which I never let out of my grasp the rest of the way. Nevertheless, both of us almost didn't make it.

About an hour and a half out over the Atlantic Ocean from Shannon, a steward wakened me and insisted on giving me a life vest, which he ordered me to put on. The plane was lurching around, violently out of control, and I immediately knew we were going to crash. The steward seemed to agree with me, judging from the way he was acting. He explained the problem as a "runaway propeller." That did not do a whole lot to alleviate my terror.

The pilot somehow got the craft under control, turned it around, and headed it back toward Ireland. We dropped to an altitude of fifteen hundred feet, dumped most of our fuel, and ships in the area were monitoring our progress. Fortunately, we made it to Shannon, where airline officials told us they'd try to secure another aircraft but had no idea how long that might take. Another man and I decided to hurry back to London to try to find a different route to the United States. I then called our British Open producer, Bill Bennington, in England, told him what had happened, and he said he would ask the BBC to help get me on a flight to New York.

The airport in London was a mess. BOAC was on strike and there were masses of people milling about everywhere. I confess I was somewhat rude, but I shoved my way to the front of a long line to reach a Pan Am representative. The woman recognized my name and told me to wait near the check-in counter. About five minutes before departure, she said, "Follow me," and I was escorted to the plane. The man who had come with me from Shannon was right alongside, and they gave us both first-class seats to New York, where we touched down about ninety minutes before airtime. I called and said I was en route, grabbed a cab, and got to the studio with just minutes to spare. I thought then that I could certainly handle the thrill of victory, and maybe even the agony of defeat, but that not getting to the post was inexcusable. (Our studio associate director that day was Mac Hemion, who went on to become a prominent ABC Sports director.)

The person most closely identified with "Wide World of Sports" over the years has been Jim McKay. Since I believe in my heart that, as The Bard wrote, the play is the thing, I am not suggesting that the program would not have endured nor thrived without him. But it certainly has been a whole lot better because of him. As time went by, it was clear that a perfect marriage had been consummated, between a unique concept and an unusually talented man with great journalistic instincts and a highly developed sense of drama. And the odd thing is that when McKay first tried to break into the business he was judged too narrow-minded to succeed.

In college, Jim McManus, as he was then known, had been sports editor of the school newspaper and president of the dramatic society, then had gone into the Navy for World War II service. Afterward, he went to New York looking for work in radio:

"I remember NBC had something called 'Welcome Home Auditions' and that any serviceman could get an audition. They gave you some copy to read and their chief announcer was sitting in the control room checking you out. They brought returning servicemen in, one after another, all day for a year or more. I was assessed—apparently by the announcer who was doing the judging—as 'too pedantic.'

"I couldn't find work in New York, so I went back to my home town of Baltimore and called the president of Loyola College and asked him if he knew anyone at the *Baltimore Sun*, because all I'd ever thought about doing was radio or newspapering. He told me to call a friend of his, Ed Young, who was the paper's city editor. I did, and Ed asked me if I was the same Jim McManus who had written a column on high-school sports for a little local magazine called *Gardens, Houses and People*. I told him I was, he invited me to come and see him, and when I did, he hired me. I started at thirty-five dollars a week as a police reporter. Ed Young really taught me everything about reporting, and, even though I spent only two years in the newspaper business, I've always believed that background played a tremendously important role in what happened to me later."

Jim went to WMAR-TV in Baltimore, where he did a three-hour show five afternoons a week called "The Sports Parade," featuring sports results, interviews, and entertainment. On it, he even sang a song every day:

"I came out of the studio one day and this guy was standing there with our general manager, who introduced the gentleman as Dick Swift from CBS in New York. Mr. Swift asked me how I'd like to do a similar show in New York. I didn't realize at the time they wanted me to do a variety show; I thought it would be sports. But when I went to New York, I found the show was called 'The Real McKay,' and that's how I adopted the name. And that was the start of it all.

"CBS had the first sports-magazine-type show, called 'CBS Sports Spectacular,' but I didn't get to do much on it. The show had only a brief run, I believe. [CBS televised the first network anthology series—"The Sunday Sports Spectacular"—which premiered January 3, 1960. The series ran for thirteen weeks during its initial airing with Jack Whitaker as host.] Then I went down to Augusta to cover the Masters for CBS. Afterward Arledge and Chet Simmons called me up and told me about the new show they were starting called 'Wide World of Sports.' It sounded like something I'd enjoy doing—as a matter of fact, I'd submitted a somewhat similar idea to *Sports Illustrated* several years before that, but nothing came of it—and so I agreed to do it, even though it was then planned to be only a twenty-week summer replacement series.

"We weren't a success when we started out," Jim recalled. "The first eight or ten shows didn't attract much of an audience, and I think we were close to being taken off the air. I'll always believe that the event that turned the corner for us was the U.S.-Soviet track meet we did from Russia. That got us some attention. The Moscow telecast persuaded Tom Moore to commit to bringing the show back on the air the following January, and to give it a shot as a regular series. To show good faith, Moore paid me all during that fall just so I'd keep myself available for it."

Jim and his wife Margaret have two children, Mary and Sean, who left NBC Sports for Trans World International in 1987. (In 1982, Sean became the youngest vice president in the history of the NBC television network at the age of twenty-seven.) The minuses are the same for McKay as for everyone else in this crazy but exciting business: the time spent away from home and family, as Jim has logged some 4.5 million miles over the years. But, McKay stresses, "It's been worth it. I'm glad it happened. No question about that."

In that first summer, the U.S.-Soviet track meet was the first telecast from Europe handled exclusively by American personnel. We transported twenty-five technicians and some twenty tons of equipment to the Soviet Union. Just weeks later, ABC featured the first underwater camera ever used to cover a swimming event, the National AAU Swimming and Diving Championships in Los Angeles.

More firsts? In 1965, the twenty-four-hour Grand Prix of Endurance from Le Mans was the first European sports event televised live to this country, and at the same time the first satellite transmission of a sports event. Six weeks later, I was fortunate to be the producer of the first live telecast from the Soviet Union to the United States; another U.S.-versus-USSR track and field competition, this time from Kiev.

The following year, the Muhammad Ali/Henry Cooper heavy-weight title bout from England was the first championship fight originating from Europe. In 1970, "Wide World" did a high-diving championship from Montreal and the Le Mans twenty-four-hour race from France on the same program and both live—which was the first time anyone had done two live events from different foreign countries.

ABC was the first network to do a sports event in Cuba after Fidel Castro took power there. Our coverage of the U.S.-Cuba volleyball match from Havana in 1971 was followed six and a half years later by amateur boxing competition between the two nations, which was the first telecast done live from Castro's Cuba.

In all, "Wide World" has presented more than 120 kinds of sports from 50 nations on six continents, and in all but three of America's fifty states plus Washington, D.C. We were the first American television network in mainland China, the first American sports department in North Korea (for the World Table Tennis Championships), and the first network to put World Cup Soccer on American television.

In the first year of "Wide World," we went to Mexico for some tennis matches, and while there Arledge heard of the Acapulco cliff-divers. He decided they would be a natural for the show, but when he met with the promoter, the demand for a hundred thousand dollars for the television rights sent him scurrying back to New York. Just one year before that, CBS had paid fifty thousand dollars for the rights to televise *all* of the 1960 Olympic Games from Squaw Valley, California. However, Arledge had barely settled back into his New York office when McKay, who had stayed behind, called to announce that he, single-handedly, had arranged television rights for the cliff-diving. Arledge quickly wanted to know how much they would cost. "I went directly to the cliff-divers," McKay informed him, "and they agreed to appear if we'll pay them ten dollars a dive.

"It's funny when you think about it," said McKay, "but 'Wide World' started out as this lousy little summer replacement show. I was nothing. The show was nothing. But things just kept growing. The show has been able to sustain itself, I think, because it's about people, rather than the record or time or distance or the final score. We focused on the individual at the beginning partly because that is what we believed in, and partly out of necessity because we were showing sports nobody really gave a damn about. Obviously, if we could get people interested in the human beings involved, then they might get interested in the sport. The classic examples of that are gymnastics and figure-skating. Before 'Wide World' you couldn't get two hundred people to come out and watch either."

I became the coordinating producer of "Wide World of Sports" in 1966 and served in that role for nearly five years. During that time, I was responsible for scheduling and formatting the program, as well as for negotiating the rights to broadcast our programming and supervising the work of the people involved in production. It was a sort of laboratory for ABC Sports, because it enabled us to experiment with camera angles, editing, all sorts of new technology, and we could do it week after week. It never got boring (which might just have something to do with winning four Emmys in five years).

Jim McKay became the first sports commentator to win an Emmy, in 1968, and he went on to win nine more to become the recipient of more Emmys than any sportscaster in history.

Dennis Lewin, now senior vice president in charge of production at ABC Sports, came to the network shortly after graduating from Michigan State University. I have always considered him my protégé, and recommended that he be named my successor as coordinating producer of "Wide World" in 1971. A long time ago, Lewin said he thought the program succeeded because it was a "people show." "The human drama," he said, "personalizing the competitors, encouraging the audience to care about the athletes' struggles, is the key to the program's success. People care about people as much as they care about events."

Although "Wide World of Sports" has been the ratings leader among the three-network anthology shows—"ABC's Wide World of Sports," "CBS Sports Saturday/Sunday" and NBC's "SportsWorld"—since 1965, the series was dealt an unfortunate blow a few years ago. A decision was made by Fred Pierce to dislodge "Wide World" from its normal time period—5 to 6:30 P.M. Eastern Time—and move it to 4:30 to 6 P.M. ET. The reason for the switch was to accommodate a Saturday evening network news program that would air at 6 P.M. ET.

While I was sensitive to the need for an early evening news program on Saturday, it was absolutely wrong for "Wide World" to be moved out of its normal time period, one that it had occupied for over two decades. I said at the time that it was akin to the "Tonight" show on NBC being asked to start at midnight but that NBC wouldn't ask Johnny Carson to make such a move.

I was concerned, not only about audience loss, since we would be on the air one-half hour earlier when fewer people were watching television, but also about the negative financial impact, as the program's costs were escalating and competition intensifying.

The dispute clearly illustrated the conflict of interest that existed because Roone Arledge at the time was president of both ABC News and Sports. Although he paid lip service to "Wide World" remaining at 5 P.M., he clearly didn't argue the position very strongly. If he had not been with ABC News at the time, the "Wide World" time-period switch would have been a "cause célèbre" for him. The change was originally planned to be implemented a year earlier than it was, and my objections helped delay the change for a year. The series aired at 4:30 P.M. starting in 1985 and while "Wide World" survives, the time-period change should never have occurred.

"ABC's Wide World of Sports," the most honored sports program in the history of the medium, is unquestionably one of the industry's true legends. It has been the flagship program of ABC Sports since becoming established in the early sixties.

Televised essentially on a year-round basis, it has therefore been a source of continuity and purpose for ABC Sports over the years. There have been a lot of victories and a few defeats, but only a relative handful of programs have been on network television longer.

5

"MR. SPORTS TELEVISION" —FACT AND FABLE

Roone Arledge Demystified

The name of Roone Arledge has already appeared a number of times in these pages, and it will occur many more times in the succeeding ones. One reason is that Roone Arledge is the most significant figure in the history of television sports in America, a true giant of the broadcasting business. Another reason is that he has created and religiously fostered, through his highly idiosyncratic personal style, as well as his talent, a mystique and a celebrity about himself that is endlessly fascinating to those in and around television and its associated industries. A third reason is that, as the man working most closely with him during his years of peak achievement and fame, I am able now for the first time to fully draw back the curtain on both the professional and the human being.

Roone Arledge's principal genius was always his impeccable programming judgment. From day one, he had an almost eerie talent for making the right decisions on what programs would be appealing to the public and how best to present them. He had an almost infallible sense of such critical factors as how long segments should last, what interviews should be aired, the order of presentation for the various segments in order to build audience attention, and particularly about the importance of the human element in sports. He realized early on that the *people* participating in the events were the essence of sports, and that we, as broadcasters, should focus most heavily on those individuals. Arledge has always been praised by the media for things like underwater cameras and slow-motion replays, but his real forte—program judgment—had little to do with the technology of the business.

Roone's background was that of a producer; therefore, when he gained control of ABC Sports, he saw to it that we were a producer-oriented network. Largely director-oriented, CBS Sports, for example, had traditionally been content merely to cover the excitement of an event without doing or saying anything to either arouse or offend anyone. ABC producers were hands-on people with the authority to direct the directors, who were and are primarily responsible for deciding picture coverage.

Over the years, so many sports events came to be covered by all three networks—plus the proliferation of cable and super-stations—that the viewer gradually became a wiser and more sophisticated individual. Then, as his enlightenment increased, he expected—even demanded—more complete coverage and more incisive commentary. It was no longer enough for the director merely to provide good pictures, and for the producer to make certain the commercials got played in their proper order.

It was a healthy change for all the networks, and it came about principally because of the vision of Roone Arledge.

His own human qualities, however, do not match his professional achievements. This highly intelligent, driven man is consumed by television, and perhaps also in later years by the mystique he had deliberately created about himself. Roone often exuded surface charm in dealing with people. This was part of his *modus operandi*, as was divide-and-conquer. His system was to pit one executive against another, one production person against another, one announcer against another. That way, no individual within the organization could achieve a level of success or prominence beyond that ordained by Roone Arledge. As Earl Sorris, a contributing editor to *Harper's*, wrote in *Business Quarterly*, "Power is gained by withholding."

I challenged Roone on this highly disruptive and unpleasant characteristic on more than one occasion, but for as long as I have known him, he has listened only to the sound of his own voice. On the other hand, we agreed 95 percent of the time on business decisions, and I must confess that when I disagreed with him in that area I was wrong most of the time.

Roone has always had a great knack for recognizing star quality, no doubt fueled by a love of stars in all fields and of all their trappings of celebrity and notoriety. This did wonders for ABC Sports over the years, as exemplified by little Olga Korbut, the Russian gymnast, at the 1972 Munich Olympics. Roone quickly grasped that she could be the top star of the entire show, and honed in on her to the degree that the American television viewer fell totally in love with her. When Pete Axthelm, the fine writer for *Newsweek,* filed a story from Munich, his desk people in New York called him and wanted to know why he hadn't written something about the famous Olga Korbut!

Four years later, it was Roone's decision to cover the downhill ski race from top to bottom during the 1976 Winter Olympics at Innsbruck. That was the great run where Franz Klammer won by one-third of a second to capture the gold medal. It was the first time the downhill had been covered that thoroughly, and through Arledge's genius ABC painted a picture the sports world will long remember. Some still say it was the finest sports coverage they've ever seen, and I wouldn't dispute that. Arledge's decision to go all out on the expanded coverage cost the network as much as two hundred thousand dollars, but when it was over, no one questioned his wisdom.

Working on a day-to-day basis with Roone was exasperating. As smart and effective as he was as a programmer, he was always an inefficient administrator. He detested making decisions and would procrastinate whenever possible and for as long as possible, often allowing a problem to go unsolved in the hope it would simply eventually go away of its own accord. He genuinely believed that, given time, most problems did indeed solve themselves. But when he was cornered to make a decision, his judgment was almost always correct, and often brilliant.

Arledge hated to be trapped by dates and deadlines. His internal correspondence was not stamped with "received" dates, and he rarely dated notes he would pass along to others. The theory was that if there were no dates involved, no one could pin him down on when he received or sent correspondence.

His reputation for not returning telephone calls is one of the odd legends of the television industry, and I'm convinced he gained some sort of strange psychic kick out of living up to it. When he became president of ABC News as well as ABC Sports in 1977, Beano Cook, the network's one-time publicity man and now a college football commentator for ESPN, cracked that, "Now Arledge has two offices where he can't be reached."

Roone had secretaries at both his news and sports offices. Some sports secretaries didn't see him for months.

One day, Charlie Lavery approached one of them and, tongue in cheek, asked if Mr. Arledge was in. "No," she replied. "Are you sure?" asked Charlie. "Yes," said the secretary. "Have you ever met Mr. Arledge?" asked Mr. Lavery. "No," replied the young lady. "Have you ever seen Mr. Arledge?" Charlie asked. "No," she replied.

Another time, one of our vice presidents heard that Roone was planning to be in his sports office that day. He then busily pretended with his handkerchief to wipe away the cobwebs from Roone's office door in front of a bemused secretary.

The jokes were funny, but the facts were not.

On the other hand, if Roone wanted to reach you, heaven help you! Once, he insisted he had tried to telephone me on a weekend during which I had never left my apartment, and was so frustrated that he urged me to get an answering service. Another time, as my wife and I were about to begin a private tour of the White House in Washington, a young lady approached me and told me it was urgent that I call Roone Arledge! When I talked to Roone, I learned that his call was indeed not urgent but it illustrated how he would go to any extent to reach you—even at the White House.

Getting Roone to show up at business meetings or sports events on a predictable basis was well nigh impossible. He seemed to think speculation about whether or when he might show up increased his stature by emphasizing his power to go his own way. I'd like to have the money expended over the years by ABC on unused hotel suites booked in the name of Roone Arledge.

Roone frequently would fall behind in filing his expense accounts. His practice was to keep getting advances from the accounting department, then do the paper work only after repeated urgings from the keepers of the books. This seemed to me, and others, yet another of his endless ways of demonstrating power.

Arledge is a man of boundless energy. He abused his body with lack of sleep; overeating and drinking; almost no exercise; and his Cuban cigars. He'd arrive at the office in late morning, usually have lunch brought to him from the executive dining room, and call meetings for the early evening hours. He seemed to have little or no consideration for employees' family needs, and also very little for his own. Roone was married and divorced twice. He is the father of four children by his first wife, Joan, and later married "Miss Alabama" of 1969, Ann Fowler.

Arledge's work has devoured him, and, because of that, others, too. Don Ohlmeyer, an extremely bright and talented producer who leaped quickly up the ladder at ABC Sports and later became executive producer at NBC Sports, maintains that he did not know the secret of ABC Sports' success until he went to another network. Says Ohlmeyer: "The work ethic at NBC was radically different than the one I'd gotten used to at ABC for ten years. At the outset, all I looked for was people who wanted to work. At ABC, the business of sports was a seven-day-a-week thing. But at NBC, if you worked over the weekend, it meant you had Monday and Tuesday off. Suddenly, it became clear to me why ABC was so far ahead of NBC. Hell, every week that went by, ABC was picking up two days! At NBC, people strolled in at nine-thirty or ten A.M., left for lunch about noon, and strolled back about two P.M., then left for home about five P.M. At ABC, people in production came in at about the same time, but they stayed until midevening and rarely went outside the building for lunch. You had a sandwich and a soft drink brought in, and you just kept working. Days off and vacations were for other folks."

Don's right. Considerable though they often were, the talents of people without the willingness to outwork and outhustle their counterparts at the other networks just wouldn't have been enough. When it all began, ABC was the new kid on the block in sports, and we caught the other networks when they were complacent and napping. Thereafter, no one outdid Roone and me and most of the other members of the team when it came to intensity, drive, and stamina.

Arledge's contract called for him to get an executive producer's credit for every show put on the air by ABC Sports. The person who legitimately takes that sort of credit has overall responsibility for the content of the show, the formatting of the program, and the supervision of the production, but it was rare for Arledge to perform these functions. Maybe a guy with six zeros in his annual paycheck simply doesn't have time for things like that—Roone's salary of recent times has been $2,000,000 a year.

Roone Arledge's great success with sports made him a logical choice to become head of ABC News, which happened on June 1, 1977, when he was named president of both divisions. However, once he was established in that dual role, it became clear he would spend less and less time on the twenty-eighth floor at 1330 Avenue of the Americas and more and more time at 7 West 66th Street, the home of ABC News. Sports was in high gear and running smoothly; ABC News long had played follow-the-leader. From the time Roone got promoted, I, as program planning vice president, was making whatever decisions were necessary and consulting with him whenever I could find him. I naturally thought his promotion might mean a move up the ladder for me, as did others in the department.

But Arledge was not about to give up any of his power or authority. Everyone knew Chuck Howard would not receive any more authority. In fact, Chuck had come close to becoming a sacrificial lamb when Don Ohlmeyer, who had engaged Howard in a long-standing battle, was offered the post of executive producer of NBC Sports in the spring of 1977. To try and keep him, Arledge offered him the job of head of production, but Ohlmeyer was lured by the attraction of producing NBC's coverage of the 1980 Moscow Olympics.

Arledge had made John Martin a vice president, too, and made it plain that Martin was special to him. Martin was given increased amounts of authority and responsibility, and came to expect more of the same, which created considerable friction within the division. In fact, John eventually became such an Arledge clone that he nearly lost his own identity, and later wisely left the network to work for Ohlmeyer after Don quit NBC to form his own company.

Then there was Jeff Ruhe. He had joined ABC right out of college and was still wet behind the ears. But he quickly became Roone's pet and everybody knew it, including, most of all, Ruhe. The world already knows of the bond that has existed for years between Arledge and the Kennedy family, and Ruhe surely didn't damage himself in Arledge's eyes by marrying Courtney Kennedy, one of Bobby Kennedy's daughters. Ruhe did a good job, but also became a major player in Roone's game of pitting person against person at ABC Sports.

In the fall of 1977, I had become so fed up with the lack of hands-on leadership, with the inability to get answers to questions that cried out for them, and with the general paralysis in the management of the division that I thought was setting in—not to mention the divisiveness that was created—that I ran out of patience. I determined at the very least to find out where I personally stood, so I sought a meeting with then ABC Television president Fred Pierce. I had been stymied in my efforts to resolve the crisis with Roone himself. When I told Arledge I thought we were inefficient, he responded: "You can't run ABC Sports like an army. You know, we're supposed to be creative, to let people think and do their own thing."

My argument was that it wasn't a matter of military discipline, but rather one of having clear lines of authority, defining who reported to whom, and operating in an intelligent, efficient, and effective manner, if only to eliminate the waste of energy we were incurring.

Roone ended that tense discussion like he ended all tense discussions—by walking away from it. I think that by doing that he believed he had won the debate.

When I met with Pierce in his office, he suggested I had earned the right to be promoted. He then buzzed Arledge and asked if Roone would be available for dinner that evening. Even Roone

Arledge has a boss, and he decided he'd better be available. When Pierce hung up the telephone and we had arranged to have dinner, I started out of his office to go back down to the twenty-eighth floor to wrap up my business for the day. Halfway out the door, I stopped in my tracks when Pierce called out: "Let me ask you something, Jim. Is Roone Arledge an honest man?"

Even now, I cannot recall how long I stood there, eerie thoughts racing around in my mind, my head fairly spinning. Why would he ask *me* something like that? Did I really want to answer that question? Could I be honest and survive the evening? What seemed like an eon must have been but five or ten seconds. Finally, I did what I believe in my heart I have always tried to do—I told the truth: "No."

And Fred Pierce said, "That's what I thought."

He told me he'd meet me in the lobby and we'd go in his car to meet Arledge at a midtown restaurant.

The trip down in the elevator was spooky. All I could think of was that here I was, coming from the office of the top man at ABC Television, who had just asked me about the integrity of the man he had promoted only months before to head ABC News. I kept wondering if I had zapped myself by telling the truth. Finally, I determined that if indeed I had done that, then so be it.

Dinner was pleasant enough. Cordial, you might say. The three of us were friendly and upbeat. The decision had been made; I would be promoted to senior vice president of ABC Sports. The interesting thing was that not that night, and never thereafter, did Roone Arledge congratulate me on that promotion.

Roone rarely came around to the sports department after that. He would drop by now and again, and of course we talked regularly on the telephone, but it was rare when he spent a full day at 1330 Avenue of the Americas. The challenge for him was at 7 West 66th Street, to show the world he could work in the news the same magic he had achieved with ABC Sports. And, to his credit, he made dramatic changes in both production and people to turn ABC News into a highly credible and competitive organization.

There are always rumors in every business, but they may be more pronounced in television since it is such a public and high-profile enterprise. For several years, there were rumors about Roone Arledge: that he would be named president of ABC Television; that he would take control of NBC; and many more along the same lines. There was one story regarding Arledge, however, that had a strong foundation in fact. The truth is that Roone Arledge came very close to being fired in late 1985, but Fred Pierce talked the Capital Cities executives out of it. We had already trimmed here and cut there, but within the industry Cap Cities was known as a very "lean and mean" organization, and it was reasonable to assume they would not only be bringing in many of their own top executives, but that Arledge, although saved by Pierce, would not be permitted to continue in control of two divisions. The rumored upshot of this anticipated development was that Arledge would be required to give up the presidency of ABC Sports. And of course I believed I had every reasonable right to think that I would be named to succeed him.

In late January 1986, my wife Lynn and I had gone to our place in Rye, New York, for the weekend. Originally, we planned to remain through the conclusion of "Wide World of Sports," then drive back to our apartment in Manhattan. But because the weather was a bit uncertain, we decided to return earlier. Besides, I was to leave the following day on an early morning flight for a Capital Cities/ABC conference in Phoenix.

We had just finished watching "Wide World of Sports" in our New York apartment when the telephone rang. It was Arledge: "I have bad news. Capital Cities has spoken. They want me to leave sports. They've come up with a new title for me. I'm to be group president of news and sports. And Dennis Swanson is the new president of ABC Sports. Dan Burke [president of Capital Cities/ABC] wants you to stay and so does Swanson."

Today, looking back on that phone call, nothing is fuzzy. I remember every word of it. I said nothing. I assumed he would continue. After a pause, he did.

"They're going to make the announcement on Monday. Since they wanted me to leave sports, I told them I would like to go out with some dignity. That's why they've created that new title. I told them they need not rush into naming my replacement, but it was already done. I guess they wanted to get everything settled before the conference started Monday in Phoenix."

I knew then I didn't have to fret about the notes I had made that day while watching the "Pro Bowlers Tour" and "Wide World." Ordinarily, I'd have talked to the bowling producer, or maybe called Bo Burton about a plug I thought he should not have given for the Showboat Hotel and Casino in Las Vegas. The bowling show had originated from there, and Bo had been shilling a bit for the place, telling viewers how fine and lovely it was. And I had made a note for us to contact Tim Brant and tell him that his energy level was too high for a bowling show. I also had made a note that Mark Breland had the "Pony" commercial brand label on his boxing trunks on "Wide World," and I thought that violated our agreement about commercial identification on fighters' attire.

Now as Arledge talked, I was busy making brand new notes.

"I wanted to call you myself with the bad news," he continued. "I waited until 'Wide World' was over because I knew you'd be watching the show and I didn't want to interrupt you. Also, I didn't want you to go to Phoenix and not be aware of what had transpired. Burke just felt I should no longer be involved in the day-to-day operations in sports. Now Swanson thinks highly of you; he told me he thinks you know more about sports than anyone in the business, and he really wants you to stay on."

I didn't have much to say during the chat. Roone was doing the talking and I was doing the listening, and when he had said his piece, I merely thanked him for calling and we hung up. I had previously decided if Roone ever left ABC Sports and I was not named as his replacement that I would leave the company.

My first call was to my financial adviser, Alan Morris, to put the wheels in motion for a quick and orderly departure. My contract went to the end of May 1986, and Alan would have to arrange the terms of the settlement. As it turned out, Capital Cities/ABC was most generous and very fair.

Next, I called my closest friends and associates at ABC Sports to tell them I planned to resign. I wanted them to hear it from me. Then I called Roone regarding the Phoenix meeting but was only able to reach his answering service.

I suppose a series of events like that might rob a man of a good night's sleep. Maybe it's in the genes, but all I have ever needed to get to sleep is to put my head on a pillow. That night, like most others in my life, I slept very soundly. The next morning, Arledge called me back and we talked briefly. I asked his permission to stay away from the office for a week, since under the circumstances I really didn't want to go there. But he was still my boss, at least officially, and I didn't feel I could simply take time off without his permission. He responded by asking, "But aren't you going to go to Phoenix?"

I thought it was amazing how casual he was about the Phoenix trip after our conversation of the night before.

"I'm not going to Phoenix and I don't want to go into the office next week. I want your blessing to take some time off."

There was a stammering "Okay."

Then he asked, "Well, then, what are you going to do?"

"I think it's probably time for me to fade away. For now, let's just leave it that way."

It wasn't MacArthur's "Old soldiers never die," and it wasn't a day that would live in infamy, but it would be a weekend I would never forget. It would take me from a company I had known a quarter of a century and set me on a new and exciting course in my professional life.

Only weeks before that, I had been at what you might call a three-stage meeting. First, Fred Pierce announced he was resigning as president of ABC. Next, chairman of the board Leonard Goldenson made some remarks. Then we met the Capital Cities people: Tom Murphy, the chairman; Dan Burke, the president; and John Sias, the newly designated president of the ABC Network Division of Capital Cities. After the meeting, I shook hands with Sias and congratulated him, and told him I looked forward to working with him.

"It's a real pleasure to meet you," he said. "You run one hell of an organization." The Cap Cities people would have heard a hell of a lot more about our organization had Roone Arledge been honest with them and fair with me. He could, and should, have told them that there was no question about who should take over as head man in sports. I had given more than twenty-five years,

90

not just to the company, but to Arledge as well. Whatever clout he had left at that moment, he should have used all of it on my behalf. But he had not carried my banner with the ABC people for years, and he was not about to give me a strong endorsement with the new bosses. I was disappointed, too, that I didn't have stronger support from Fred Pierce. While I'll always be indebted to Fred for seeing that I was promoted to senior vice president, I deserved more from him after Capital Cities took over, despite his being influenced by Arledge, the man whose integrity he himself had questioned.

On Super Bowl Sunday, Lynn and I went to my office to clear out my personal things. Then we came back home, watched the Super Bowl, and speculated what the future would bring.

Roone Arledge came out of all of it with his dignity intact, a new title, and a deal to head up coverage of the 1988 Calgary Olympics. I came out of it disappointed and chagrined but not bitter. My resignation took effect February 3, 1986. Because I quit, Cap Cities could have cut me off without a cent, but as I said, they were extremely fair.

Two months later, I accepted an invitation to honor the twenty-fifth anniversary of "Wide World of Sports." There was no question that I would go. After all, I had watched that program being born, seen it become the show with the greatest impact in the history of television sports, and some of me would always live within that series.

Dan Burke was there, too, and after some opening pleasantries he apologized for the way my situation had been handled, then made a remark I believe speaks volumes:

"We didn't know the [ABC] people. We need you."

He didn't need to remind me about the thrills of victories and the agonies of defeats, nor the human drama of athletic competition. Nor corporate competition, for that matter. It was a great run—those twenty-five years—and I wouldn't trade those experiences for anything in the world. That's why a piece of my heart will forever be with ABC Sports.

6

TWO KINDS
OF COURAGE

*The Most Unforgettable
Characters in My Quarter Century
of Sports Television*

Growing up as I did near Pleasantville, New York, I was of course well acquainted with *Reader's Digest,* which is published from that town. One of the *Digest's* successful features of long standing is something called "My Most Unforgettable Character," and there is a wild assortment of these characters in the archives of the magazine.

In twenty-five years at ABC Sports, I can narrow my list of "most unforgettable characters" to two: Muhammad Ali and Evel Knievel. For sheer color and excitement, no one can match them. At this writing, Ali has made sixty-three appearances on ABC Sports, Knievel nineteen. Evel's motorcycle jump in Ohio in 1975 received a 22.3 rating and a 52 percent share of audience, the highest-rated program in "Wide World of Sports" history. Ali's third fight with Joe Frazier, which aired in 1976, achieved the second highest "Wide World" rating to date—a 21.0 and a 43 percent share—while the second Ali-Leon Spinks fight, televised as a special in September of 1978, received the highest ABC boxing rating ever—37.2 with a 61 percent share of audience.

Not only did Ali and Knievel have courage and color and charisma, they shared another trait that was vital to their success: knowing that they had those things. No athletes in my experience have had more of a sense of themselves.

Babe Ruth had it, but he didn't have television to help him get it across to the public. Joe Namath and Reggie Jackson have it and so does Arnold Palmer and Sugar Ray Leonard. Earvin (Magic) Johnson also has it, that acute awareness of self and the passions one can arouse in others.

Evel Knievel is one of the most courageous individuals I have known in sports, if you categorize what Evel did as "sport." Evel—his given name is Robert—made his first appearance on the ABC Television Network in 1973. So colorful was he that his failures were as spectacular as anyone else's triumphs.

Every manner of study has been made on why people do the seemingly crazy things they do, like rock-climbing, flagpole-sitting, tightrope walking, cliff-diving, free-fall-parachuting, and so many other feats that clearly don't involve much common sense. And there have been studies about why people watch such stunts. Do people go to, say, the Indianapolis 500 automobile race to see people crash, get hurt, get killed? Did people want to see Evel Knievel get mangled? I don't think so. I think fans are fascinated by the sheer courage of daredevils, stunt men, race-car drivers, and boxers—those who engage in what the world considers death-defying feats, men who put their lives on the line and who are willing, not always for a price, to risk the ultimate sacrifice. Maybe these men have courage the common man lacks. Maybe the ordinary man wishes he could do similar things. Whatever, I think most fans identify with the man who tests himself by going all the way to the ragged edge, and sometimes beyond.

If he crashes and walks away from it, wonderful. If a man takes a fearful beating in the prize ring, gets knocked cold, then rises from the floor to wave to the crowd and fight again, hooray for him! Let's face it, whatever their other appeals, most of the time there isn't a whole lot of danger in baseball, or golf, or tennis.

Knievel, born Robert Craig in 1938, acquired his nickname while spending a brief period in jail. One of the guys in jail with him was named Knoffle. The jail guard thought it was pretty funny—"Evil Knievel in one cell and Awful Knoffle in the other." Later Knievel changed the spelling of his name from E-v-i-l to E-v-e-l.

Knievel was a paradox. One day he came to our offices, following one of his many accidents, along with his son Robbie. He didn't actually walk into our offices, it was more of a hobble, and he needed a cane to hold himself upright. We assembled in the conference room to talk about his next jump, and naturally he wanted ABC to televise it. On one hand, he seemed so fragile, almost like a wounded sparrow battered by a car windshield and trying to fight off crippling injuries to be able to soar into the clouds once again. On the other, he had this aura of invincibility about him. Obviously, he had a tremendous ego, and it was almost of the swaggering kind. Yet just beneath that brassy exterior, there was a goodness and a great sensitivity about him. He had great charm and was always very nice, most accommodating, in all his dealings with us.

Evel was careful always to give warnings to the fans before his jumps, describing himself as a professional daredevil and explaining that he had chosen this way of making a living and that what he did was for him alone, and that the stunts should not be tried by anyone else. I cannot tell you that I was perfectly comfortable with all the deals we made with him, or with every stunt he pulled, but I supported our involvement despite those reservations. My main concern was that, despite Evel's words of caution before each stunt, we were fostering daredevil activity on the part of the public, particularly young people. It was always in my mind that it was possible that our showing of Evel's stunts might result in crippling injuries or death to some kids who would be watching "Wide World of Sports."

I'd be less than candid if I did not add that this is an example of the kind of programming we sometimes did in order to attract ratings. Sure, the jumps were fun and exciting, and had ABC not televised them another network surely would have. But that doesn't make it right. We took a lot of criticism for demolition derbies and things like that, but they were happening before television came along, we didn't create them, and I had no problem in such cases even though the critics got on us about some of them. But to this day, I still question our judgment about putting Evel Knievel on television. Okay, so this guy jumped over cars, and there was that huge jump over the English buses at

Wembley Stadium in London. I ask myself if he would have done all those things had television not put money in his pocket and cameras at those locations. Of course, it was Evel who created the monster. Television, ever receptive to ways to attract audiences and to make dollars, merely helped it grow.

Dennis Lewin was involved with many of Evel Knievel's performances, some as the in-the-field producer and others as the in-studio coordinating producer. He recalled:

"Evel Knievel is one of the world's all-time-great promoters, and I honestly feel he has never been given enough credit for putting his life on the line the way he did. After all, not even the doctors know how many bones he's had broken over and over again, and maybe Evel would have to spend a full day examining X rays to count the fractures.

"No matter what you think of the man, and regardless of what you may think about his morals, there's a big part of him that you have to like. Under all that braggadocio, he is a very decent human being. He drummed up so much interest in himself that people came to regard him as the ultimate con man, and they somehow ignored, or at least tended to minimize, the daredevil part. After all, he put his life on the line every time. And he always delivered. He never pulled the wool over anybody's eyes.

"Sure, he came up with outlandish schemes, but he always performed. He never backed out. He never altered his planned course. He didn't advertise one thing and then do another. There were no last-minute surprises with Evel. He promised he'd try something wild, and, time after time, he'd do it or almost kill himself trying. Right to the end, with that leap he tried over the Snake River Canyon in Idaho in that thing that looked like a rocket, there were skeptics who thought it was all just a fraud. Not so! Some people even said he knew from the start it couldn't be done, and that he was afraid, and that he went down intentionally. That's not true, either!"

Failing to get U.S. government approval to jump the Grand Canyon, Evel embarked on the Snake River stunt in 1974 in a contraption he called the X-2 Skycycle. Denny Lewin again: "The truth is that when he got into that capsule, there was about one chance in the world that he could save himself, and that's exactly how it developed. There's no way anyone could have preplanned what took place. When the parachute popped, if Evel had floated backward he'd have gone into the river below and surely drowned. When he went to the other side of the canyon, if he had hit the canyon wall hard enough, he'd have been like a pogo stick with nowhere to go. That way, he'd have been a goner, too. The only thing that could have happened to save his life did, indeed, happen: The wind blew him back into a bush. It was the *only* bush at the bottom of the ravine and, believe me, it was a long, long way down to the bottom of that ravine.''

The leap that first put Evel Knievel on the map was the one he did in 1967 over the fountains at Caesar's Palace in Las Vegas. It took all of his promotional genius first to get it set up, and then to get anyone to pay attention to it. Dennis Lewin was involved in that one, too:

"When we first met, he'd never been on network television, but I assumed he'd already made the deal with the people at Caesar's Palace. As it turned out, the way he talked Caesar's Palace into letting him do it was by telling them he'd closed a deal to get it on ABC! When he proposed the deal to me, I told him only that it was something we'd consider, nothing more. He caught me at a very busy time, and I may have told him I'd get back to him on it, but that was the only time we discussed that particular feat. I made him only one promise: You do the jump and have it filmed or videotaped, and I'll at least take a look at it. To Evel, I guess that meant a sure deal. Anyway, on the strength of it he convinced Caesar's to go ahead.

"That's the jump that put him on the map. He did it, all right, but lost control of his motorcycle and rolled over and over, and then over some more. And all the time, he was having it filmed, at his own expense. He had it filmed at regular speed and at high speed (slow motion), so there was some pretty spectacular footage of that awful crash. He broke about every bone in his body, but it got big attention, and from that minute forward you couldn't hear the name Evel Knievel without seeing pictures of him splattering himself all over Las Vegas. And that's the thing that sold him to ABC."

Ash Resnick, then assistant to the president at Caesar's, said

Evel came to Jay Sarno, one of the hotel's owners, and assured him he had a deal with ABC. "He told us it'd be the greatest event in the history of the world and that we'd get all the publicity," said Resnick. "There was an absolute mob there that afternoon. We had to block off the streets. I watched it from the rooftop and he cleared the fountains, but he couldn't control the bike. It went one way and he went the other, bouncing like a rag doll. I don't understand how he lived through it. The man's got guts. I love him. He's beautiful people."

Unwittingly, Evel Knievel created some production magic on the twenty-eighth floor at ABC. We had made a deal with him for a jump at the Los Angeles Coliseum, and Ned Steckel was assigned to produce the show.

"When Ned came back with the footage," Lewin remembered, "I took a look at it and felt something was missing. Suddenly, I drew a parallel between Evel Knievel and Conrad Birdie in *Bye Bye Birdie*. So I told Ned to get the music to *Bye Bye Birdie* and put it on the piece. Evel simply had all these people mesmerized, just like Conrad. Here he was, climbing this daredevil platform, speaking to the crowd, putting everything on the line. Ned was reluctant to have music accompany the piece and reminded me that 'Wide World of Sports' had never used music with such events. I was adamant, we did it, and it worked beautifully. That started a long series of events where we always used music alongside Evel's stunts. One time, we used 'Bad, Bad LeRoy Brown' and that worked, too."

ABC producer-director Doug Wilson calls Evel Knievel the greatest promoter, the greatest tub-thumper, he's ever known. Doug Wilson was at ABC, even before Arledge, Chuck Howard, and I joined Sports Programs, Inc., and Doug is still there. Probably best known in the industry for his utilization of music during ABC Sports' programs and his sensitive work with our figure-skating telecasts, he did a lot of shows with Evel.

"Evel had unbelievable instincts," said Wilson. "What he did was very simple, yet at times very complex. There were so many gray areas in the world about that time—Viet Nam and all that—but this man did his thing cleanly and simply. He went out and risked his life just for the hell of it—for the glory more than for the money, I'm sure of that.

"I was assigned to do his big jump from Wembley Stadium in London in 1975, and when Evel got there, he was terribly disappointed to learn they'd sold only a few thousand seats in this place that seats ninety thousand people. First thing he did was to fire his publicity man. Then he called a news conference and told the English he was delighted to come to that country since he was an American and, after all, Americans had gone out and won the war and saved the English asses. Then he made some off-the-wall remark about one of the English generals of World War II having had an affair with the wife of a German general, and we were off and running. In a matter of hours, the whole country was talking about him. And he sold the tickets!

"Then he hired the best-known photographer in England, but when the guy began telling him about the magnificent ideas he had for publicity shots, Evel told him to hush up. He ordered him to take only one picture—of Evel standing on top of the thirteen London buses that he planned to leap on his motorcycle. That picture made every newspaper in England.

"Evel had brought this customized red Cadillac pickup truck over from the States, and he rode it all over London, drawing huge crowds wherever he traveled. When he'd meet up with a British motorcycle gang, he'd warn them not to do the things he did and he'd advise them to wear helmets.

"But the capper came at one of his two news conferences. Some female British reporter asked Evel if his failure to jump the Snake River Canyon had damaged his credibility. Without missing a beat, Evel snapped, 'Lady, no canyon and no woman I ever jumped did any damage to my credibility.' The crowd loved it. When he did his thing, after personally taking charge of the publicity, there was a throng of eighty thousand at Wembley Stadium.

"About half an hour before the jump, Frank Gifford and I went into Evel's van and spoke with him. Frank had been assigned to do the show for 'Wide World.' Evel was lying down with his feet propped up. He told us his circulation was bad, and that the healing process was very slow because of the hundreds of fractures he'd endured. He made mention of the crowd. 'Can you imagine that,' he said, 'there are more people out there waiting to see if I break my neck than there are in my hometown of Butte, Montana.' Then he went out there and broke practically everything but his neck.

"After he crashed, Frank was trying to help him. It was a pathetic sight, just awful. He was about half out of it and telling Frank that he didn't want to be carried out; he didn't want to be put in an ambulance where people could see it. He said he had walked into that arena and he would walk out. I didn't see how he could crawl, much less walk. But walk he did. He kept waving to the people and eighty thousand of them were on their feet, cheering him and yelling, 'Hip, hip, hooray.' It was some sight, all right, and one I'll never forget. Right after the crash, he told Frank and me that he knew going in that he would never make the jump. He said he realized at the outset that he would surely crash.

"He said he'd been waiting for a certain gearbox to arrive from the States, and it simply didn't arrive. He and his mechanic knew that the gearbox he was forced to use wouldn't be enough to get him over the thirteen buses. So I asked him why in hell he did it, and he just looked at me with a sort of half smile and said, 'What do you want me to do? I'm the world's greatest daredevil. Do you think for one minute I'm gonna go out there in front of eighty thousand Englishmen and stand on those buses and say excuse me, folks, but do you mind if I take a bus away because my gearbox didn't arrive? I can't do that. I'm Evel Knievel. Don't you understand?' For the first time, perhaps I did.

"Evel's one of a kind. I mean, when he had all that trouble later, he fired his lawyers and took out after a guy with a baseball bat and whacked him something awful. He just believes in the old-fashioned system of frontier justice. You hurt me, fella, I'm gonna hurt you back. Now there's no justification for belting a guy with a baseball bat, but when Evel did it, he didn't hire some hotshot lawyer and deny it. He stood right up there in front of the judge and admitted not only that he had done the dirty deed, but that he'd do it all over again. He took his medicine like a man. There is a consistency about him. He's incredible."

Evel was still trying to talk himself back onto ABC not long ago. He called Dennis Lewin once more, suggesting a daredevil stunt with himself and his son Robbie performing.

"We passed on it," said Lewin. "I simply said, 'Not right now.' I really have had mixed emotions about it. Maybe we ought to do a feature story on him, though. He's been through hell, he's had all sorts of lawsuits against him, and at one time he was trying to make a living selling paintings. I doubt that he ever saved a dime. He lived for today. His tomorrows were always so up in the air. But he was a happening, and an incredible performer. He's one I'll never forget."

Nor will I. Nor anyone else, I suspect, whose life he touched.

It seems altogether natural that Evel Knievel and Muhammad Ali should have hooked up, if only briefly, as they did in the summer of 1987. Whether Ali enlisted the help of Evel or whether the daredevil considered it just another stunt is not clear, but they teamed up to try and solve a marketing problem. It seems the former heavyweight champion got involved in a shoe-polish business in which he sought to gain nationwide distribution through Kmart. The test-marketing hadn't impressed Kmart and distribution was suspended in all the company's twenty-two hundred stores.

When Kmart's officers and shareholders got together a little later in Troy, Michigan, for their annual shareholders' meeting, what dynamic duo should make a surprise appearance but Muhammad Ali and Evel Knievel? They not only attended, they made it a media happening, arriving in a convoy of white limousines, escorted by police cars. While Ali did not address the stockholders, Evel read a brief statement attacking Kmart's decision. The company's vice president for public relations, Bob Stevenson, commented, "They've made their point, let's say with something other than usual business procedures."

No one ever accused Muhammad Ali or Evel Knievel of being orthodox.

Only by traveling the world could one begin to comprehend the enormity of Muhammad Ali's notoriety. In my time, only soccer immortal Pelé drew attention on a world scale of anywhere near the same scope as Ali, and in truth he pales by comparison. I think Ali was and perhaps still is the most recognized figure in the world. And there can be no question that he played a very significant part in the early success of ABC Sports. Early on, Ali and Howard Cosell formed a relationship that linked them forever in the minds of the American television viewers.

It would be absurd to suggest that this relationship spilled over into a personal thing, simply because the two men are so dissimilar. But there can be no question that they helped each other greatly professionally, first because their stars were on the ascendancy in unison, and secondly because each sensed the link they had and the importance it had to the other. And, of course, both are grand masters of public relations and self-promotion.

It matters not whether Ali could have stood in there against Jack Dempsey, or held his own against Joe Louis, or have been able to withstand the bull-like rushes of the swarming Rocky Marciano. What counted was what he did, in another time, in *his* time. Here was a brash, good-looking kid out of Louisville who became an Olympic champion, embraced a curiously different religion, changed his name from Cassius Clay to Muhammad Ali, went ''bear hunting,'' as he called it, against the scowling Charles (Sonny) Liston, and somehow wound up with the heavyweight championship of the world, only to sacrifice it by refusing to be inducted into the U.S. Army, and uttering those never-to-be-forgotten words, ''I ain't got nuthin' against them Viet Congs.'' By turns brash and boisterous and deeply solemn, occasionally he'd be moved to a kind of childish but joyful doggerel, and it all combined to make him surely one of the most entertaining and intriguing figures of the age.

It was ABC's custom to secure the rights to Ali's fights, and televise them either live or on a tape-delayed basis. When we did a delayed broadcast, we'd bring him—and sometimes his victim—into the studio to do commentary on the battle. One of Ali's appearances cost ABC a great deal more money than we had anticipated. He fought Chuck Wepner in 1975, and, as usual, it was a one-sided affair, and he had then joined Cosell in the studio for the postmortem. Ali had been ''knocked down'' in the fight—at least, it was ruled a knockdown by referee Tony Perez—but Ali had claimed that Wepner had stepped on his foot, and that his going to the canvas was actually a slip, and that should not have been counted as a knockdown. Dennis Lewin remembered the incident:

"By the day of the taping, I finally had tracked down a wire-service photograph that showed Wepner stepping on Ali's foot just before Muhammad went to the canvas. It looked like Wepner was actually standing on Ali's foot. We showed that photograph during the taping and Ali was at his uproarious best. He was doing his thing, and part of his thing was to say some things about Tony Perez.

"The end result was that Perez sued Muhammad Ali for slander, which raised the question as to whether I should have deleted the allegedly slanderous portion from the show. My position was that Ali was the one who had said those things and not ABC. As an interviewee, Ali certainly had a right to his opinions. To me, his comments were just a part of the Ali act. I don't think anyone who watched that piece could ever have concluded that Ali was serious. He was just mouthing off, being Ali, doing his thing.

"Ali won the lawsuit, but then—and for as long as I live, I'll never understand it—an arbitrator ruled that since Ali was in the ABC studios as an entertainer he was covered by the agreement between the American Federation of Television and Radio Artists and the American Broadcasting Company. The arbitrator ruled that ABC was liable for the attorneys' fees. It wound up costing us a six-figure sum."

Once, while Ali was in exile from boxing because of his refusal to enter the military, we thought it would be good to have him do commentary on the U.S.-Soviet amateur boxing competition from Las Vegas, and I sent word for him to telephone me at my home. He called soon thereafter and I told him what we had in mind.

"I'd like very much to do that," he said quickly.

I explained that we'd pay him a fee plus his expenses. He paused, without replying, and didn't even ask how much money we had in mind.

"Muhammad, we normally pay fifteen hundred dollars for something like this."

His reply stunned and saddened me.

"Whatever you want to pay me is fine, Mr. Spence. I really need the money."

"Tell you what, Muhammad. We'll pay you twenty-five hundred dollars plus your expenses; that's round-trip air fare, your hotel and meals and other expenses."

"That's really nice of you, Mr. Spence. Thank you. What I'd like to do, though, is drive out there."

He explained that he was in Chicago at that time and would prefer to drive to Las Vegas. When he arrived there, the producer called me and said Ali didn't seem to have any good clothes with him. We bought him a jacket, and I wondered if, in the days since he was stripped of his title, anyone had had to buy clothes for the greedy people who took so much of Muhammad Ali's money.

Ali fought for extraordinary sums of money, pulling down monstrous purses, much of it frittered away or taken from him by those who took advantage of his loyalty and good nature. It brought to mind Sugar Ray Robinson, often described as the finest fighter, pound for pound, who ever crawled through the ring ropes. He made lots of money, too, and traveled with quite an entourage. He had his personal valet, his own hair stylist, and assorted other hangers-on who called him "Champ" and feasted at his table while he was on top, then deserted him when his skills diminished.

But no one had more leeches than Muhammad Ali. He may never have produced the loaves and fishes, but he surely fed the multitudes. Then, as his talents thinned, so did his flock. Sadly, he got to a point where he was fighting from memory and was doing it because he needed a payday, or because he was being almost pushed into the ring by the greed of others. Out of skills, out of work, and not nearly as wealthy as he should have been, that was the latter-day story of this superb fighter and equally great showman. And then, of course, he also lost his health.

It was Ali's showmanship that caused ABC Sports to hire him as an expert commentator when we decided to do the "Foreman

Versus Five" extravaganza on "Wide World of Sports." The show was a farce going in, and we knew it. Putting the former heavyweight champion of the world, George Foreman, in against five opponents was one of those promotions that probably never would have come about had it not been for the magic of the television set. We looked at it more as entertainment than sport, but it became more of a farce than we anticipated. In fact, it was an embarrassment.

The deal was set for April 26, 1975, in Toronto, and Foreman was scheduled to go three rounds (or less, if he could work it out) with each of five fighters: Boone Kirkman, Terry Daniels, Charlie Polite, Alonzo Johnson, and Jerry Judge. We thought that somewhere along the line, maybe late in the show when Foreman got tired, he might have a good battle with one of the fighters. It didn't happen. Foreman disposed of all of them, and it was more wrestling than boxing.

The show brought to mind the retort attributed to the late Joe Louis, when the former heavyweight champion turned to professional wrestling to make a buck or two. "It beats stealing," Louis was quoted as saying. So did the "Foreman Versus Five" thing, but not by much. The *real* show happened just outside the ring and involved Muhammad Ali.

We took every possible precaution to safeguard against the afternoon becoming a circus. We told Ali his role was to be that of a serious commentator, not a comedian. Dennis Lewin was the producer and he'll never forget what happened:

"We were staying at the Westbury Hotel, just across the street from Maple Leaf Gardens, and we called everybody together for a production meeting. Ali was there, and Cosell of course, and Roone Arledge made the trip to Toronto. The one thing I stressed more than any other in that meeting—and I was aiming my remarks more at Ali because I was concerned with what he might say—was that he was reporting as a guest commentator, and that we wanted him to conduct himself as an analyst. Knowing him, there was always the chance he'd go off the deep end, that he'd start thinking *he* was the show.

"So I kept going back to that point during the meeting, and Ali assured me that he understood. I even remember saying I didn't want any clowning around. That was the exact term I used. From the very beginning, we all knew there was this built-in danger and that the whole thing could deteriorate into a carnival. Roone got up and reinforced what I had said. And Ali kept saying, 'Don't worry, I understand. I'll just analyze what's going on in the ring.'

"Well, let me tell you that no sooner did Foreman get into the ring with the first guy than Ali started taunting him. And he taunted Foreman from the beginning to the end of the telecast, and it drove Foreman bananas. The whole thing turned into something that was, well, not very pretty. The more Ali taunted, the madder Foreman got. It kept snowballing and the thrust of the telecast, unfortunately, became the yelling and the taunting going on between Ali and Foreman. It was out of control. There was no retrieving it into anything resembling sanity. Conceptually, it wasn't all that bad going in, but in actuality it was terrible. I know. I produced it. It was a joke. We caught a lot of flak for it. And we deserved all of it."

It could have been worse. Believe it or not, we once considered a battle between Muhammad Ali and Wilt Chamberlain, the basketball superstar. The idea had been kicked around by the media, and Wilt himself had suggested it, saying he had given boxing some thought and wouldn't mind getting in the ring with Ali if the price was right.

We brought Wilt and Ali into the studio and put Howard Cosell between them for an interview on "Wide World of Sports." We used a measuring tape to do one of those tale-of-the-tape things to see how they compared physically. With Ali it was reach; with Wilt it was more a matter of wingspan. Ali was a very large human being, tall and erect and broad-shouldered, and as imposing a physical specimen as you could wish to find, but he was dwarfed by Chamberlain. I've seen lots of seven-footers, but, unless you have actually stood alongside Wilt Chamberlain, you can have no conception of what big really is. He is not only very tall, but his upper body is beyond belief. He may well be the strongest athlete this country has ever known. It impressed Ali, too. But it didn't stop him from sticking it to the big man. The two were bantering back and forth in the studio—Wilt had this little goatee at the time—and suddenly, and this was vintage Ali, the champion reached across Cosell and tugged at Wilt's goatee and remarked with a chuckle, "I ain't fightin' you. I ain't fightin' no billy goat."

A lot of boxing people didn't take Wilt's fight talk seriously, and I can't be certain Ali did, but I honestly think Chamberlain was leaning that way. And while lots of people would have considered an Ali-Wilt matchup a farce, it's safe to say ABC would have gone for it and put the fight in prime time.

Fame is fleeting and sports fans are fickle, and because Ali fought well past the time when he should have retired, his stature has been diminished in some eyes. True, he fought stiffs and bums in some inglorious mismatches, and because they fought in different eras, we could never determine what would have happened had he gotten in against Dempsey, Louis, or Marciano. But the three of them combined never brought as much dash and excitement and, yes, controversy to the prize ring as did the man who broke in as "the Louisville Lip." He gave ABC Sports some of its finest and funniest moments, in the ring and out of it.

For as long as there has been the recording of the human experience, either on film or audiotape or videotape, the "outtakes"—those not-intended-for-public-viewing mistakes and flubs and blunders and bobbles that are as inevitable as night following day—have provided almost as much entertainment as the events themselves. An Ali fight was the basis for one of the best in ABC's archives, and someday perhaps someone will unearth this classic and put it on one of those shows that takes the bleeps out of the cutting room and places them in our living rooms.

Ali was preparing to fight the British heavyweight Brian London, and Howard Cosell went to England to interview the challenger. This is how it went:

"Brian, certain members of the written press are saying this fight is a mere farce, that you are an unworthy contender, that this contest with Muhammad Ali is really no contest at all, that the fight has no business taking place, and that you, in fact, are a bum."

"Fuck you, Howard!"

"Cut, *cut*! No, *no*, Brian, you don't seem to understand. That's what is being said by the *written press*. I'm not saying that. Let's begin again. All right?"

"Very well, then."

"Brian, certain members of the written press are critical of your upcoming bout with Muhammad Ali. Certain members of the written media are describing you as an unworthy contender, and saying that this fight should not come off. They, in fact, describe you as a bum. Just how do you respond to that, Brian?"

"Fuck them!"

7

HAZARDS
OF SPORTSCASTING

Chris Schenkel, Keith Jackson,
and the Woody Hayes Debacle

Roone Arledge had hired Chris Schenkel in late 1964 with the promise that ABC Sports would get back into televising football. We reobtained the rights to NCAA college football in 1966 and ABC has televised college football every year since.

Schenkel and Bud Wilkinson had become our "A team" on ABC's college football, Chris was the anchor performer on our golf telecasts, he hosted the "Pro Bowlers Tour," and on top of that handled various "Wide World of Sports" assignments. He had become quite a star, and deservedly so.

An extracurricular chore that Chris volunteered for, and enjoyed, was taking Arledge to the Masters golf tournament each spring. Chris was solidly entrenched at the Augusta National Golf Club, originally through his connections with some of the Masters corporate underwriters, and he was always hired to narrate the tournament's highlight film. Sadly, it was at the Masters, in 1971, that Chris Schenkel discovered that Roone Arledge had found a new attraction.

His name was Frank Gifford.

Chris and Roone had adjoining rooms in Augusta, and Chris recalls the conversation:

"Roone tapped at my door and I told him to come in. I don't

think he even sat down. He just said, 'What would you think if I brought Frank Gifford over from CBS?'

" 'What the hell for?' I wanted to know. I knew right off there were no openings. But Arledge didn't anymore want my opinion than the man in the moon. He had already made up his mind. Frank was his hero. Gifford was doing some work for CBS, nothing really major, and he was the golden boy from California. He'd been a star in the National Football League and, more importantly, he'd been a star with the New York Giants. When I asked Roone what Gifford would do for ABC, he blurted right out that, of course, he'd do 'Monday Night Football.'

"Now that series had just finished a very successful opening season with Keith Jackson doing the play-by-play. But the die was cast. Arledge knew right then and there he was going to dump Keith Jackson and put Gifford in his place. Gifford was glamour, you see, and Arledge always wanted glamour. He's always been the kind of guy who does flip-flops over celebrities and Gifford was one, in his mind. I asked Roone if he had called Keith to talk it over and he said he hadn't, because he hadn't really made any decision yet. I knew him well enough to know that was a lie, and I urged him to call Keith. I didn't want Keith to have to read about it in the newspaper. But that's exactly what happened. And it happened because Roone Arledge has always been insensitive to other people's feelings. At the time, I guess I never gave a thought to how all this might affect me. But by that day I was out of favor with Roone, and for reasons I still don't understand."

Arledge obviously never gave a thought to, nor did he care about, the long-standing relationship Keith Jackson had enjoyed with Elton Rule, then the president of the American Broadcasting Company. Keith had worked for Elton when Rule ran ABC's local television station in Los Angeles. The quickest rumor to make the rounds on the twenty-eighth floor was that Jackson— and he really did have to read about the demotion in the newspapers—placed a hurried call to Elton Rule, and that Rule, in turn, called Arledge and demanded that he do something to assuage Jackson. Keith denies that he called Rule, and Rule verifies that version. But just what transpired is a bit foggy.

Elton Rule, who became vice chairman of ABC, was a popular and effective network president, and one not given to interfering in the day-to-day operations of the divisions. But he said he may have called Arledge about this matter:

"I know I was very upset about the way Keith was treated, and I may have picked up the telephone and called Roone and expressed my concern. I honestly don't remember.

"I had come to know and respect Keith when I was vice president and general manager of KABC in Los Angeles, and when I was called to New York to be president of the ABC Television Network, one of my first involvements with Roone was the development of 'Monday Night Football.' We were at our first affiliates' meeting, and we hooked up the telephone to a speaker and announced that we had obtained the rights to televise 'Monday Night Football.' There was great excitement about it. These were tremendous times with moments of great glory and examples of great creativity.

"Arledge? There can never be any question about his genius. You just knew that going in. He had a style, a touch, almost, that was unmatched, and it flourished particularly during Olympic Games' telecasts. But when it came to dealing with people, well, that's a different matter. Roone had tremendous freedom. He was allowed to do more than he should have. He had too much power. And he set the people working for him against each other. He made adversaries out of them. It was counterproductive and it was wrong. I have nothing against Frank Gifford, nothing at all. But Keith was treated shabbily and so, too, were others over the years."

Keith was in Milwaukee, doing a bowling film, when word of the change hit the newspapers. When he got back to his hotel room late that day, a stack of telephone messages awaited him. None was from Arledge, although Roone swore up and down that he had repeatedly tried to reach Jackson to tell him the news before it became publicly known. Roone had been busy scurrying about, making deals to scrape together the dollars necessary to persuade Gifford to jump networks. Gifford wound up with deals to do shows for WABC Television in New York and the ABC Radio Network, in addition to his network television assignments, with each division under the umbrella picking up a part of his considerable salary.

When Keith returned to his home in the Los Angeles area, he and Arledge finally had a chilly conversation on the telephone, and arrangements were made for Keith to fly to New York for a face-to-face meeting the following week.

Once in Roone's office, Arledge reiterated that he had tried to reach Keith, that he had left word with the hotel operator. Without batting an eye, Keith reached into his pocket and extracted a huge stack of telephone slips—he said there were more than thirty of them—and dropped them on the desk under Arledge's nose.

"Find yours," he said.

It has taken all of Keith's courtly southern-bred manner just to maintain a civil attitude toward Arledge. Some of our dirty laundry over that deal was aired in public, and we were fortunate that Keith elected to say very little to the media.

A few years later, perhaps to mollify Rule, Arledge decided to give Jackson the number-one college football spot occupied for so long by Chris Schenkel. Chris was relegated to doing games of secondary importance, which naturally had a ripple effect all the way down the line of football broadcasters working for ABC at the time.

There are two inescapable observations to be made here. The first is that Keith Jackson was, and is, a very good play-by-play announcer and deserved a primary football role. The second is that Chris Schenkel's career had been set on an irrevocably downward path.

No announcer ever cared more about ABC Sports, nor did more for ABC Sports in a business sense, than Chris Schenkel. He came to symbolize the home-God-mother-country-apple pie mood of Middle America. He had this great voice and friendly manner and made a terrific appearance, and he'd go anywhere and do anything to help us with sponsors. In the early days, when the concentration was more on event coverage than journalism, he was a terrific image-builder for ABC Sports. As the industry evolved, we had to be more sophisticated and wanted a greater degree of journalistic involvement from our commentators. That doesn't mean we wanted them to be editorializing all over the place, but it was time for change. And Chris simply could not change.

Here he was, a genuinely kind and caring person, who found himself hamstrung by his own industry, and by the times in which we were living. The nation was in a state of unrest and confusion, and in some cases mild rebellion, in the mid and late sixties. Kids were tearing about wildly, burning their draft cards and in some cases ROTC buildings, with college campuses becoming havens for radicals, sanctuaries for anyone who wanted to protest about anything. The people were out in the streets; our leaders were being shot and killed. The mood was antimilitary, antiestablishment, as American kids were being killed and maimed in some godforsaken country halfway around the world. And here was Chris Schenkel, telling viewers each Saturday during football season, "What better way to spend an autumn afternoon?"

No two people ever represented "the establishment" better than Chris Schenkel and Bud Wilkinson. In the booth, it was Mr. Nice Guy sitting alongside Mr. Nice Guy. Bud Wilkinson is as knowledgeable as anyone we've ever had work a football telecast, but he always pulled his punches. And so did Chris. Their performance was akin to what Billy Graham said some years ago about a developing trend in our religious lives: "The modern church has become a nice place where nice people go to hear a nice man tell them how nice they are." Chris and Bud were simply out of step with the way sports television, particularly at ABC, was developing.

Critics had begun to really snipe at the two of them. Schenkel was far and away their favorite target, and he took some particularly devastating shots from Gary Deeb, a syndicated columnist who worked out of Chicago. Early on, Arledge appeared to rally to Chris' defense, issuing some supportive quotes and doing a radio show with Howard Cosell. But the damage was done. And Chris took the shots, as he has taken everything down through the years, without flinching.

HAZARDS OF SPORTSCASTING

"There's always been the criticism that I never knocked anybody," said Chris. "Well, I've done mostly amateur sports over the years, and I just always feel I'm not about to knock some college kid just for dropping a pass, or missing a block. After all, they're students. They're just kids, like yours and mine. But the criticism got to Roone, I know that. He started reading all the clippings and damn near suffocated. He loved all the good publicity, but he couldn't tolerate any of the negative things. And he'd always overreact. Every once in a while, he'd tell me, 'Chris, you just have to change. If somebody doesn't do something right, just say it.' But I just told him I'd never change. And I won't.

"One Saturday afternoon, he happened to be in the studio in New York and I was on a remote, getting ready to do a bowling telecast. He could see me on the monitors in the control room and I was wearing my glasses. He sent word through the New York studio to my producer in the truck for me to take off my glasses. I told him I couldn't see without them. 'Then get contact lenses,' he barked. I sent word back that I'd tried to use them but couldn't. And I've worn my glasses ever since.

"But all in all, I don't have any regrets. I've always tried to do my best. The times changed, I guess, and I didn't. I could have gone back to CBS a couple of times, and I was tempted. So I'd meet with Arledge and tell him I was thinking about leaving. He'd tell me, 'Chris, you're the dean. You can't leave.' He'd make some more promises, I'd believe them and I'd stay on, and he'd never keep his promises. But Roone Arledge has to live with himself, and I have to live with me. I don't know about him, but I can handle my part of that deal."

College football enjoyed a tremendous growth in popularity starting in the late sixties. Despite the unrest and the talk by the amateur psychologists—and maybe the professional ones as well—that football players were no longer the heroes on the college campus, we found quite the opposite to be true. Fans embraced college football as never before, with the telecasts of games enjoying unprecedented success.

When professional football began its tremendous rise in popularity, Don Canham, Michigan's longtime athletic director and one of the brightest minds in the history of college sports, said the colleges had pretty much lost a generation of fans because of the impact of the pro game. But Canham didn't blame the pros. He called the National Football League the best-merchandised happening in sports history, and hailed NFL commissioner Pete Rozelle as a visionary. While the NFL was being promoted and merchandised, the colleges and universities, according to Canham, were sitting on their butts and wringing their hands. The colleges thought their product would sell itself, so while the pros thrived, the colleges went into a period of stagnation. ABC Sports helped bring the college game back. Special contributions were made by commentators Ara Parseghian, former great Notre Dame coach, and Frank Broyles, athletic director, and former outstanding coach at Arkansas, who performed so ably for nine years as our college football expert. (Frank shares my love for the game of golf and we once played 101 holes in three days at Augusta National.)

And thank God for people like Bear Bryant, who brought flavor and imagination to the sport. In my book of memories, the likes of him will never again be seen.

I first encountered him as a young impressionable production assistant during a stop on the "Professional Bowlers Tour" in Birmingham in 1962. About a half hour before air time, I was busy with my chores when all of a sudden things came to an absolute standstill. To a person, everyone rose and gave a rousing round of applause. I asked someone nearby, "Why the applause?" The quick reply was, "It's Bear Bryant!" I instantly learned about the great affection for "the Bear" in Alabama.

No one was more cooperative nor more accommodating to ABC Sports. Sometimes we'd be scrambling around, asking schools to move games in a schedule they'd drawn up eight or ten years before, or we'd want them to change their starting time to suit our television needs. Many were very accommodating, some were not at all, but Paul (Bear) Bryant, the legend of Alabama, was always the greatest.

"You folks are payin' us folks a whole lot of money," he'd

drawl, "and, by God, if y'all want us to play at two o'clock in the morning, well, that's when we'll tee it up."

The late Bear Bryant probably had more power than any coach in the land. He was not only the coach and the athletic director, he earned such affection from the legions of Crimson Tide fans that the political officials of his state turned to him for counsel and support. He enjoyed such autonomy that he could make decisions on provocative issues and never have to worry about being second-guessed. He was a dictator, for sure, but a friendly and benevolent one.

At one time, Bryant made it known he would like to do some television work for ABC. We used him on one game as an expert commentator, but he mumbled and drawled so much in that deep voice of his that it was well nigh impossible to understand him. He called me later and suggested that he would be a mighty fine addition to the announce booth for "Monday Night Football." Can you imagine it, Bear Bryant in the booth with Howard Cosell? When I reminded him that he was still coaching at Alabama, that it would not only present a conflict between the pro and college games, but would be impossible for him to juggle his coaching schedule with his broadcasting commitments, he assured me he could juggle both careers. I told him I appreciated his offer, but left no doubt that we would go in another direction. He never brought it up again. I always suspected that when he made that call he might have been a little bit into the bourbon and branch water, just like the time he jokingly complained at a Sugar Bowl dinner that I hadn't even sent him a Christmas card after he had carefully "arranged" the New Year's Day bowl games to favor ABC. From that time until he died, I always made sure to send him a nice card at Christmastime.

For a brief time, we used the late Duffy Daugherty, former Michigan State coach, as a college football analyst. Face-to-face, Duffy was one of the funniest storytellers in the land, but it was hard for him to insert his material and make it funny between plays. The man was a yarn-spinner, and, with only twenty-five seconds to get the ball in play in college football, his stories were often hurried, or left hanging.

One of Duffy's great banquet stories tells of the time he went fishing with Bear Bryant in Alabama. Sometime during the lazy summer afternoon, with just the two of them in the boat and the fish taking the day off from biting, Bryant drawled: "You know, Duffy, there's a passel of folks down here in Alabama who believe ol' Bear can walk on water."

Duffy said he understood, what with Bryant's record and the affection felt toward him in that neck of the woods.

"You know, Duffy, it might sound kinda silly, but, by God, I've always wanted to kinda try it. You know, jes' to see if I could, one time."

"Well, Bear, there's no one around except the two of us. I can't think of a better time to try it."

The lake was clear and shimmering, with hardly a ripple from the boat to the tree-lined shores. Bryant stood up in the back of the boat, took a giant stride, and plopped into the water. As he went under, bubbles began to gurgle to the surface. Suddenly, the Bear reappeared, coughing and sputtering, and spitting out what seemed to Duffy to be gallons of water. Duffy was overboard in a flash, grabbing the larger man by the neck and assisting him back to the craft, where he half-pushed, half-dragged him into the boat, then crawled back in himself. The two legendary coaches crouched there on opposite ends of the aluminum boat, sopping wet and totally spent by the ordeal. Bryant spoke first:

"Duffy, you son of a bitch, if you ever tell anybody ol' Bear tried to walk on water and damn near drowned, I'll never speak to you again. You heah?"

"On one condition, Bear. Don't you ever tell anyone I pulled your ass out."

Surely the most controversial incident in the long history of ABC's involvement with college football was the coverage—or, more honestly, the lack of coverage—of the Gator Bowl flare-up involving then Ohio State coach Woody Hayes and a Clemson player, Charley Bauman. The date was December 29, 1978.

Clemson had the lead, but Ohio State was putting on a late drive and appeared to be headed for what would have been the winning touchdown or field goal. Suddenly, Bauman, the Clemson player, intercepted an Ohio State pass and was driven out of bounds near the Ohio State bench. In a flash, Woody Hayes grabbed the Clemson player and took some punches at him. It was all over in a matter of seconds. A semblance of order was restored and Clemson won the game. In that instant, Coach Hayes had wiped out much of the goodwill he had generated through twenty-seven seasons of coaching the Buckeyes. By losing his temper, he had disgraced himself and embarrassed his great university. The whole nation had seen the ugly incident, and there could be no question that Woody would be fired. He had left OSU's then athletic director, Hugh Hindman, no choice, even though there are some Buckeye diehards who still think Coach Hayes was only being himself and that Hindman had no business firing a legend. It would be an inglorious departure, a sad ending, indeed, to a coaching career few men could ever match. Woody died in 1987.

The trouble was, ABC never properly covered that sideline melee, either with pictures or words. There's an excuse for the lack of pictures; none for the absence of words.

I had gone to New Orleans for the Sugar Bowl, and so watched the Gator Bowl telecast from my hotel room. Like the rest of the audience, I'm sure, I was stunned when Coach Hayes grabbed the Clemson player and starting flailing away at him. But I was even more shocked when our announcers, Keith Jackson and Ara Parseghian, didn't say a single world about it. I immediately got on the telephone to Bob Goodrich, the producer, who was in the control truck at Jacksonville, Florida.

My first question was, "Are you people aware of what happened?"

"Yes, Jim, we know about it."

"Well, we haven't said anything."

"Keith says he didn't see it."

"Well, he's the only person who didn't see it, then. It's perfectly clear that Woody struck the player. We simply must have Keith deal with this."

Goodrich assured me he would take care of it. I went back to my chair and waited for Keith to explain what had happened.

Still there was no explanation. It was as though the incident just hadn't happened, yet the whole country had witnessed it. Back to the telephone I went and, again, Bob Goodrich and I conversed.

"Bob, please listen. This is a *major* incident. Woody Hayes has struck a Clemson football player. We *must* deal with it. And we must do it *immediately.*"

Bob explained that Keith insisted he had not seen the slugging. Technically, there was no way to show it on instant replay. (I'll explain why in a minute.) Bob told me that Keith was absolutely refusing to comment on something he had not seen. Keith told Bob he was looking at the Gator Bowl scoreboard when the supposed event occurred. By that time, I was boiling.

"Bob, listen hard, please. We simply *have* to find a way to deal with this. It's a major story and we have a journalistic responsibility to treat it as a major story."

I hung up, sat back down, and again waited for Keith's explanation. Again, he said nothing. I went right back to the telephone for my third call to the truck.

"Bob, I do not want to order Keith to say it, but please relay my message to him right now that this must be dealt with. Get someone on the sidelines—get an official—get someone who witnessed it. If Keith says he didn't see it, get the attribution from the field. But get it!"

For the third time, Bob assured me he'd take care of it.

The tragedy of it all is that ABC went off the air and never once alluded to the obvious fact that one of the best-known, most successful, and most volatile coaches in the world had slugged an opposing team's player.

The following morning, Goodrich left Jacksonville to return to his home in California. On a stopover at the Atlanta airport, he phoned me at the hotel in New Orleans and told me he had read the Atlanta newspapers and that there didn't seem to be such a big flap over our part in what had taken place.

"Trust me on this one, Bob, this is a huge story and we have a huge problem. We're going to have every major newspaper in the country on our case about this."

You didn't have to be psychic to make that kind of forecast. It was inevitable it would happen, and our defenses weren't very well constructed. The truth of it is that we *could* not show an instant replay that night. Here's why:

Ohio State, in an effort to catch up, was passing on every down. The producer had three videotape machines available to him, which meant that he could key on three players. He chose to key on the receivers. (Goodrich would later say, "I know it was the conservative way to do things, but I didn't want there to be a pass interference call and then miss it. Also, I didn't want to blow it if someone made a spectacular catch. If that happened, I wanted to have it on isolation.") As things developed, it was our end-zone camera that was isolated on the interception. As is always the case, at the end of a play, when somebody goes out of bounds, we stop recording the end-zone camera; the guy operating the video-tape machine in one of the trucks punches it out of the "record" mode and takes the machine back to the beginning of the play. That's simply standard operating procedure, and has been for as long as I can remember. After all, you can't anticipate that a coach is going to jerk some player around and try to punch his lights out.

Goodrich again:

"I was looking at the tape-machine picture. I saw the interception, so I began to look to see where I had it best. I never actually saw what the people at home were seeing. But Terry Jastrow, who was directing the telecast, and our NCAA media director, Donn Bernstein, who was also in the truck, both started yelling, 'Holy shit, he hit him!' I immediately asked them what they were talking about, and they explained that Woody Hayes had slugged a Clemson player. My next move was to tell the tape operator to take his machine down to the end of the play so we could see what pictures we had. What we had was zero, because, remember, the tape operator had stopped recording before Hayes hit Bauman. The other tape machines had nothing, because they were keying on the receivers.

"I wasn't recording line ["line" is what the viewers at home see] because I was trying to be conservative and cover all the players I possibly could on isolation.

"Besides, at that time, we hadn't purchased what we call 'net return,' because we considered it too expensive. Net return means a routing of the network feed out of New York back to our mobile unit, in this case at Jacksonville. That meant our New York studio couldn't take the pictures of the slugging and send them back down the line to the game site. The bottom line was that we had no pictures for Keith to see, so he could comment; we couldn't make the whole thing unfold again. I'm sure viewers would have liked to have seen it again. Hell, we'd have liked to see it, too. There I sat, with nothing.

"On the headset, I told Keith Jackson that I'd been told that Woody Hayes had hit the kid and that he should say something. All I got was silence. As I recall, we went immediately to a commercial, and right away Jim Spence called and wanted to know what in the hell was going on. I told him the situation, that I didn't have a replay. While I had Jim on the phone later, I told Keith that Jim was on the line and insisting that Keith say something. Keith's response was that he hadn't seen it and wasn't about to say anything about something he hadn't seen.

"I hung up with Jim, then we came out of a commercial and continued on with the game. Billy Edwards was our sideline guy who coordinated commercials with the officials, and I urged him to try and find out what had taken place, and get additional confirmation. Ara Parseghian said he hadn't really seen anyting. As I remember, he said he had noted a scuffle on the sidelines, but couldn't figure out what had taken place. But Ara also heard me tell Keith that we had enough confirmation and that we should go ahead and comment on it. *Still* Keith made no mention. Then Spence was on me again, telling me to relay exact words to Keith—that we must deal with it *right now*. The reply from Jackson was that no one sitting in front of a television set five hundred miles away could tell him to say something about an incident he had not seen with his own eyes. Case closed.

"And so we went off the air looking like assholes. To this day, I believe that if Keith had merely said, 'Ladies and gentlemen, there has been an incident, apparently involving Ohio State coach Woody Hayes and one of the Clemson players. We cannot show you a replay of that because of some technical problems we have encountered, and I never saw it with my own eyes. But I understand that you all saw Woody Hayes strike one of the

Clemson players. And so, obviously, there is a major problem with Coach Hayes and it'll have to be dealt with.' If he had just said that much, that would have done it. Boom! It wouldn't have been ideal, because we didn't have the pictures to show it on replay, but it would have saved a hell of a lot of embarrassment.

"The way it happened, I looked bad, Keith looked bad, ABC looked bad, and it's for damn sure that Woody looked bad. That night, I was certain I was going to be fired. After all, I was the producer and it ultimately was my responsibility. The buck stopped with me, and I figured it'd make ABC look good if they fired me. So I went on back to California assuming my career, at least the ABC part of it, was over.

"The following day, I had a couple of conversations with Jim, and then I refused to answer my telephone for several days. People, mainly sportswriters and television critics, were calling day and night, but I either had my wife answer the phone or I took it off the hook. I just laid low. And I mean *low*. But I figured ABC certainly would say something about it during the Sugar Bowl telecast. Keith had flown directly to New Orleans to do that game, and I just naturally assumed they'd have shipped the tape from New York to New Orleans, cued it up and let Keith smooth things over, saying here's what happened a few nights ago at the Gator Bowl, and we couldn't show you the replay at that time because of technical problems. Nothing. Not a picture. Not a word.

"Chuck Howard was producing that game, and to this day I can't tell you why it wasn't done—whether Keith wouldn't say it or whether Chuck wouldn't push it—but again it was left undone. The whole thing wound up in Roone Arledge's office not long after that, and I was seated right next to Keith. We all told our versions of what had taken place and when Keith said, 'No one ever said anything to me,' I shot right back so everyone could hear me, 'That is not true.'

"Parseghian didn't come to the meeting but rather, as I recall, sent a long letter to Arledge telling him what he remembered, or didn't remember. Ara's memory got a little fuzzy between the time he left the press box and when he wrote that letter. The fact is, Ara heard every word I had spoken to Keith on the headset. He knew Keith was under instructions to say something about what had happened on the sideline. Ara's an old jock and he just didn't suck up his guts. I guess he's the kind of guy who wants to be everybody's friend and didn't want to take sides. So he chose not to recall, exactly, what went on.

"The whole thing was a bad scene. I came out of it scarred but all right. And I think Arledge believed me. I admitted that I was screwed up, that I had made a mistake and that I should have been recording the 'line.' They tried to tell me it had always been SOP to record line, but, if it was standard, everyone ignored it. No one ever told me it was standard. But, failing that, I did everything I could. I guarantee you that now no one is confused about policy. You simply record the line, every time out of the box, and that's all there is to it. In the unlikely event another coach ever slugs another player, we'd probably have a replay of it."

Both Keith Jackson and Bob Goodrich are talented people. Both have contributed immensely to ABC Sports. Both are friends of mine. That night, I was very disturbed at both of them. I was mad at Bob for not getting the job done, and I was mad at Keith for refusing to do the job. But, mainly, I think the fault in that instance lies with Keith Jackson.

It was awkward when he came to New Orleans for the Sugar Bowl. We were in the same car, going to a dinner with the Sugar Bowl people. It was inevitable the subject would come up. Keith was sitting in the front seat with our driver. My wife and I were in the back seat. Keith stared straight ahead. After a period of silence—and without turning around—Keith said, "Jim, I couldn't do it. If my own mother had told me that Woody Hayes had struck an opposing player, and I hadn't seen it, I wouldn't have said it on the air."

Keith wasn't going to budge, and neither was I. He had taken a strong position and was prepared to defend it—and still has that same position, and still defends it. On the other hand, I thought then, and I think now, that his position was indefensible.

Perhaps we should have done something on the subsequent Sugar Bowl telecast, and I take full responsibility for the decision there. Looking back on it, all we could have done was show the slugging incident one more time. But by that time, I think everyone in the free world had seen it more than enough. We could have explained our situation and the technical problems we had encountered in Jacksonville, but ask yourself how many football fans cared about, or could have understood, those problems and the conversations that took place involving the truck, the announce booth, and my hotel room.

The bottom line is that we blew it, and blew it big. We took our lumps and we had them coming. But in college football over the years, the thrills far outweighed the agonies.

8

THE MAN WHO BUILT
THE COLLEGE
MONSTER

*Walter Byers and His Once
Impregnable Empire*

Television cannot merely shrug and absolve itself of all the blame for some of the major problems facing college athletics today. The vast sums of money we handed out helped create the monster, and we must take some responsibility for that.

There was all the hoopla and the fanfare of college football and its newfound exposure to the national television audience, and everyone got caught up in the excitement of it to the point where they lost perspective on what they were creating. The colleges and universities were getting those handsome checks in the mail, and the newfound wealth did to some of them what newfound wealth often does to people: It made them, in some cases, greedy and corrupt. Most athletic programs at our major colleges and universities are legitimately run and honestly operated, but we have a number of individuals who believe the old chestnut first attributed to the late Herman Hickman when he coached at Yale: Winning isn't everything; it's the only thing.

Thankfully, some of the terrible abuses are now at least being aired and addressed, if so far not solved. I believe the key to handling the problems is the total involvement of the presidents and chancellors of the various schools. They simply have to retake control of athletic programs; take them out of the hands of certain athletic directors and coaches. At many of our institutions, the football coach has become a demigod, and sometimes is also the athletic director. In other situations, a powerful coach will operate virtually autonomously, either ignoring the athletic director or having such a sweet deal that the athletic director practically works for him—especially when, as in many cases, he has been handpicked by the coach. As often as not, athletic directors at some of the powerhouse schools perform only the duties of a business manager, while the coach makes the really important decisions. In a few instances, the athletic department is operated as a separate corporation, thus enabling the people in it to create their own rules and standards with only token reference to a higher authority.

The trouble is that presidents and chancellors see the huge stadiums that need to be filled, and they know that you fill them only by winning and that you win with people (*You Win With People* was the title of the late Woody Hayes' book), and that you get the winning people with aggressive and often overzealous recruiting. The tragic result is the intellectually impoverished recruit getting into school, sometimes with altered transcripts; then once there, taking Mother Goose courses without being required to attend classes with any degree of regularity; then being handed passing grades until, once eligibility has expired, he is turned out into the world no more educated than the day he arrived, and with precious little preparation for meeting life on any level other than that of playing one particular game.

Many people believe this cannot change. They think that alumni pressure is so massive that presidents and chancellors cannot take strong positions without the risk of getting fired, and they argue that the average president is no different from the average guy in the street when it comes to covering his own backside. These university executives have seen the studies that prove there is a direct correlation between the number of football victories and the amount of money the old grads contribute, and they know that sports is the single best rallying point for any school. Not many old grads come back to campus to celebrate the dedication of a new science building.

The lack of any definitive reform as a result of the NCAA special convention in Dallas in June of 1987 raises serious questions regarding the resolve of presidents and chancellors of institutions involved in major college athletics.

The NCAA (National Collegiate Athletic Association) has no real control over presidents and chancellors, so reform must come from within the institutional framework itself. The networks would be delighted to assist by paying less in rights fees, but how many times have you heard of anyone agreeing to a pay cut? And yet the problems now are extending well beyond that of the uneducated or ill-educated "student." The television advertisers are beginning to have serious concerns. Where they used to look at college football as this marvelously wholesome activity, with the beautiful campus with its shady walkways, ivy-covered walls, pep rallies, bonfires, cheerleaders, and tailgate parties, with all those healthy young Americans out there competing on what the late General Douglas MacArthur called "the fields of friendly strife," the people who purchase television time and those who put up the cash for them to do so now look at college football with at least an honest eye, and once in a while with a jaundiced one.

Now what they see is that the strife is not merely on the field, but everywhere in ugly headlines and uglier stories. They watch and read the news and they hear about steroids and other drugs, and cheating on grades and admission tests, and about free automobiles and apartments and stereos and credit cards and bank accounts, and sometimes even sexual favors, and about coaches who coldly walk out on valid contracts without so much as an apology to the aggrieved school. Most advertisers are not too eager to be associated with a program that breeds headline stories about some seventeen-year-old whose recruiting enticements included a job for his father, the company of a prostitute while on his campus visit, and the promise of a signing bonus of twenty-five thousand dollars.

The graduation rate of athletes at some of the schools that annually produce powerful football and basketball teams is nothing short of a national disgrace. There are schools that have not had more than a relative handful of players obtain valid degrees. Some of the schools you consistently find near the top of the weekly ratings would do almost anything rather than go through the embarrassment of showing you the academic standing of their athletes.

The NCAA's position has always been that it has never had sufficient manpower to police what goes on at major universities. Why didn't the NCAA take some of the enormous rights fees television has paid out over the years and simply hire more people? The NCAA has never been what you'd call understaffed in any other area; thus, to claim undermanning in the area of enforcement always struck me as ludicrous. I don't deny that policing is a tough problem, or that you'll have violations no matter how many people you have working in that area. But it's long past the time for everyone to recognize the size of this problem and to see cheating for what it really is—the erosive force that could undermine everything everyone involved has worked for so long to build. Indeed, I believe that the scandalous behavior by a limited few, combined with insufficient enforcement practices, could destroy the very fabric of American college sports. I'm no Pollyanna, but surely it is impossible for any rational person to deny that young people should be in college first and foremost to get an education.

There are some gung-ho sports junkies who'll argue that taking a normal course load, or even going to classes, is not the important issue. Their argument is that it's "the college experience" that counts, especially for student-athletes who are products of impoverished or disadvantaged environments. College, the argument goes, places these youngsters in a pleasant atmosphere where they are able to assume a different attitude and posture about themselves and about life in general. It is contended that just being in college, merely seeing life at a different level, meeting people from other backgrounds, enables such "students" to grow socially, if not intellectually. In my opinion, that's absolute nonsense! In the first case, it is customary at some of our athletic factories for the athletes to be purposely isolated from the academic community, sleeping in athletic dormitories and taking their meals at training tables. Unless they go to class, just where do they rub elbows with the other students? The truth is that in many of the worst cases the athlete is pampered and sheltered in what amounts to more of a cloister than a college.

And that, along with all the other evils, has to change before the whole thing strangles itself. Hopefully, the so-called "death penalty" meted out by the NCAA to Southern Methodist University in 1987—SMU was barred from playing any football in that year, and restricted to seven away games in 1988 (it decided not to play the 1988 season)—will send a strong signal throughout the land.

An observer of college athletics would have to say that Walter Byers exerted more control over college football than Pete Rozelle has had over the professional game. To my mind, Walter Byers, who stepped aside in 1987 after thirty-six years as executive director of the NCAA, has been the most powerful man in American sports. His departure leaves me with mixed feelings. The NCAA certainly will be a more democratic organization from here on in. Byers' successor is the highly regarded Dick Schultz, who had been athletic director at the University of Virginia and chairman of the NCAA Division I Men's Basketball Committee.

Walter Byers considered the NCAA the alpha and omega of his life. Indeed, it could be argued that it shoved all else, and everyone else, out of his life. You could set up any committee you wanted within the framework of the NCAA, and the bottom line was that somewhere along the way you would have to deal with Walter Byers. This short, gray man could be absolutely charming over a cocktail—and he always enjoyed a good healthy drink—but in another setting he could sometimes do such a one-eighty that you wouldn't want to even have a drink with him. The NCAA had a television committee, and a negotiating committee, but by whatever methods it took, the whole ball of wax invariably wound up being precisely whatever Walter Byers wanted it to be. Walter was a dictator, and not always a benevolent one. Walter Byers, the loner, austere, very bright, calculating, a man who asked good and hard questions, was tough to figure. People who worked with and for him for many years say that not once have they been invited to his home.

The first time I felt the fullness of Byers' wrath was when ABC ventured into NFL football. Make no mistake about it: the

National Football League was *the enemy*. To Walter this meant all-out war, and he was quick to let us know about it. Confessions, while they may be good for the soul, can sometimes be embarrassing, but I have to admit that on more than one occasion ABC Sports was unduly influenced by Walter Byers.

Walter mistakenly thought he had Roone Arledge's assurance that as long as ABC had college football rights it would never dabble in NFL football. He was furious about our NFL deal, and we almost lost college football because of it. Walter insisted that ABC's "Monday Night Football" package never be mentioned on the college telecasts. At first, we didn't promote "Monday Night Football" either during the college telecasts or during the scoreboard shows following the college games, although later we had one promotional message during each half. Also, we could not use footage of any NFL play in these promos. Additionally, Walter was very sensitive about the announcers we would use, as became obvious later when Paul Hornung finally went to court and won a lawsuit against the NCAA, claiming he had been unfairly kept off college football telecasts done by Ted Turner's superstation in Atlanta. ABC had kicked around the idea of using former pro quarterback Fran Tarkenton on some college games; even though the NCAA did not have announcer approval—only consultation rights—we dropped the idea. (Fran was not really interested anyway.)

Another example of Byers' influence involved our coverage on "Wide World of Sports" of the dedication of the new NCAA executive office in Shawnee Mission, Kansas, in April of 1973, certainly not in keeping with the "Wide World" programming concept.

Walter Byers wielded great control, more than Pete Rozelle, because he didn't have as many strong personalities and egos to deal with in imposing his will on colleges and universities as Rozelle did with pro team owners. Additionally, with more than one hundred schools involved in what the media likes to refer to as big-time athletics, the whole thing tends to become very fragmented, further helping Walter gradually gain almost total control. While he pretty much disdained the spotlight, no one could ever accuse him of turning his back on power. The late

Charles E. Wilson, when he was chairman of the board of General Motors, had said that what was good for General Motors was good for the nation. Walter Byers believed that what was good in his mind was good for college athletics. He seized, sometimes ever so gently, the important powers involved in the college game. I have learned that people will share their talents, and often their money, but rarely do people share power. At times, he allowed his power to blind him.

An example is the television contract we negotiated with the NCAA for the rights to televise college football from 1982 through 1985. This was the contract that later was voided by the United States Supreme Court. We had gone back and forth in 1981 and Walter was being extremely tough. He did a great job getting a lot of money for the schools over the years. I never met a tougher negotiator. The cordial guy who'd join you for a drink turned tiger around a conference-room table. It almost seemed as if he became a different person. A former newspaperman, Walter never trusted television people. A midwesterner, he never trusted easterners, and particularly New Yorkers. More than once, he let us know how much he hated the city of New York.

The fact that during any NCAA negotiation you were dealing with Walter more than with a television committee was made abundantly clear to me in 1981. Charlie Lavery was working with me during the negotiations, and we hopscotched all over the country, meeting in five different cities before getting the thing settled. And even then, it took a near fist fight to get the deal done. We had our first session with the NCAA Negotiating Committee in Columbus, Ohio, another meeting in San Francisco, a third get-together in Kansas City, and a fourth in Denver before nailing down the agreement in Newport, Rhode Island.

There was a formal negotiating period—the legal time we had been granted to complete negotiations—and it expired during the Denver session, with the whole thing covering thirty days, clock running. We got embroiled in the roughest verbal exchange in Denver. We had agreed at the Kansas City meeting that we would consider midnight local time the stopping place, regardless of the city. Here it was, a quarter to twelve, and we were still arguing.

Walter had been upset all day. He was grouchy and argumentative. He wanted to catch a flight back to Kansas City, and he kept
questioning the deadline. He figured he had done the negotiating
over a thirty-day period, did not have a signed deal, and, by
golly, he was antsy to catch the first thing smoking to Kansas
City.

I reminded him that we had a pact to continue until midnight,
Denver time.

"There is no such agreement," Walter roared.

I insisted that there was, and besides, I said, "We're talking
about something that is vitally important to both the NCAA and
ABC Sports, and I think we owe it to ourselves to spend every
minute we can to try and reach an agreement."

Never a man to melt quickly, Walter was adamant that he
knew of no such agreement. I told him that Tom Hansen, now
the Pacific 10 commissioner, and then television program director, knew of it. Hansen was there in the room, and although he
never responded, Walter realized from his silence that we had
made such a deal. At one point, Walter became so furious that he
leaped out of his chair as he was trying to make a point and stuck
a finger right in Charlie Lavery's face. Charlie was a pretty good
athlete in his day, a running back at Virginia Military Institute,
and I honestly thought Charlie was going to deck old Walter right
then and there.

Still, I had only fifteen minutes to reach Fred Pierce and Roone
Arledge back in New York—and it was almost two o'clock in the
morning in the East. At this point, for the first time in its history,
the NCAA was talking about a split network deal involving ABC
and most likely CBS. While I headed for the telephone, Charlie
was to try and hold the committee together. As it turned out, the
midnight deadline arrived before I was able to complete my
discussion with Pierce and Arledge. When I returned to the
meeting room, Walter Byers was gone.

It was then up to the NCAA to give us a final proposal, and a
few days later the NCAA package arrived on my desk in New
York. Their proposal was for a four-year deal for $131,750,000!
We scheduled the showdown meeting for Newport, where
Walter and the entire NCAA committee were on hand. We made

up our minds we were not about to lose college football under any circumstances, but it was important for me to take something—a crumb, if you will—back to New York. I wanted to be able to tell my superiors that we got the NCAA to knock off $250,000 from its final offer.

I didn't beg, but I came damn close to it. And I recall saying, "Walter, I think we are ready to make a deal. If ABC Sports will commit one hundred and thirty-one and a half million dollars, do we have a deal?"

Walter never flinched. He never budged, either. Not one lousy penny.

"No, you know what the number is."

I went at him one more time.

"You're not willing for two hundred fifty thousand dollars to bend just a little bit?"

"You know the number. The number is one thirty-one seven-fifty!"

Did you ever try to get a sphinx to compromise? Walter was absolutely rigid. I looked around the room at the members of the committee. No one uttered a word. I thought that by their steely silence they were saying, "For God's sake, Walter, give it to him. Don't be such a hard-ass."

Walter liked his position. He was dealing from strength. If that meant being a hard-ass, tough!

There would be not one single crumb for me to take back to New York. Strike one for the cowboy from Kansas City. He had made his point. He had once again stuck it to the television hotshots from New York.

"Walter, if ABC Sports commits $131,750,000—just so we're clear on this—do we have a deal?"

"Yes."

"All right. You've got your one thirty-one seven-fifty."

CBS was also meeting with the committee in Newport, and we had managed to stick a favored-nation clause into our contract. It specified that the NCAA couldn't sign a deal with another network for a smaller figure without our figure being reduced. With NBC having alienated the NCAA by having aligned itself with the rival College Football Association, I'm surprised that CBS didn't drive a harder bargain with Walter. That, of course, would have driven the ABC price down. The only explanation that makes any sense is CBS's desire to maintain a solid relationship with Byers, particularly as it pertained to their retaining the rights to the NCAA Basketball Championship. They had just acquired the rights to the college basketball championship starting in 1982 after NBC had televised this event for a number of years.

As it turned out, we shared that contract with CBS for the first two years. I predicted openly, in interviews with the press, that the ratings would go down as exclusivity was eroded. And they did, each season. Then came the historic Supreme Court decision that determined that our NCAA contract covering college football telecasts was illegal, and in violation of the nation's antitrust laws. And every bit of it could have been avoided had Walter Byers been a man of greater sensitivity. This debacle helped me to better understand the meaning of the old saying that "there is none so blind as he who *will* not see." The College Football Association had been formed in 1977, and the organization made no bones about why it was organized—because many of the major schools didn't think they were being fairly considered. It was looking more and more like some of the schools would pull out of the NCAA, and no one was more vocal than Joe Paterno of Penn State. One night in 1981, I spent more than an hour on the telephone with Paterno, discussing the various problems in college football.

When we hung up, I was more convinced than ever that Joe and his allies in the CFA were deadly serious about their concerns and their aims, and I could see a major schism in the very heart of college athletics. Further, I had similar discussions with Chuck Neinas, the executive director of the CFA since 1980, and I don't know of anybody who has more knowledge about college football as it pertains to television. I quickly placed a call to Roone Arledge.

"These people in the CFA are for real," I told Arledge. "I think we ought to call Walter Byers. I'm not at all sure that Walter fully understands that these people are very, very serious."

Roone agreed, and we set up a conference call that involved the two of us, Charlie Lavery, and Walter. We made it clear to Byers that we were talking as "friends and partners."

"In my judgment," I told him, "you have to address this problem now. These people have asked for a special convention, and I think you ought to grant their request and try to work things out."

He told us he appreciated our concern, but with Walter it was always difficult to figure out whether he really appreciated it or whether that was his subtle way of telling you it was time to hang up. The NCAA did call a special convention, though, and at that session in St. Louis addressed some of the CFA concerns—but not enough to keep the University of Georgia and the University of Oklahoma from filing the lawsuit that upset everybody's apple-cart. Walter knew that in 1981 the CFA had actually signed a contract with NBC, but the deal didn't get final approval. So, you see, for a guy who was as masterful as he had been for so many years, Walter failed to heed the many warning signals that were being sent out. In my judgment, he could have avoided most of the trouble simply by hopping on an airplane and having lunch or dinner with the president and chancellor, respectively, at Georgia and Oklahoma and pointing out that the NCAA recognized that Georgia and Oklahoma, as haves, believed too much emphasis was being placed on the have-nots. Walter could have told the Georgia and Oklahoma people that flexibility in terms of additional *money and exposure* would be forthcoming—although the NCAA was not going to provide all they wanted.

The truth is that, all the while, the NCAA had itself been operating in violation of antitrust laws. In fact, as the storm was building, Walter addressed a meeting of the chief executive officers of the Big Eight Conference. Instead of easing their fears and relieving some of their tensions by telling them that he understood their problems and would address them, he was arrogant and abrasive and accomplished just the opposite of what he should have set out to do. At a time when he should have been listening to others' points of view, he was insensitive and inflexible. It was as though his sole message was: I know what's best for all of you, and that's the way it's going to be.

To my dying day—or his—I will never fully understand Walter Byers. And I don't think anyone else will, either. Talk to some college presidents and athletic directors around the country and they will tell you he has done an outstanding job for college athletics. Others think he has been petty and dictatorial, and that he has operated in such a high-handed way as to assure that the world of college athletics served *his* purposes rather than the other way around. I know he confused the hell out of me at times.

As for the resultant dramatic decrease in college football television-rights fees, that must leave Walter chuckling. The total amount of television revenue had climbed from $1.2 million in 1952 to more than $78 million for the 1984 season, before the court decision in June of 1984. After that decision, which eliminated the exclusivity that existed via the NCAA, revenues nose-dived by over 50 percent and since then have not come close to the level of the voided NCAA contracts. The major schools gained control of the rights to their properties, all right, but in the process they created a significant revenue shortfall.

Walter Byers has rarely been openly flattering about anyone. But during the preliminary NCAA meetings in February 1981, which led to the eventual agreement in Newport, Walter made what you might call a "minispeech" about me. It was the nicest talk anyone ever gave about me. Usually, one has to die before that sort of praise is uttered. He told about my positive relationship with the NCAA and how easy it was to have meaningful dialogue with me. He said I really had the NCAA's best interests in mind, and that I conducted difficult negotiations in a straightforward, sincere manner. He topped off his remarks by mentioning that my task had been particularly difficult since I had replaced Roone Arledge as the lead ABC Sports executive in dealings with the NCAA.

During those same meetings, I had talked with Walter about the upcoming negotiations for the NCAA basketball package and affirmed ABC's interest therein. I had previously expressed to him that we did not want to get into a bidding contest, as a matter of principle, but at the same time we wanted the championship and were prepared to negotiate in good faith.

Walter Byers looked me straight in the eye and said: "Jim, we are going to do it your way. We are going to meet with all the networks in Tampa later this month, and we are going to pick one entity and negotiate with that one entity."

To make sure, I asked him again if we'd be expected to have a specific dollar figure ready when we got to Tampa. He assured me we would not. "You won't prejudice yourself if you don't discuss numbers in Tampa," was his response.

Later that month, our delegation met with the NCAA Basketball Championship Committee in Tampa, and I remember we flew back to La Guardia in a blinding thunderstorm with lightning flashing all around us. When I finally got home, I had an urgent message to call Walter's assistant, Tom Jernstedt, in Tampa, who told me the committee would need a financial proposal from ABC by seven-thirty the following morning. I was dumbstruck. I just couldn't believe what I was hearing. Jernstedt repeated the conditions: "The committee needs your figure by seven-thirty in the morning. We have met with the other networks and we have proposals from them and we need your proposal."

All the time trying not to blow my cool, I reminded him of my conversations with Walter, and how I had been promised there would be no bidding. I told him it would not be possible for me to get together a bid by that deadline. He told me he'd relay my message to members of the committee. It didn't take him very long to call me again, and this time he said that the committee would wait until 10 A.M. for ABC's offer.

Arledge and I were in Fred Pierce's office early the next morning, and, while there was concern about the financial commitment that would be necessary, we were not prepared to enter into something like this on such short notice. We also had to work out a conflict with an Academy Awards telecast. I called Jernstedt and told him our decision. Then Walter Byers got on the line:

"Are you guys going to make a proposal or not?" His manner was curt, his voice stern.

"Walter," I protested, "you and I went over the ground rules. We talked about the procedure and this is not what we discussed. We don't think we should be involved in a bidding situation. On the other hand, we would like very much to be able to sit down with you and try to negotiate a deal, and we think it would be good for you and good for us. But I repeat, you and I discussed all this thoroughly, and we are not going to get into a bidding war."

Walter Byers hung up on me. Astounding! Just weeks before, I had been one of his favorite people of all time. The long and short of it is that Walter Byers' only consistency is his inconsistency.

Byers was always consistent on one issue, though. Over the years, we discussed the feasibility of a national championship playoff system for college football, and Walter always spoke of the problems involved. Someday there will be a true national collegiate football championship, but there is strong, organized opposition. Walter's point was always that the promoters of the bowl games, including the conferences aligned with major bowls, are united against such a playoff. Their fear is that the value of the bowl games as attractions would be sorely diminished. CBS has taken the position that if bowl games were to be included in the playoff system, the games would remain valuable properties. NBC has pretty much adopted the party line put out by the Rose Bowl people, since theirs is such a happy marriage and NBC isn't about to take a public stance that would offend the organizers of an event that is right at the top of the list among major sports happenings in this country. And it doesn't matter that neither the Pacific 10 nor the Big Ten has had a team acclaimed national champion in recent years. Tradition is what sets the Rose Bowl apart. It's a big slice of Americana.

Through the years, ABC made several attempts to get the Rose Bowl, but I don't think anyone ever really got close to wresting the contract from NBC. In the late seventies, both ABC and CBS were advised that the Rose Bowl committee would welcome our involvement in competing for the rights to televise the game, and naturally we were eager to take part. The meeting was held at the Bel-Air Country Club in Beverly Hills, and Roone Arledge and I made the presentation and proposal for ABC. Once we got back to New York, we learned to our astonishment that the CBS bid was identical to ours, right down to the last penny. The plot thickened when we learned that the exact amounts of our bids had been leaked to NBC. Obviously, NBC had a bed partner at the Rose Bowl, just as ABC Sports did during some of the Olympic negotiations. So NBC came in with a higher bid and got the deal once more.

A few years later, it was much the same story. I went out and made the proposal for ABC, but I never allowed myself to believe, even for an instant, that we would be successful. We couldn't ignore the event, and so to show good faith I went, but with only the faintest glimmer of hope of being successful. The Tournament of Roses Association had made it clear that there was great fondness for ABC, since we were the network of college football. Too, members of the committee thought highly of Keith Jackson. I'd had a meeting in Pasadena with Bill Nicholas, of the Tournament of Roses Association—he was chairman of the football committee—and told him that, since NBC had a first refusal clause in its present contract, the way for us to do business would be for the Rose Bowl to sign a one-year deal with NBC. That would free the committee, after one year, to do whatever it liked, and it surely wouldn't have hurt Pasadena's bargaining position. CBS was hot for the deal, too, and both of us wound up making substantial bids. I don't think either of us ever had a legitimate shot at it, and the Rose Bowl folks wound up signing a multiyear deal with NBC. I think ABC and CBS were used. It wasn't shabbily done, but we were used, nonetheless.

When that multiyear deal was winding down, there came the usual gesture to ABC about getting involved in the bidding for the next contract, covering the 1984 through 1986 games. This time, we decided not even to do any flirting. Instead, we issued a press release stating that it "would not represent a responsible business decision" for us to engage in the Rose Bowl bidding process.

Two bad experiences had taught us a lesson.

I've believed for years that you could retain the postseason bowl picture pretty much like it is, and still have one game to determine a national champion. Years ago, ABC Sports made such a proposal.

A blue-ribbon panel of sportswriters and sports broadcasters would select the two teams it believed merited a shot at the national championship. All this would be done after the January 1 bowl games. You'd have time for preparation and promotion, and play the game the weekend before the Super Bowl.

Naturally, the bowl promoters are opposed to this, and a lot of the coaches are, too, because the way it is now, they can get into a bowl game if they have even a half-decent team, and you wind up with eighteen different winners, whereas with one championship game, the coaches who don't win the title are considered losers. The academicians are opposed to it because of the way it would lengthen the season. Actually, the season would be stretched out for only two schools, and many college athletes involved in basketball and baseball spend a lot more time away from the campus and the classroom than football players do. I think you would generate, in time, Super Bowl–type television revenue for such an event. ABC paid $17 million for the 1988 Super Bowl. Give the participating teams a million dollars each and earmark the rest for academic scholarships and divvy it up among all the colleges.

Call me a dreamer if you like, but remember that a lot of things thought to be dreams in 1960 have become realities in sports over the ensuing years. Would you have thought that tennis players would be playing for a hundred thousand dollars per week in tournaments all around the world? Would you have believed that Super Bowl tickets would sell for a hundred dollars each, and be scalped for as much as two thousand dollars? Would you have believed there could be a sports team with an "average" salary of half a million dollars per man? And that some college coaches would take home more than three hundred thousand dollars a year, or four times as much money as the presidents of their schools?

So I ask you to believe that, yes, there will come a day in the not-too-distant future when, in mid-January in Pasadena or

Miami or New Orleans, two college football teams will square off in a national championship game, and the networks will be slugging it out to determine which of them gets to televise the game, and sponsors will be lining up and scrambling to take part. All this, naturally, is predicated on the optimistic thinking that our colleges and universities will clean up their acts and decide not to destroy college sports. The NCAA Football Postseason Subcommittee endorsed a one-game playoff in January 1990, the Sunday before the Super Bowl, but the NCAA membership, the colleges and universities, voted against a national championship game during their convention in January 1988. Some day such a game will be approved.

9

THE HALFBACK, THE QUARTERBACK, AND THE LAWYER

*An Uneasy Mix Makes
Prime-time Magic*

Years before Andy Griffith became sheriff of Mayberry, when he was just a face in the crowd, he had a hit comedy record called *What It Was Was Football*.

That was long before the night of September 21, 1970, in Cleveland, Ohio, when ABC Sports kicked off a unique series that would sometimes generate more headlines off the field than on it, would cause much of the nation to change its Monday night routine, and could create more elation—and chagrin—in corporate corridors than any series in the department's history.

Almost in an instant, ABC's "NFL Monday Night Football" became much more than just a game. It was an event, a happening, a larger-than-life phenomenon that quickly exceeded the network's highest expectations in every respect. And as you may know, television people are notorious optimists.

What other event could generate so much curiosity that a network could unceremoniously remove its finest play-by-play man from the series after its inaugural season, replace him with a counterpart so inexperienced he sometimes had the same player playing for both teams, and gain points in the ratings? What other event could prominently feature a performer who became known as "the man you love to hate," who inspired such fierce feelings that the grand prize in some saloons around the country was winning the right to throw a brick through a television screen with his face on it, and climb even higher in the ratings?

What was it Shakespeare said about greatness? That some men are born great, some men achieve greatness, and still others have it thrust upon them? ABC Sports had professional football success thrust upon it.

The year 1970 would be a significant one in many ways in the world of professional football. It was the first year after the merger of the leagues that the teams would be playing a common schedule, and National Football League commissioner Pete Rozelle was searching for ways to expand both exposure and revenues. That meant going beyond the regular Sunday afternoon telecasts on CBS and NBC. And because those networks were the incumbents in pro football, Pete went first to them. Both CBS and NBC were then highly successful in prime time and did not want to further involve themselves in pro football. Their theory was old and normally sound: If it ain't broke, don't fix it. When it was suggested to CBS Network president Bob Wood that CBS should take on "Monday Night Football," he said, "Preempt Doris Day? Are you out of your mind?"

Rozelle than turned to ABC, but the initial reception was cool. Management at the network level had serious concerns about the viability of professional football at night. There was a feeling of uncertainty, and even fear. But give Roone Arledge credit; he believed in "NFL Monday Night Football" from the very beginning. The first factor in ABC's favor was that it was then solidly entrenched at the bottom of the heap in nighttime programming. (In those days, comedians joked that if you wanted to end the war in Viet Nam, put it on ABC in prime time and it'd be canceled after thirteen weeks. They also made cracks about there being more people listening to police calls than there were watching ABC at night.)

What eventually persuaded ABC executives to roll the dice with prime-time pro football was the concern that if ABC said no, the league would go into syndication with the series, and thereby further damage the network's image and financial condition. Roone Arledge became certain of this intention in his discussions with Rozelle, and it was a scary prospect. There's no telling how many stations along the already weak ABC lineup would have dumped out of network prime-time programming to take a chance with the NFL, because they surely weren't getting rich by taking what ABC was offering. Thus, in the end it became a crapshoot, and one in which ABC promptly started on perhaps its greatest roll of sevens and elevens.

ABC Sports already knew how to televise a football game from a technical standpoint, but we were all aware from the outset that a Monday night game had to be different. Prime time is always somehow different. It's not that you don't bear down during daytime telecasts, but there is a certain extra awareness that comes from doing anything in prime time. You just know you are almost certain to have more people watching, and maybe that factor keeps you more on your toes.

There would be no question as to the man we'd pick to do play-by-play. You put your best foot forward in any new venture, and it was a certainty that we'd go with Keith Jackson, who I believe will be remembered as one of the finest play-by-play broadcasters in the history of the game. As previously noted, from the start Arledge also wanted Howard Cosell involved, and Rozelle thought Howard was worth a try. Arledge had, by then, become good friends with Frank Gifford, and it was Gifford who recommended Don Meredith as the third man in the booth. The thinking was that Meredith, with his Texas drawl and cornpone humor, would play well off Cosell. It happened exactly that way, although not without a few struggles.

I don't think Cosell ever had any major problems with Keith Jackson. Howard respected Keith and the combination in the booth worked well, despite what some of the critics were saying. As for Meredith, Cosell has always said he anointed Don, made him the hit that he became. I think it was simply a successful merging of very different personalities, a rare combination that clicked. True, Cosell brought out the best in Meredith, but Cosell played well off Dandy Don, too. As for the best, and the worst, that was within Cosell, no one could have kept all that under control. He would have shone through if nestled between Abbott and Costello.

It was written in those days, and has been since, that there was considerable emphasis at the network on the marketing and promotion of the Monday night games. The truth is that we never had to cultivate much of anything to make it go, although we did heavily promote the series. Sure, there were gatherings for sponsors, and with more of a festive atmosphere than there would be for Saturday afternoon or Sunday afternoon football telecasts, but the package largely sold itself, for a number of reasons. First, there was the sheer novelty of pro football on weekday evening prime-time television. Here we were, intruding, if you will, on Monday nights, traditionally a down time for people who normally have had the weekend off. For a lot of them, it was a real pick-me-up. Second, the games were mostly good ones, and they were mostly well announced by a team whose collective and individual personalities quickly hooked and held a lot of people. Then, I'd be remiss if I didn't mention the bettors and the bookies. Monday night games gave the gamblers all across the country a chance to get even, or to reduce some of their weekend losses, or in some rare cases, to get deeper into the bookies' pockets. Add it all up and, almost overnight, ABC's "NFL Monday Night Football" became a major happening. People changed their habits to become committed viewers, nationwide, while bars and restaurants added television sets so patrons could watch the games over a cool one or two.

Howard Cosell getting overserved and sputtering out "Phhhiiillll-aaahhh-delll-ppphhheee-aaahhh" didn't endear him to the Women's Christian Temperance Union, but it hardly affected our ratings adversely. I don't subscribe to the theory that every knock is a boost, but the widespread publicity that attended Howard getting drunk on the air created even more attention for our new venture.

The NFL liked it, and why not? Three networks being involved meant $44.9 million into the league's coffers. By 1974, when

ABC signed a second contract for "Monday Night Football," the revenue to the league and its teams increased to more than $60 million. Eventually, the three-network dollars went to more than $2 billion for the 1982–86 package, the biggest money deal in the history of television, entertainment, or sports, and "NFL Monday Night Football" has become the second longest-running prime-time series on network television after "60 Minutes."

Moving Keith Jackson out after the initial season as play-by-play man was a curious and, as we've seen, a poorly handled maneuver. It was terribly hard on Keith, lucrative to Frank Gifford, his successor, and in the end probably worked well for the network. No one could argue that Gifford was, then or now, a better play-by-play broadcaster than Jackson, but Keith has a hard, straight style, and in some ways a no-nonsense manner about him, while Gifford is a much softer personality. I think, because of that, both Cosell and Meredith were able to gain more attention for themselves; in other words, Gifford's presence brought more of an entertainment side to the broadcasts. But I was opposed to making the change.

Arledge brought it up for the first time when we attended the NFL's winter meetings in Palm Beach, Florida. He suggested we have dinner, and told me there was something specific he wanted to discuss. We spent the entire evening going back and forth over that one issue. I told him I thought Frank Gifford would be good for ABC, but not on "Monday Night Football."

"In my opinion," I said, "Keith ought to continue as play-by-play man. He did a fine job last season, and I see no reason to change. With all due respect to Frank, I think it'd be a disservice to Keith and not in the best interests of the NFL series."

There simply was no reason to make the change. Arledge told me it was in "the thinking stage," and I knew right then it was a *fait accompli*. Gifford's star status was what Roone was after. In some fifty years on this earth, more than half of it in television, I've rarely encountered anyone more celebrity-conscious than Roone Arledge. Make someone a star, whether of the overnight or time-tested variety, and Arledge wants to meet him/her, have dinner with him/her, and, if possible, put him/her on television. Figure-skating star Carol Heiss Jenkins totally captivated him;

Ethel Kennedy and her family made him do flip-flops (along with, some would tell you, making him alter his news judgment). Frank Gifford would become part of Roone Arledge's famous-people collection.

Gifford met every qualification. He was the All-American halfback from Southern Cal. He'd become all-pro with the New York Giants. He had a huge recognition factor in New York City, which made him a darling of the advertising fraternity. He was good-looking, positive, and charming. Finally, he was a close personal friend of the commissioner of the NFL, which meant he was definitely good enough to be Roone Arledge's friend and hero, too. The Gifford-Rozelle relationship began when Pete was doing college publicity in California and Frank was a Trojan star, and it continued when Rozelle went to the Los Angeles Rams as Gifford was making it big in the pros. I always had the feeling that on Pete's side there was a touch of hero worship in the association.

There is no doubt that Howard Cosell, from day one, was jealous of the friendship between Rozelle and Gifford, and of the respect they had for each other. It was also plain as day to anyone in our office who had any association with the Monday night package that Howard also suffered a deep envy of the warm personal relationship between Gifford and Arledge. Here Cosell always felt he was on the outside looking in. It was Frank Gifford who traveled with the jet-setters to the "in" places, who went to the beautiful-people dinner parties, who was always mixing socially with Commissioner Rozelle and his wife and friends. With Pete and Howard, it was almost strictly business.

Gifford, in Howard's view, was the epitome of "jockocracy" and the moment Gifford began doing play-by-play in the 1971 season, Cosell began to complain to me. He never pussy-footed around about it; he called Gifford embarrassing and incompetent. Gifford originally did have a lot of difficulty doing play-by-play, misidentifying players, stumbling over things like the down and yardage. But no one ever worked harder to try to improve; he prepared and did his homework and concentrated on the job, and eventually became a competent play-by-play man. Although an extremely nice man, his weaknesses were camouflaged when he was able to concentrate purely on calling plays. At times, he was almost suffocated by the other talent in the booth. That analysis and perspective are not Frank's strong suits quickly became apparent when his "Monday Night Football" role was changed to that of analyst in the fall of 1986. With Arledge no longer having real authority in sports, Gifford had lost his principal supporter. Despite statements in the press, Frank was extremely upset at being forced to give up play-by-play, considered quitting, but eventually reached a new and more lucrative financial arrangement with ABC.

Ratings and revenue climbed steadily through the early years of the series, as did Cosell's complaining about Gifford and Meredith, and the critics' carping at Cosell. Meredith emerged as a strong player and developed a good following. I think the guy sitting there in his easy chair really identified with Don, saw him as a good old boy with a pretty good outlook on life who loved his mom and dad, Jeff and Hazel, and took neither the game nor himself too seriously. After all, he wasn't doing surgery up there in the booth. This was just your average Monday night across America, and all Dandy was doing was watching a game right along with you, sitting there between this nice gentleman from California and that obnoxious know-it-all from New York. The public loved it when he gave Howard the needle, which he did whenever Cosell gave him an opening.

But in the end, it was all too perfect for Don, and he got out after the 1973 season. He wanted "to grow as a performer"; he wanted to act; he wanted to do more than be the middle man on a football broadcast. He definitely did not want to leave ABC, but the network offered him no opportunities outside football, whereas NBC did. Don was a hot property and we did not want to lose him. And we surely didn't want the mess that followed his departure.

The first person we tried to fit in as Meredith's successor was Fred (The Hammer) Williamson. Fred had made something of a name for himself as a rugged defensive back for the Kansas City Chiefs, and was involved in a career making second-rate movies. Following Dandy Don would have been a tough job for anyone; it was impossible for Williamson.

Chet Forte, who directed the series telecasts so ably through 1986 was the member of the production team who stayed with "Monday Night Football" the longest. He reported to Roone that Williamson wanted merely to waltz in and waltz out; he didn't think any preparation was required. This lack of homework showed badly, and Fred's was a test run only during the preseason telecasts, as he failed to make the cut into the regular season schedule.

When we knew Fred Williamson wasn't the answer, we turned to Alex Karras. He, too, was untried on live television but had done some movie work. Also, we knew he had sufficient sense of humor not to take himself too seriously. There was no organized opposition to him, although we knew the league did not look too kindly on his hiring since he and Paul Hornung had been suspended for a year for betting on football games. Alex stayed through the 1976 season but was never really more then adequate. His funniest line came during a game involving the Oakland (now Los Angeles) Raiders. As one of the cameramen got a shot of Otis Sistrunk of the Raiders on the sidelines, his bald head glistening in the lights, Alex cracked, "Otis is from the University of Mars."

The following year, Sistrunk's shiny pate again showed up on our screen and Alex used the same line, but it wasn't nearly as funny that time. I think Karras worked fairly hard during the first season or so, then became content to come up with cute little quips that sometimes worked and sometimes seemed terribly strained.

No one could ever match Don Meredith's line when, during the early years at a painfully tedious game at Houston, with the Oilers getting blown away, the camera showed a close-up of an Oiler fan who was obviously bored stiff with the whole affair. When he realized he was on camera, the fan flipped the bird to America's "Monday Night Football" faithful. Was he really telling us what we thought he was telling us? Not at all, Dandy Don assured the television audience: "He's just telling us we're number one."

Meredith returned to the telecasts in 1977 and stayed through the 1984 season. He would have you believe he never worked, never really prepared for a broadcast. That's not true of his first stint, but I don't think he put in a comparable amount of effort when he came back for his second tour of duty. There was a lack of freshness to his commentary, and what he said often lacked impact. He was no longer unique.

By then, prime-time pro football was no longer confined to Monday nights, but had spread to Sundays and Thursdays. Concurrently, we began to have contract troubles with Meredith. He wanted considerably more money to do games other than the normal Monday contests, and we refused. We were paying him over thirty-five thousand dollars a game. We thought that was more than fair and we called his bluff. Our final answer was to hire Fran Tarkenton to do the "other" games. Meredith would never admit it, but I believe the introduction of Tarkenton shook him up and made him work harder. Fran did a decent job and was always well prepared, but he was too much like Cosell; there wasn't enough diversity between the two commentators—both were providing critical commentary. "Monday Night Football" had to be different; it had to be as entertaining as it was informative, and with Meredith out of the booth the telecasts lacked both humor and warmth.

We then turned to O. J. Simpson after the 1982 season. Some years before, I'd had the distinction of signing O. J. to an unusual contract when he first joined ABC Sports in which he got no guarantee but was simply paid a fee when we needed him for an event. But that's not to suggest he came cheap in 1983, because he didn't. So in 1983 the nation was treated to Gifford, Cosell, and either Meredith or O. J. Simpson—not to mention the United States Football League in the spring.

Just as I believe that a certain amount of the criticism directed at Cosell arose because he is Jewish, I think some of the sniping at O. J. came because he's black. Granted, Simpson has significant problems at times with grammar, and there are words that give him fits. But in terms of the quality of his commentary, I think he made good contributions. He had something interesting and incisive to say on almost every telecast. He did his homework and studied hard to try to get better at the job, including everything he could do to improve his speech. And we probably should have done more to help him.

Cosell is correct in his criticisms of what he termed the "jockocracy." Far too many people have been plucked out of some sports arena and thrust into a broadcast booth with no training and precious little preparation. Somehow we have expected that because they have performed well in a particular sport, they will automatically be able to talk about it brilliantly to the guy in Peoria. It ain't necessarily so—in fact, it is rarely so. Unfortunately, ABC Sports was the ringleader in this practice of taking athletes and throwing them to the wolves. Some of them have been extremely bright human beings, but they simply were not broadcast professionals and we made very little effort to assist them in becoming such. Marquee value is what we wanted, and that's what we got. Most of the time, we got little else.

O. J.'s first season was Cosell's last. And O. J. remembered that the climate going into that season was anything but healthy: "It was a big step for me anyway, since I'd never done anything like that, and I knew it would be tough. I had always dreamed of doing 'Monday Night Football,' and I had known Howard since my college days and we'd always gotten along very well, and he sort of took me under his wing. But Howard was very bitter, and Chet Forte was going through whatever it was he was going through, and everybody was sniping at everybody else. It wasn't a friendly atmosphere."

This situation wasn't improved by the game in Buffalo when Howard remarked that one of the teams, trailing by only ten points, could "get right back into this game by scoring." O. J. chuckled and said, "Once again, Howard, you've proved yourself to be the master of the obvious."

That was too much for Cosell to take. O. J. Simpson could not, *must not*, criticize Howard Cosell, and particularly not over the air. Bob Goodrich, who was producing that game, said, "We knew Juice was just trying to be funny, and everyone thought he was, but Howard took it personally. He shut up for about the next ten minutes. In fact, I think he was so mad he left the broadcast booth."

Some time after Cosell permanently left the "Monday Night" booth, he and O. J. had words on the telephone.

Simpson: "He got on my case because he said someone told him I'd been rapping him. That's ridiculous. He and I have kidded back and forth for years, at places where we'd both be asked to get up and talk, at press conferences, anywhere. He'd put me down and everyone would laugh. Then I'd say that Howard was helping me with my diction, and I was helping him with his knowledge of the game, and we had done that, back and forth, for years. Wherever I spoke, I'd always say nice things about Howard, and tell how we played gin rummy, how he'd come to the studio when I'd be doing 'Wide World of Sports,' just to keep me company. He knew I was nervous and he'd help settle me down. I always told people how he supported me. So I was shocked when he got on my case. And I was mad. Here's a guy I had called when I heard he was leaving 'Monday Night Football' and I pleaded with him to stay on. I told him not to let those suckers think they beat him."

Cosell criticized Simpson in his most recent book, writing that O. J. telephoned him and cried over the phone and apologized.

"That's simply not true," said Simpson. "That bothered me when I read it in the book. I mean, it really bothered me. I cried when my father died, and not long ago a good friend of mine lost his mother, and I got a little emotional with him. But I sure didn't cry over the phone with Howard. I told him he was believing hearsay. He wouldn't even tell me where he got his information. I told him he knew me better than that, and that whoever was coming to him with stories like that wasn't his friend. He kept telling me I was no friend of his, then his wife got on the phone, then Howard would get back on, and . . . well, it was a mess. But it's all right now. We're buddies. I understand Howard. It's over and done with. We got together later in New York and I got some things off my chest and that takes care of it.

"After his book came out, he autographed a copy for me and I read it. All I know is I've had a good career, and I try to be positive about things. It was upsetting when he wrote those personal things about people. After all, you can find something negative to write about anybody. I have to try and understand

Howard. The man has a lot of bitterness. Maybe he has a right to it, I don't know. I just try to be straight with everybody. My mother instilled in me the philosophy that you should treat people the way you want to be treated, and I've tried to do that. I don't have any ex-friends. And Howard is still my friend."

And O. J. is a friend of mine. He's a constructive, positive human being and I cannot imagine anyone not liking him.

Cosell left "Monday Night Football," as he had threatened to do, after the 1983 season. The following season it was Gifford-Meredith-Simpson, and sliding ratings. Cosell would have you believe that every lost rating point was directly attributable to his departure. Actually, we had suffered a larger rating decline in 1983 than we did in 1984.

Just as you don't tune up a car when it is running well, you begin to take action when the engine starts sputtering, and Roone made the decision not to renew Meredith's contract. Since I didn't want Don to read about it in the newspapers, as Keith Jackson had done, I called and told him the bad news, saying simply that we thought it was time for a change. It was a tough call, but I don't think Don was surprised, and he was a pro and a perfect gentleman about it. He said he understood, and that he'd had two great runs with ABC Sports and had enjoyed both of them. He made it very easy for me that day.

So now none of the original cast was in the booth. Jackson had lasted one season, Cosell made it through fourteen, and Dandy Don had two stints covering a dozen seasons. The new team was Frank Gifford, embarking on his fifteenth season, with O. J. Simpson, heading into his third year, and a newcomer—Broadway Joe Namath.

The hiring of Joe Namath had more to do with the entertainment part of broadcasting than anything else. It was pure hype; we had looked at our ratings coming off the 1984 season and realized we needed a shot in the arm. That didn't mean we thought Namath was going to be terrible on the air; on the contrary, he had done movie and television work, along with commercials, and even had some stage experience, which gave us reason to believe he might be pretty good. Also, having spent so much time around New York and Los Angeles, he was no stranger to media pressure.

While we were in the process of hiring Namath, Frank Ramos, the director of public relations for the Jets, called me and said, "Jim, you're going to be pleasantly surprised with Joe. He's the hardest-working guy you'll ever meet. I know he has that 'Broadway Joe' image, but, believe me, I know the guy and I'm telling you he will work his fanny off for you and he'll be a terrific commentator."

Joe did work hard—and he certainly had plenty of inspiration with a salary of $850,000—but nevertheless he was disappointing. We explained to him what kind of input we expected and the role we wanted him to play. We wanted him for his glamour, true, but we also expected him to impart his considerable knowledge of the game, to let viewers know *why* certain things were happening. Right away we knew it wasn't working. And the critics did, too, giving him only a tiny bit of breathing room before they lit into him. It was the kind of criticism that is hard to ignore. Sometime during that first season, I got hold of Jimmy Walsh, who's represented Joe for a long time, and told him we had to do something to upgrade the quality of Joe's commentary. I told him that Joe had indeed brought us the glamour we wanted, but now we just had to have more insightful commentary.

Walsh was defensive about my remarks. He said it was difficult for Joe to work in the environment that existed in the booth; it was tough for Joe to get in his comments. At the very least, he implied that Gifford had let it be known that he, Gifford, was the main man in the booth, and that he was not eager to share the microphone with either Namath or Simpson. To me this was nonsense, because I don't think Frank Gifford did anything other than try to make things work for everyone in the booth.

The 1985 season was a curious one. The ratings were up 15 percent, which can be attributed to several elements: The schedule was good, the games were exciting, we had oddball happenings like the wild snowstorm in Denver and Joe Theismann's broken leg, plus the tremendous game between Miami and

Chicago and the added excitement of the Bears, Walter Payton and William (The Refrigerator) Perry. It was a positive season, and I saw no need to make wholesale changes. I thought O. J. had improved as a result of his hard work to make himself a better contributor to the telecasts, and I thought he deserved to come back in 1986. With some more work, I believed Namath could have gotten a lot better, too, and our deal with him called for him to work another year. Nonetheless, based on Namath's performance in 1985, the decision was made by Dennis Swanson to buy out his contract in 1986. Namath then made some candid remarks about his former broadcast partners at ABC that Swanson deemed in violation of Joe's agreement and refused to pay Namath his full nine hundred thousand dollars. Joe filed a lawsuit in order to obtain his money.

William Taaffe of *Sports Illustrated* took a pretty good shot at Namath, and I couldn't really quarrel with that. Michael Goodwin of the *New York Times* simply wondered if the sparkle had gone out of the Monday night telecasts; if they had become "just another" football game. To my mind, "Monday Night Football" was not then, and is not now, as special as it once was; inevitably, after so many years, it has become tired in some ways; however, it is still an attractive and strong broadcasting and advertising package, and for those reasons if no others will be with us for a long time to come.

But back then, we searched ourselves thoroughly, asking what more we might do. From the beginning, we'd tried to make it more than just a Sunday game moved thirty-two hours later by involving our top producers and director and our best camera people, along with ever greater technical resources. After fifteen years on the air, we needed to keep the series as fresh and innovative as possible.

As the 1985 season was winding down, ABC held its affiliate board of governors' meeting at the Arizona Biltmore Hotel in Phoenix. Every one of the major ABC executives would be there to meet with the affiliated station representatives, and I arranged for the "Monday Night Football" team—Frank, O. J., and Joe—to attend. As it turned out, O. J. had to cancel out because of his father's illness, but Frank, Joe, and I got together with

Arledge for a breakfast meeting to go over some last-minute details about our presentation. Roone was running late, Joe was engaged in a conversation with a waiter, so during the lull I turned to Frank and asked him how he felt, in retrospect, about Howard's book and particularly the way we handled it at a press luncheon at the Tavern on the Green in New York's Central Park in October. At the luncheon, I had made no secret of my disappointment with what Cosell had said in his book concerning Frank and our other announcers in light of the fact that Howard was then under contract to ABC. To his credit, Gifford didn't lash out at Cosell for the terrible things Howard had written about him, but he made no secret that he'd been very hurt by it all. And he was hurt, too, by the fact that neither Arledge nor Fred Pierce said anything publicly in Frank's defense. The fact is, neither said one word in public either attacking the book or defending the people Cosell lambasted.

"Under the circumstances," Gifford told me, "I think it was handled okay. But I'm still extremely disturbed that neither Fred nor Roone ever made a statement about Howard's book. Frankly, I think they let me and a lot of other people down."

And so do I.

As for Namath, I'm delighted that he landed on his feet and signed with NBC to do NFL games again. He's being teamed with Marv Albert, and I think Joe has a chance to be very good as an analyst.

How Gifford went from being the play-by-play voice of "Monday Night Football" in a three-person booth to color analyst and second banana to Al Michaels in a two-man setting (it went back to a three-man setting after just one season with the addition of Dan Dierdorf, whom I had first suggested we hire, back in 1985) is a story in itself—although it may be more soap opera than mere story.

In 1984, Michaels was making $425,000 a year but was very unhappy because he didn't have a headline role on either of our football packages. Keith Jackson had college football and Gifford had pro football, and Michaels was sufficiently jealous of both of them to be making noises that he might jump to CBS Sports. So Roone, Irwin Weiner, vice president, talent and financial affairs for ABC News and Sports, and I sat down and discussed a plan whereby Michaels would be given half of the major games in our college football package. If it took this extreme measure to keep Al at ABC, then I was very reluctantly in favor of the plan, but we agreed to discuss this point further before a final decision was made. It seemed very unfair to hurt Keith another time. After all, he'd been taken off "Monday Night Football," while Michaels had already been given the "Monday Night Baseball" package that long had featured Jackson as the number one announcer. However, Roone was still harboring a grudge over the terms of Keith's long-term contract, and despite not showing much respect for Al until after the Lake Placid Olympics, he now was firmly in Al's corner. I was strongly opposed to splitting the college football package in 1985, the last year of Keith's contract. Roone finally agreed, so we delayed the potential college football commitment to Michaels until 1986, when we'd be negotiating a new contract with Jackson.

I was leaving on a business trip to Hawaii, and on a stopover in Los Angeles I called my office to check on the status of the Michaels deal. I learned that agreement had not yet been reached. When Arledge arrived in Hawaii a few days behind me, he informed me that the Michaels deal had been completed and that it included Al's getting half of the college football package in 1986. I was infuriated that Arledge had not spoken about it with me before authorizing Weiner to finalize things with Michaels' agent. Since the commitment to Michaels was a *fait accompli*— and not wanting to disrupt our trip with a confrontation—I waited until we got back to New York to confront Roone about his failure to contact me prior to the deal being closed.

"We tried to reach you in Hawaii," he said.

I told him I hadn't received any messages at my hotel. Just to follow up, I called his lead secretary, Nancy Dobi, and asked her if Roone had tried to reach me in Hawaii. She confirmed that he had not tried.

Soon after that, I called Jackson to tell him about the change in college football, that he'd be sharing the package with Michaels. Keith was hurt, angered, crushed, you name it. He told me he had no intention of accepting our decision and that he'd leave ABC

Sports at the end of his contract. I wanted to rectify the situation, and got the chance to do so when I went to Las Vegas in April 1985, for the Marvelous Marvin Hagler/Thomas Hearns fight. Al was doing the closed-circuit telecast, and over lunch with him I asked him to relieve us of the commitment we had made to him for college football starting in 1986. I told him we stood a pretty good chance of doing major-league baseball on Sunday afternoons, as well as on Monday nights, in 1986, and that I'd appreciate his accepting the Sunday baseball assignment as a substitute for the college football games. Al was magnanimous, saying he didn't want to hurt Keith nor see him leave the network. He decided to go along with me, although I know he later was disturbed that he had made that decision. The whole thing became academic when Al was assigned the play-by-play role for "Monday Night Football." His deal gave him the main role in both pro football and baseball at a salary of more than $1 million a year!

Meanwhile, Jackson said he was considering retirement when his contract expired in January of 1986. Offered a deal not as lucrative as his previous one, he turned it down. Then the new ABC Sports president Dennis Swanson flew to Los Angeles and made him a new proposal, which he accepted. By re-signing Keith, the network reattached itself to a real pro, who has always been loyal and reliable.

The working arrangement of the television networks with the NFL has always been a solid one. The NFL is an efficient organization, although very protective about its image and perhaps a little oversensitive in some areas. But ABC's relationship with the league has been remarkably smooth, and, other than perhaps "Wide World of Sports," the NFL games clearly have been the most significant series televised by ABC. Some people have suggested that ABC made strong scheduling demands on the league, but we actually had minimal consultation rights. From the beginning, the league and the network understood that "Monday Night Football" was vastly different, that being in prime time put us up against strong entertainment competition at the other networks. But the power clearly always was entirely in the hands of the NFL. We would "suggest" to the late Bob Cochran, who was broadcast coordinator for the NFL, then to his successor, Val Pinchbeck, the league's director of broadcasting, or to Pete Rozelle himself, that it would be nice if we could open up the Monday night schedule with a particular game. A few times, the NFL gave us the choice of two games on a particular date, but that's as far as it went.

Rozelle, who possesses an astute public relations mind, knew the importance of an attractive schedule for a successful prime-time package, but he was doing business with all the networks and couldn't show favoritism. Once in a while, though, word would filter down that CBS and NBC were screaming about some of the good matchups we had on Monday night. When our ratings tumbled in 1984, the NFL requested more input on the 1985 schedule, and I put together a list of potential team appearances we would have liked, jotting down which teams we'd like three times, the ones we'd want twice, those we'd like once, and the ones we wouldn't care at all about seeing. We also informed the NFL what teams we'd like on the non–Monday night games, emphasizing that intradivisional games were highly attractive to us. This emphasis did lead to a number of intradivisional games on the 1985 Monday night schedule, and, I think, contributed, in turn, to a dramatic upturn in ratings that year.

I was sorry it took me so long to get to know Pete Rozelle better. Roone Arledge jealously guarded his relationship with the commissioner, and it was apparent from the earliest days he was in awe of the man. In fact, Bob Cochran told me that ABC Sports could have had the Super Bowl one contract before it finally happened, if Arledge had been tougher in negotiations. But you don't tough it out with one of your heroes. According to Cochran, the NFL's plan was for ABC Sports to televise the Super Bowl, and also to retain exclusivity in prime time with both the Monday night games and those televised on other evenings. Pete offered Roone an either/or deal, but Cochran said we could have had both if Arledge had been stronger.

I regretfully was never an integral part of the NFL-ABC contract negotiations, and it was only in my last five years or so at ABC that I developed a relationship with Rozelle. The whole thing was climaxed by my testimony in the USFL-NFL trial. Right after I had testified—and the upshot of it all was that the NFL had not put pressure on my network to damage the USFL in any way—I got a very nice letter from Carrie Rozelle, Pete's wife, in which she referred to my honesty and dignity while on the witness stand.

The commissioner of the NFL surely is entitled to deal with the number-one guy at a network, and I wasn't that guy. But down deep, I resented the way I was systematically excluded from the inner circle. Roone was at the core of my exclusion; Rozelle didn't grasp initially that I was handling the day-to-day operations in sports after Roone assumed his ABC News responsibilities. Early on, I think there may have been an uncertainty about me, but in the decade of the eighties, we came to know and respect each other. Indeed, I don't know of anyone in any sport, in my time, who has done as thorough a job of stewardship as Pete Rozelle. Although his record is not impeccable, the NFL will be hard put to find someone to measure up to his record when he retires.

10

CHALLENGING THE BIG BOYS

The Sorry Saga
of How the USFL
Committed Suicide

The first word I heard about the United States Football League was in December 1981 when a gentleman named Mike Trager called me out of the blue and told me he represented the league and wanted to chat with me about it. The league had not even been formally organized at that time, but we talked briefly and he invited me to a meeting of the owners. The meeting was set for early 1982, but I told Trager I thought it was premature, and I didn't go.

A few months later, I met with five of the owners at ABC Sports. I explained my concerns, which were chiefly questions about the financial viability and the staying power of the owners. I was also concerned about the image of ABC Sports and what our dollar commitment would be should we deal with this bold new venture. The league made the decision to begin operations in the spring of 1983, and ABC made plans to televise the games, after concluding a deal in May of 1982.

I had by then become convinced that the league could make it and that our image would not be impaired. I was assured the owners had sufficient financial staying power to weather the storms certain to arrive in the developing years. One of the most convincing arguments presented to me came from the late John

Bassett, who owned the Tampa Bay Bandits and who served as chairman of the USFL's Executive Committee.

"In the old World Football League, I was the richest owner," he told me, "but in this one, I'm the poorest."

ABC Sports had a programming need in the spring and early summer months, and in this regard the USFL was something of a godsend. No one was thinking the new league was going to rival the National Football League; it was, simply put, triple-A football in the off months, with a few stars scattered here and there, but that was enough for us to make a commitment for $9 million in each of the first two seasons, $14 million in 1985, and $18 million in 1986. We'd checked advertising agencies and received interest from some potential sponsors. It was risky, but ABC Sports had built its success on taking chances.

Before I went into that first meeting with the USFL owners, I called Val Pinchbeck of the NFL and told him about it. I don't remember Val having much of a reaction to the news, but I can't imagine the NFL being overjoyed about the prospect of a competing league's games on ABC. As a courtesy, I called Val again just before we publicly announced the network's involvement.

At a luncheon at "21," Walter Duncan, the owner of the New Jersey Generals, asked me what I'd think if he signed Herschel Walker, the University of Georgia running back. Herschel had played only three years and was a virtual cinch to win the Heisman Trophy, and it was considered unethical to sign a player before his college class had graduated. I told Duncan I was opposed to it, and that it would create bad blood between the colleges and the USFL. Walter signed him anyway.

Herschel Walker made his debut in the kickoff game, on the first Sunday of March in 1983. We got a 14.2 rating (approximately 42 million viewers saw at least a portion of that telecast), which far exceeded anyone's expectations. Duncan later told me he signed Walker to avoid probable litigation on grounds he would have deprived Herschel of the opportunity to earn a living. The Generals paid the Georgia star $1 million for 1983, $1 million for 1984, and had an option on Walker's services in 1985 for $1.25 million. Herschel also got a loan of $750,000, plus some lucrative endorsements.

ABC Sports made money, too—about $12 million in 1983, some $14 million in 1984. In both those years, the USFL was the network's most profitable sports property, exclusive of the Los Angeles Olympics. But then the league started to make some critical mistakes, the biggest one being the abandonment of cities like Chicago, Philadelphia, and Detroit after the 1984 season. Cities of that size are critical to television ratings, and the ratings were down in both 1984 and 1985, with ABC taking a $4 million loss on the USFL in 1985.

The league's announcement that it would switch to a fall schedule after the 1985 campaign hurt, too. That made it, in effect, a lame-duck league merely going through the motions until it got set to bang heads with the NFL. The two main players in that scheme were the New York real-estate developer, Donald Trump, by that time calling the shots for the New Jersey Generals, and Eddie Einhorn, co-owner of the Chicago White Sox and a major figure in the new league as owner of the Chicago franchise. Of course, Einhorn's reason for pushing the fall was that he didn't want his football team competing for attention with his baseball team. As for Trump, I'm persuaded that all he ever cared about was getting into the big game with the big boys, the National Football League. Nothing else mattered even a little bit.

Donald Trump had come on board with the Generals just prior to the 1984 season, and our first meeting was in the executive dining room at ABC. At the table for four on the fortieth floor were Trump and the USFL's then commissioner, Chet Simmons, with Charlie Lavery and me representing ABC. We had no more than exchanged pleasantries when Trump made it clear how the rest of the meeting would go if he had his way: "You guys don't have a contract, you know."

From that opening salvo on, it would be Trump and I doing most of the talking, Simmons and Lavery listening. I told Trump I didn't know what he meant.

"I mean just that. You do not have a contract. All you have is a memo."

That meant, in Trump's way of thinking, that the USFL was free to negotiate higher rights fees. To me, it meant no such thing.

We had a valid contract and I had to make it clear to him right off the bat that we would not be intimidated.

"Hold on, Donald," I told him. "I think it's great that you're involved with the league, but if we're going to do business together, there must be clear recognition that the United States Football League is committed to ABC Sports. We have two years firm and two options for 1985–86, then a first refusal for 1987. And I'm not going to talk about anything else unless you recognize our signed contract."

Simmons had no option but to affirm the agreement, since he was the one who had signed it—and I wish he had been as strong then as he was in our subsequent dealings with the USFL. Only then did the New York real-estate billionaire concede that there was a binding agreement between the USFL and ABC. Had I allowed Trump to bully us that first time, he surely would have done so in the future. That's the way the man operates. Just ask New York mayor Ed Koch.

Trump had a second salvo for me, though. He informed us that he felt the league had to go to a fall schedule in 1987. Here we were, not even kicking off season number two, and the new boy was hell bent on moving things to the fall to go head-on against the big-leaguers. And he made it clear he'd prefer to do it sooner, as early as 1985, if he could pull off a major miracle. (During a subsequent phone conversation with me, which he said was the longest call he'd ever had—over ninety minutes—Trump emphasized how important he thought it was to play during the normal football season. I think he thought he had to go head-to-head against the NFL in order to convince a jury of the USFL's plight, or to force a merger. Incidentally, he paid for the call.)

It was time for my salvo: "Tell me, Donald, do you really want the USFL to operate on its own, to be a separate entity, or do you want only to get into the NFL?"

Trump assured me he wanted the new league to stand on its own. His long-range plan, he said, was to have the winner of the USFL play the Super Bowl winner in a game called the Galaxy Bowl. There had been no mention of such a thing back on April 21, 1982, when I first met with owners Peter Spivak, Bill Daniels,

George Matthews, John Bassett, and Walter Duncan, and heard them tell me how each had committed $6 million and that there were seven other owners out there who had done the same thing. Now, on January 27, 1984, there could be no question that Donald Trump would be doing most of the talking and getting most of the publicity for the USFL.

Trump left me with something else to consider, saying, "You know, Jim, we're aware of the closeness that exists between Roone Arledge and Pete Rozelle, and we know Pete is putting pressure on Roone." Right then I saw that we were likely heading down the wrong road with a project whose original aims had been badly twisted by a man who considered himself so powerful that he could single-handedly determine its destiny.

The USFL wanted more regional telecasts in 1984, and asked us to pick up the option for 1985 even before the 1984 campaign started. The feeling was that the publicity would give the league both more credibility and more exposure. We did do more regional telecasts, which added about a quarter of a million dollars to our costs each time we did them. We also exercised our option for 1985 during the 1984 season. In the final analysis of the USFL in 1984, we had done more telecasts and spent more money, but had gotten smaller ratings and saw a decline in revenue in the offing. The picture was not a pretty one.

In a memorandum to fellow owners, Myles Tanenbaum, one of the owners of the Philadelphia Stars, had proposed a strategy whereby the USFL would adopt "an uncompromising, rather irritating attitude with respect to ABC"; provide the network with a sham schedule of "the poorest matchups for Sunday afternoon"; and in all other respects make itself "an unpalatable party to deal with."

Tanenbaum obviously felt the USFL package would look very pretty to another network and wanted us out of the picture after 1984. NBC had at one time been involved in several preliminary meetings, and at one juncture had made an offer that topped the one ABC eventually tendered. But Tanenbaum couldn't have been more wrong.

No matter what network had landed the new league, Donald Trump would have taken the project down the tubes. He once sent out a long-winded telex to league members, urging a move to the fall, criticizing ABC Sports, lambasting some of his fellow owners, and generally second-guessing the leadership of his league. "We all know that no one controls this league," he wrote, "and, perhaps that is its greatest weakness." He concluded by proposing an immediate meeting of league owners to institute antitrust action against the NFL.

People can say whatever they like, but no one will ever convince me that Donald Trump got into the USFL for any reason other than to try and get into the NFL. He didn't give a damn about what might happen to his fellow owners. When the USFL barged ahead and announced the move to the fall prior to the beginning of the 1985 season, despite a study commissioned by the league that showed such a move would be ill advised, it created major problems for ABC with the network's affiliated stations, with advertisers, and with the public. Their reaction was understandable; they were asking why they should support the USFL this time around when it would be moving out of the spring months the next time around. The more pressing question then became, Will there even *be* a USFL after the 1985 season?

ABC could have canceled the USFL contract when the Chicago team decided not to play in 1985. Our deal had a clause in it that stated that we had the right to terminate if there were no teams in the three major cities—New York, Los Angeles, and Chicago. We opted not to exercise that termination right, based on the league agreeing that we would negotiate a reduced rights fee for the season. As it turned out, ABC withheld $7 million in rights monies in 1985. There had been so many franchise shifts, and such a reduction in the size of the league, that both its complexion and the value of the television contract had been dramatically altered. In our view, the USFL simply wasn't living up to its obligations. However, attempts to renegotiate failed, so the league filed suit for the $7 million. The dispute was settled out of court in early 1987, and I'm told ABC eventually coughed up $1.975 million to put the thing to bed. I later learned that the USFL had been willing to settle for $250,000.

The USFL was also upset about our decision to use Lynn Swann as expert commentator in 1985. The league felt that Joe Namath should be our expert and that we were withholding Joe for "NFL Monday Night Football." The truth is we felt Lynn, who had been our expert commentator during the first two USFL seasons, deserved to continue with the series in its final year on ABC.

John Bassett struggled diligently to work out an extension of our agreement for spring football beyond 1985, but was frustrated by the growing support within the league for a move to the autumn months. In June 1984, Bassett wrote that he was removing himself from the "continuing renegotiations with your company and your department in regard to the games of the United States Football League." He said in his letter:

> I want you to know that from the beginning of our negotiations some months ago, I have never ceased to respect the integrity, knowledge and willingness to accommodate our league that you brought to the table. Hopefully, the partnership that the United States Football League and ABC Sports enjoyed over the first two years of the league's existence will continue in a manner that best suits the profitability and flexibility of both organizations. I am sorry that the time and effort we put into the negotiations did not achieve the resolution that was satisfactory to both parties, but I do want it on the record that I respect and appreciate your efforts. . . .

Now contrast that with the attitude of another of the USFL owners, Marvin Warner of the Birmingham Stallions. Warner accused ABC Sports of contracting with the USFL so we could sink the league, and twice threatened to bar us from Legion Field in Birmingham unless we blacked out the Birmingham market. We acquiesced once, then, the second time, Arledge was prepared to give in primarily to curry favor with then USFL commissioner Harry Usher, but our Birmingham station squawked so much we went ahead with the telecast. Warner once threatened to file legal action against Roone Arledge, Charlie Lavery, and me, and at the USFL championship-game banquet in Tampa in July 1984, he rekindled those fires. After we spoke briefly at the dinner, he made a point of asking me where I lived, and asked Charlie Lavery the same thing. We were certain he just wanted to know where to file the lawsuit. He also fumed at Lavery about an ABC News feature story comparing the Super Bowl with the USFL championship game. It was a man-on-the-street segment done in Tampa, in which half the people interviewed didn't realize the USFL title game was being played in their city and the other half didn't care. To Warner, ABC News had done the feature to deliberately degrade the new league.

A former U.S. ambassador to Switzerland during the Carter administration, Marvin Warner since then has been convicted of "unauthorized acts" and "securities violations" in connection with the failure of the Home State Savings and Loan company in Cincinnati, Ohio. He once owned that savings and loan association, and thousands of depositors got their money back only after long and anxious months of waiting when it was taken over by another bank. After all that happened, Charlie Lavery said, "I suppose this means Marvin will never file that suit against us."

Another unpleasant incident involved Trump, when he called me and requested that our announcers no longer refer to his team as the New Jersey Generals. He wanted them called merely the Generals, since in his view the team represented the New York metropolitan area. He owned the team and so, I guess, he could call it anything he wanted. If Lew Alcindor could change his name to Kareem Abdul-Jabbar, if Cassius Clay could become Muhammad Ali, and if the New York Giants could move to another state and still be called the New York Giants, I saw no good reason why we should not abide by his wishes. Next time out, our announcers called his team the Generals. However, that didn't set well with a New Jersey legislator, who made loud noises about the designation. When asked for comment, Trump denied ever having made such a request.

The lawsuit filed by the USFL against the NFL need never have happened. Conjecture and hindsight are two of the marvelous gifts we give ourselves, but I think the USFL could have survived had it stuck to spring play. My eventual hope was for the league to become a nighttime series in the spring. But a handful of owners, led by Trump, refused to stay in the shallows. They insisted on going into the deep water with the sharks and the barracuda, and they got devoured. They wound up with nothing—unless you call the three dollars they won in the lawsuit something.

The best ally the United States Football League had was Howard Cosell. Here was a man who spent a goodly portion of his adult life saying despicable things about newspaper reporters—"Those two-hundred-dollar-a-week clerks," was his favorite epithet—and then suddenly he joined them. He became a columnist, doing two pieces a week for the *New York Daily News*. You could say—and he has since said it—that it's not the medium but the message. But for him to join the ranks of those he had so severely castigated as "hacks" struck me as the ultimate hypocrisy.

The minute Howard joined the newspaper fraternity, he began to take pot shots at the NFL. It figured. He could no longer suppress his deep resentment of the league and its commissioner. Just as boxing wasn't corrupt until the Cosell coffers were full, the National Football League was sacrosanct as long as he was in the broadcast booth on Monday nights.

Before the long-awaited USFL-NFL trial began, Cosell set up his own ground rules in a column on May 4, 1986:

"I have been deposed by both parties as a potential witness in this case and will, therefore, be under proper legal constraints in my reporting. But I promise you that within the bounds of legal propriety I will never sacrifice a journalistic principle. Don't forget, I never played the game and I never will."

Howard is a lawyer, and he reminded the world that he could not make any comment that might be construed as prejudicial. Then he proceeded to take one cheap shot after another at the NFL before becoming a key witness for the USFL!

Here's one of the salvos he fired in his column:

"Without question, the NFL is the most powerful and politically wired sports organization in the nation. . . . One can even reasonably infer that the NFL has the ability to speak persuasively to the office of the attorney general of the United States. . . .

And the point of it all, of course, is to bypass the courts, where the NFL has done nothing but lose case after case, and to secure for itself an antitrust exemption: The freedom to operate without the usual constraints or competition that businesses such as Macy's and Bloomingdale's and Ford are run by . . . the NFL knows Congress is the way to go, not only because of the league's poor record in court, but also because its much vaunted propaganda machine is collapsing, wheezing and gasping. . . ."

He was eager to remind his readers of the NFL's court loss to Al Davis and the Raiders, of the drug problems in the NFL, and of the fact that the husband of an NFL owner had been involved in scalping Super Bowl tickets.

"All of this negative publicity," Cosell wrote, "has materially muted the great propaganda machine."

It certainly didn't mute his. Smack dab in the middle of the trial, he used the Bo Jackson story to again spank the NFL, praising the former Auburn football star for then spurning the NFL and selecting a baseball career. Then, while the fires of the court system were smoldering, he again dragged up the drug scandals, and his pal Al Davis and the lawsuits, and the various Heisman Trophy winners who had spurned the NFL (going all the way back to Army's Pete Dawkins for that one), even resurrecting the well-known fact that the Heisman has never been won by a black athlete who attended a predominantly black school. Just what that had to do with the NFL and the USFL lawsuit is beyond my capacity to understand.

Then Howard wondered "just how long the public will continue to subscribe to the league's self-proclaimed exalted status. The NFL would have you believe that it is everyone's prime goal, the dream of every boy's lifetime, to be drafted into their service. To be chosen by the Bucs, or the Bills, or even the Bears. Hogwash. But the NFL's public relations machine grinds on and on and on, and too many members of the media willingly aid it. Until a Bo Jackson comes along and shows the public what a sham it all is."

On the last day of court proceedings—and prior to jury deliberations—Cosell's column was as blatantly unfair to the NFL as his testimony at that same trial was inaccurate. He spent six paragraphs and more than two hundred words defining perjury, explaining the foundation for the American judicial system and the basis for that system as it was formulated by the Founding Fathers. The next ten paragraphs and four hundred more words he spent scandalizing those truths in a scurrilous attack on television and the sports institutions it covers. He spoke of the pressures imposed on television and those who exert them. He alluded to the "control" and the "clout," and described the commissioners of baseball, football, and basketball as the most powerful men in sports.

"Fail to respond to these men and you risk losing baseball or basketball or football," he wrote. "If your business is sports television, you cannot fail. You cannot risk losing their business. Without them, you have no product. You go out of business."

All this hit at the time a jury of six would be sifting evidence and rendering a verdict in a $1.69 billion trial. Whatever verdict the five women and one man delivered, it would have a profound effect on sports as we know it. No matter what instructions Judge Peter K. Leisure might have given those jurors in United States District Court, there is a good chance the jurors either read or heard about Cosell's own informal summation.

"The fact is," Howard concluded, "no major sports league can survive without a television contract. The fact is, all three major sports leagues exert enormous power and pressure on all three television networks. The fact is, television responds, time and time again, to that pressure. The fact is, perjury is a crime."

I'll buy that last part, and add that there is a strong case to be made for Howard Cosell having perjured himself. He totally lost his objectivity toward the NFL and could not suppress his hostility. He had testified that the NFL did exert pressure on ABC against the USFL, that I was guilty of "interfering" with his "SportsBeat" show's presentations dealing with the USFL because of "NFL attempted influence" over the show. That is a flat out lie.

As soon as I heard Cosell's testimony about my alleged interference with his shows, I called Ed Silverman, who was the managing editor of "SportsBeat" and the chap running its day-to-day operations. I asked him straight out if I ever applied any pressure to anyone at that show as to what would be said, or not said, on the program. He and I both knew that I had called a few times to make certain we were being fair and presenting both sides of an issue. And this is what Ed Silverman told me, even after his boss, Cosell, had testified under oath about NFL influence and so-called pressure:

"Jim, you called a few times and asked that we give balance to our stories, and to make certain that we gave the NFL a chance to be heard, that we present both sides of the issue fairly. I believed then and I believe now that you were seeking only journalistic balance."

Reporters later would describe Cosell's testimony as "rambling and often raucous," and "bombastic." On several occasions, his testimony drew laughter. I might have laughed, as well, had the whole thing not been so pitiful.

There are four milestones in the relationship between ABC and the USFL, and to my knowledge not once, anywhere along the line, was there any pressure put on ABC Sports by the NFL—although that's not to suggest that Pete Rozelle and his colleagues were elated that we got in bed with the fledgling league.

Milestone number one was when we agreed to televise the first two USFL seasons in 1983 and 1984. Milestone number two came when we exercised our option for the 1985 season and still there wasn't a peep from the NFL. Milestone three was when we offered the USFL $175 million to extend the contract for spring football and the league refused. Milestone four was when we rejected USFL demands that we move with them to a fall schedule beginning in 1986. The NFL was never any kind of a factor in any of these four major decisions.

No one in his right mind could dispute where Cosell's sentiments were, and are. He desperately wanted the USFL to win the suit, just as he had rooted for Al Davis to win his lawsuit against the NFL. And that's a twist, too, since Cosell had long strongly opposed franchise shifts in any sport. He justified his support of Davis as a matter of law. For my money, the way the USFL lost the suit was wonderful—getting three dollars was perfect!

Although the NFL was found to be a natural monopoly, the jury found—and the decision was upheld—that the NFL had not willfully acquired or maintained monopoly power in the television submarket, and, further, that the NFL did not even attempt to obtain it. The jury determined that, even if the NFL had so tried, it did not have the power to deny the USFL access to the networks. In fact, the jury went further in determining that the NFL's actions were not "the substantial cause of the USFL's failure to acquire a national broadcast television contract," and that the networks' refusal to enter "into a broadcasting contract with the USFL was based on uncoerced, independent business judgment."

The summing up by the court of the USFL's subsequent request for an injunction was nothing short of marvelous:

"In sum, when a firm which has committed myriad blunders in the marketplace seeks to gain benefits through [injunctive relief] that it could not acquire through fair competition—courts should [not] be condemned for obstructing such an effort."

In short, the USFL committed suicide. (The USFL later filed an appeal with the U.S. Court of Appeals for the Second Circuit.)

Pulitzer Prize–winning reporter and celebrated author David Halberstam wrote in *Playboy* in December 1982 about the "early" Howard Cosell: "Howard in those days seemed only mildly excessive, no more out of control than a number of the interesting figures on national television, and he seemed, as well—and this was at the core of it—to be ABOUT something. . . . Howard was not an owner's man; he was a winner's man. He wanted, needed, to be with the winners, as if their success might rub off on him. Correspondingly, he did not want to be with losers, fearing, I suspected, failure by association."

Halberstam said he had wanted to meet Cosell and was excited when it happened, and there was talk that Halberstam might ghostwrite Howard's first book. After their second conversation, Halberstam said he realized it would never work. He described himself as one who once "had been favorably inclined toward him but who now saw him in a new light, as a symbol of the excess that television had wrought upon sports, of the assault upon civility and texture that the tube, with its need for action and the event, demanded."

Halberstam describes himself as "a serious sports freak," and none can question his brilliance. He wrote that "the Howard who emerged in that decade as 'Monday Night Football' became more and more successful was a monster. His insecurities, which had once made him interesting and irreverent, now made him seem heavy and ponderous. The bully in him was more evident now.

"Where once he had challenged the sports establishment," Halberstam continued, "now he was a principal figure in it. . . . Now he shilled shamelessly for his network, for its principal event, 'Monday Night Football', and for his boss, Roone Arledge. Now no major figure in sports, no matter how questionable his values or practices, could appear on Monday night with Howard without being referred to as a dear or close friend. Usually, it would turn out, Howard had dined with him just the night before. With the powerful, he flattered and was flattered in return. . . . Howard, first and foremost, was about Howard."

Five years after the publication of that article, Halberstam was asked if he had changed his opinion about Cosell:

"No, no, it's stronger than ever. The narcissism is interesting. The moment he left football, football became bad. 'Monday Night Football' especially became bad. There's too much violence, too much scoring. When he was there, nothing was more wonderful than 'Monday Night Football.' They were the three musketeers there in the booth; all great buddies. Once out of the booth, he turned on ABC. The ugliness and the darkness started. He turned on Gifford and Meredith and Simpson, and then the NFL and the entire world. The football that once was perfect now became an evil thing. He's a sad man who turned on all those around him. The sad man overstayed his welcome. His ego inhaled him.

"When he went down, he wanted to bring the NFL down with him. It's the same thing as saying that World War III is good only if I get to cover it. . . . About the time this was happening, I saw Roone Arledge and I told him, 'Hey, this is terrific what's happening to Howard. No good deed goes unpunished.' He became a tele-celebrity who acquired a larger audience and at the same time, more insecurities. His success didn't bring him peace.''

It seems a curious coincidence that both Howard Cosell and the United States Football League, in a sense, strangled themselves.

11

FOREVER
A MAN'S WORLD?

*Why Women Sportscasters Are
Still So Far from Winning
Equal Air Time*

Phyllis George has been the most prominent of women sports broadcasters to date. Her entry into a world dominated by men was a symbol for aspiring women. When she failed to gain widespread acceptance, the cause suffered greatly.

CBS must shoulder much of the blame for Phyllis George's failure. She was thrust onto network television sports programs because she's a pretty, personable former Miss America. She never developed credibility as a sportscaster.

ABC and NBC have been less exposed in this area, because their women were not as pretty nor given roles as prominent as those Phyllis tried, but all three major networks are to blame for the failure to develop female talent within the industry. The major problem all three networks face in this area is that women have lacked depth in dealing with what is essentially a man's domain. It's a credibility gap that discerning viewers can spot in a minute.

Let there be no question that the predominantly male audience has some resistance to hearing its sports from a female. That's male chauvinist piggism at its worst, but it's a fact. On the other hand, there is no reason why an audience, whatever its makeup, should be required to tolerate an announcer with a very shallow level of knowledge of or feeling for sports. And that, of course, is the main reason we have had 99 percent of our sports dealt to us by men.

More and more women are becoming interested in sports, and no doubt some of them have done so, at least initially, in self-defense. It is true, too, that we are hearing more of a demand for women in positions of prominence in sports broadcasting. But I believe that, even among female viewers, any lack of under-standing or knowledge by a female sportscaster immediately comes through. With your true sports aficionado, superficiality jumps right off the screen and into the television-viewing room.

Over the years, ABC Sports hired a significant number of women, and some played important roles at various events. Dating all the way back to Carol Heiss Jenkins, the champion figure-skater, there was no reluctance to hire women simply because they were women. Carol was obviously a very talented person, and we decided to put her on the air as an expert commentator. I produced the National Figure-Skating Champi-onships in Cleveland in 1964 and we did a segment we called "Girl Talk." We placed Carol in the stands with Peggy Fleming, who was fourteen at the time, and put spectators around them, and they sat there and chatted about skating and life in general. Carol was very good at it. She was pretty and vivacious, and it worked well from a programming standpoint. Later, after Peggy Fleming had won five national championships plus the only United States gold medal at the 1968 Winter Olympic Games, she joined ABC Sports as an expert commentator on figure skating.

Of course, the hiring of Carol and Peggy was partly tied to Roone's penchant for celebrities. He had to have them on his team, personally and professionally. (And how he loved to tell others about his well-known friends and associates! Once, head-ing to Georgia on vacation, I asked Charlie Lavery to stay close to Roone on an important matter and keep me informed. As the time for decision-making neared, Charlie notified Roone that we might have to reach him on the weekend. Roone said he planned to spend it at his place on Long Island, but gave Lavery the name of a posh restaurant where he'd be if he didn't pick up the telephone at home. "I don't know if the reservation is in my name or not," Charlie said Arledge told him, "but if it's not, it might be in the name of Swifty Lazar or Irwin Shaw or Ben Bradlee. I'll be with them Saturday night." As I said to the queen, I'm no name-dropper.)

When Billie Jean King began attracting national publicity, not just for her tennis but for her involvement with women's rights, Roone felt we had to hire her, and so we signed her to a contract for a hundred thousand dollars a year. Unfortunately, she was ill equipped for television commentary and rarely went on the air. She'd dispute this and claim no one at ABC Sports took her aside and tried to work with her, but the main problem was that she was off playing tennis, and very involved with other activities, and simply not sufficiently available to us. Then, a couple of times when we planned to bring her into the studio to cohost "Wide World of Sports," she simply couldn't get a hold on things. She's a sports fan, and I think has good knowledge of a variety of sports subjects, but she lacked the ability to transmit that information from the studio to the audience. Commenting on tennis was one thing, but beyond that Billie Jean King simply was not equipped to be a sportscaster. Further, when stories about her life-style surfaced, they hurt her with the public. Talk all you want about alternative life-styles and choices of sexual partners and individual freedom and all the rest of it, but there's an old line they used to use in vaudeville: "Does it play in Dubuque?" Being gay is still not the way to wow them in Dubuque.

Billie Jean King is the perfect example of what Howard Cosell talked about when he used the term "jockocracy." She was hot as an athlete, and on top of that she was a feminist, and a leader, and a very prominent person with the nation's media. I was a part of the decision to hire her, and I was personally wrong, as we in the sports department were collectively wrong in our approach to things from a professional standpoint. Just as CBS hired Jayne Kennedy because of her looks—she's a very beautiful woman with precious little talent as a sports broadcaster—ABC Sports hired Billie Jean King because of her headline value. What we should have done, if we had had patience and available staff, and if Billie Jean would have devoted enough time to it, was to provide her with instruction and then assign a producer to her and let her do events off the air into a videotape machine. Then we should have critiqued her and helped her get ready to perform on actual events for television. The really sad thing is that the same thing can be said of a lot of the people ABC, CBS, and NBC have hired, and so many times later discarded when their marquee value was diminished.

We televised Billie Jean's "Battle of the Sexes" tennis match against Bobby Riggs in 1973: the middle-aged hustler against the Grand Slam champ. Jerry Perenchio is the guy who brought it to us. He's bright and aggressive, and he persuaded us to pay seven hundred fifty thousand dollars for the television rights. We did it live from the Houston Astrodome, and, with a ton of hoopla attached to it, the event took on an immediate circuslike atmosphere. I thought it would be a fun thing, and good for ABC, so long as we approached it less as an athletic contest than as a happening. The show did well and got big ratings, the participants and the promoters made lots of money, and so did ABC. We took a little heat in that it was critically described as a made-for-television thing, but nonetheless it provided a couple of hours of wonderful entertainment for the American viewing public. The match was watched by over 37 million people. Billie Jean and Bobby sparked emotional involvement, the match helped build interest in orthodox tennis, and nobody got hurt.

The same cannot be said when it came to putting Billie Jean on the air as a broadcast performer. She got hurt and so did sports television; it was a setback for her as a person and as a professional, and a step backward for the women's movement in broadcasting.

ABC also could have hired Phyllis George. Eddie Elias, the founder of the Professional Bowlers Association and one of the finest human beings I know, represented Phyllis and spoke with me about the possibility of her moving over to our network. I'd met Phyllis and knew her husband, a former governor of Kentucky and one-time owner of the Kentucky Colonels and the Boston Celtics, John Y. Brown. They're nice people, but I saw no place she could fit on ABC.

Thankfully, there have been a few women who have become good commentators, or expert analysts—people who add real insight when dealing with a specific sport or discipline. For example, Cathy Rigby McCoy is an extremely capable broadcaster about gymnastics. She isn't good at it just because she happens to know the discipline, because it's something she did herself very well, but because she's taught herself how to communicate all that knowledge, how to deal with a television audience. Diana Nyad, the long-distance swimmer, has a natural quality about her that I find appealing, but I'm not convinced she has the ability to grow into a major performer. Peggy Fleming is a lovely and knowledgeable person, but she's just too mild on the air, doesn't have enough bite in her commentary. It's a lot like her skating: graceful and elegant, but with a need for more flavor and incisiveness.

You may ask why the networks, having hired such people, don't work more with them to try to make them better. I'm for that; both parties have the money and time to do it. (NBC Sports has made such an effort by engaging Marty Glickman to coach its announcers.) But there's another argument: Why should a national network be a training ground? There is a school of thought that holds that sportscasters, including star athletes, should follow the traditional pattern of starting at local stations and learning the business there before achieving network roles. Unfortunately, many athletes are at a distinct disadvantage in that they've spent so much time honing their sporting skills that little or nothing has been left over for growing in other ways. Frankly, too many of them are so emotionally stunted as to be ill-equipped for life outside their particular arena, and therefore often very late in maturing—if they mature at all.

A figure-skater, for example, in order to attempt to become an Olympic champion or world-class performer, must spend vastly more time skating than doing anything else, ofttimes including sleeping. The skater is at the rink before dawn, back in the rink after school, and, many times, back there again in the evening. I remember how curious it was to see Nadia Comaneci holding a doll, as a four- or five-year-old child would hold it, at the Montreal Olympic Games, and here she was in her teens! What such dedicated performers do requires so much time and effort, and often such large amounts of money, that the average sports-watcher cannot even begin to comprehend the sacrifices involved. But such performers often miss out on, or are delayed in getting to, the other parts of life essential to making them into well-rounded personalities. Too often, young star athletes are comfortable only within the confines of their own little worlds, and frequently come off as aloof and one-dimensional in the presence of "outsiders."

Probably no woman wanted to succeed in broadcasting more than Donna de Varona. She was the darling little kid of the 1960 Olympic Games in Rome, who then came back and won two gold medals in swimming as a seventeen-year-old in the 1964 Tokyo Games. She was an attractive, athletic, California girl with a refreshingly breezy and carefree air about her, and it was inevitable that Roone Arledge would have her in his stable. She was used early on only as a commentator on swimming events, and, after some awkwardness that was understandable, she became a capable performer in that role. But she wanted more, and she simply was not capable of handling more difficult assignments. Again, there was the lack of depth and the problem of credibility. Unfortunately, we had given her a taste of life in the big leagues of broadcasting, and you could hardly blame her for wanting more of it.

Donna de Varona's was another classic case of an oft-repeated theme: There's a star out there, so haul out a contract and let's make a deal, and hope that people will be attracted to his/her personality. No training, no experience, no preparation, and no guidance beyond the little a busy producer can provide on the spot. It was the old story of taking an adroit performer in one field and throwing him/her, unschooled, into another totally different field, and thereby often to the wolves. Athletes, in the main, are eager to undertake that bold step, most of them believing in their hearts that broadcasting is easy—until they're on the inside looking out. Check your newspapers at the end of any season, and you'll read plenty of stories about athletes who are thinking about retiring. When asked about their future plans, as often as not the response is something like, "Oh, I don't know. I've been thinking about going into broadcasting." That is, of course, if they can't find legitimate work!

The author *(right)* preparing for an "ABC's Wide World of Sports" telecast in the early days. Alongside is the late Sonny Diskin, who directed ABC's early boxing programs.

Howard Cosell *(left)* and Muhammad Ali enjoyed a unique and mutually respectful relationship, but the champ took the kidding to the ragged edge by threatening to remove Howard's toupee.

Ed Scherick was the founder of Sports Programs, Inc., the predecessor organization of ABC Sports. Although he seldom received the credit, he created "ABC's Wide World of Sports."

The multi-million-dollar "Monday Night Football" announcer line-up featured Dan Dierdorf *(left),* Frank Gifford *(center),* and Al Michaels *(right)* starting in 1987.

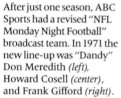

After just one season, ABC Sports had a revised "NFL Monday Night Football" broadcast team. In 1971 the new line-up was "Dandy" Don Meredith *(left),* Howard Cosell *(center),* and Frank Gifford *(right).*

The pregame gatherings before "Monday Night Football" were special and often attracted celebrities, like actor Robert Urich *(far right)* with Cosell, Spence and wife, Lynn *(far left),* before a Redskins' home game.

NFL commissioner Pete Rozelle *(right)* with Jim Spence at an NFL winter meeting in Arizona.

Ali, always the center of attention, became almost a regular on "ABC's Wide World of Sports."

When you say "Wide World of Sports," you say Jim McKay. He hosted the series' premiere in April 1961.

Spence and Arledge, who was outstanding in executing the "Wide World of Sports" concept, with one of the series' many Emmys.

No one dared "mightier" deeds than Evel Knievel. He was the ultimate showman.

ABC announcers' meeting, May 1985. Back row *(left to right)* F. Gifford, D. Lewin, K. Jackson, J. Spence, A. Michaels, J. Whitaker, and C. Howard. Seated *(left to right)* A. Trautwig, J. Lampley, J. McKay, and C. Schenkel. H. Cosell was unable to attend due to family illness.

Frank Broyles *(left)* and Keith Jackson became college football's most effective broadcast team. Keith has been ABC's principal college football play-by-play announcer since 1974 and Frank worked on ABC's telecasts for nine seasons.

Former Boston Celtics' great Bill Russell *(left)* and Jackson enjoyed unusual rapport when ABC Sports televised NBA basketball.

Chris Schenkel *(left)* and Nelson (Bo) Burton, Jr., are a hit team with the popular "Professional Bowlers Tour." Chris has been host of this series since its inception in 1962.

Donna de Varona, shown here in Los Angeles, site of the 1984 Summer Olympic Games, has been on network television for over two decades.

CBS Sports' top announcer Brent Musburger *(left)* with excellent basketball analyst Billy Packer.

Dick Enberg *(right)* and Merlin Olsen have attained star status at NBC Sports.

ABC baseball broadcasters Al Michaels *(left)* and Jim Palmer.

Tim McCarver, outstanding ABC expert commentator on baseball.

Spence *(left)*, Arledge *(second from left)*, along with two USFL figures—Judge Peter Spivak *(second from right)*, then acting chairman, and Walter Duncan *(right)*, of the New Jersey Generals—in May 1982, when ABC Sports announced its agreement with the new football league. The press conference was held at "21" in New York.

The U.S. Boxing Championships brought Cosell, Arledge, and Spence *(left to right)* before Congress.

Donald Trump *(right)*, with Jim Spence, has a string of successes, but his venture into USFL football was not one of them.

(Left): Dave Marr, a former PGA champion, and also a winner in the booth.

(Right): Former PGA Tour standout Bob Rosburg provides incisive commentary on ABC.

ABC's Jack Nicklaus (left), NBC's Lee Trevino.

Nicklaus and Arnold Palmer, living legends.

(Left to right): Spence, with former golf executives Mark Cox and Joe Dey.

Gordon Johncock's Indy 500 victories were memorable events for ABC Sports.

Foolish Pleasure, with jockey Jacinto Vasquez aboard, won the 101st Run for the Roses when ABC Sports televised the Kentucky Derby for the first time in 1975. The Derby had been televised by CBS since 1948.

Jim Craig *(left)* and Captain Mike Eruzione with Arledge and Spence at ABC affiliates' meeting after 1980 Olympic hockey triumph.

J. McKay *(left)* and C. Schenkel, Olympic hosts.

Arledge presented 1972 WWOS award to Olga Korbut.

Nadia Comaneci won three gold medals in 1976 at Montreal.

Sugar Ray Leonard, outstanding performer in Montreal.

Carl Lewis won four gold medals in Los Angeles, equaling the legendary Jesse Owens' feat.

Olympian Mary Lou Retton won the Women's All-around gold medal in gymnastics in 1984.

The Olympic Flag continues to fly as the modern Olympic movement approaches its 100th anniversary in 1996.

When Donna de Varona began talking of spreading out and doing shows other than swimming, Roone Arledge pushed the ABC Sports staff to find some kind of vehicle for her, with the result that for one tediously long Saturday afternoon she sat alongside Dave Diles on the "Prudential College Scoreboard" show. Now Diles had been involved with the show for many years, and over that span of time had worked with eight different cohosts. Donna de Varona set the record for the shortest amount of time spent on that show. Bob Goodrich was the producer in those days, and about the third time Donna pronounced Clemson with an extra syllable (she made it "Clem-en-son")—this following some other embarrassing mistakes—Bob determined that she was ill-suited for that line of work, and said so to management. Donna then complained to Arledge that Goodrich gave her no help, no guidance, but just let her hang out to dry.

"Not at all true," said Goodrich. "Donna's a nice lady, but I knew we had trouble going in. So I set aside an entire rehearsal day on Friday and did a run-through with her, including giving her tapes of previous shows to watch. We did that with only one other person on that show, Warner Wolf. It just wasn't Donna's cup of tea. She just couldn't cut it."

Donna's sister is Joanna Kerns, star of ABC's "Growing Pains." She resented Donna's golden-girl status, and, when Joanna played a dumb sportscaster in the television movie *The Four Seasons,* using her maiden name, a bitter sibling dispute evolved. I understand that the two are now close again.

Donna is a nice woman, and a friend of mine, but she has limited capabilities in television. She sat around most of the time, got work when we had a swimming show, and waited for a break that would never arrive. Finally, when NBC was getting ready to do the Moscow Olympics—the Games that never got on the air in 1980—Donna left ABC for what she perceived to be a better opportunity. Perhaps it would have turned out that way, had NBC televised the Games.

When it came time for ABC to prepare for the 1984 Olympic Games in Los Angeles, Roone Arledge decided to bring Donna back to ABC, and he and I promptly had a falling out over that decision. Arledge not only gave her a six-figure-a-year commitment, but made promises to her that the network could not realistically keep. And I told him just that. He didn't consult with anyone about it. As president of ABC News and Sports, he certainly didn't have to check his every move with me, but I didn't have to remain silent, either. He had come to me with the deal in hand, explaining that Donna would perform some duties as his special assistant, and urging me to see that she was assigned frequently as an on-air commentator, then adding that he wanted her to have an "important role" in ABC Sports' management.

I told him: "That's just not possible. Donna's a fine lady and I like her, but I don't see how she can play a significant management role. For her to be in a meaningful position, we'd have to assign her duties already being handled by others. I don't think it's right to take responsibilities from other people who've worked hard and been very loyal and productive. As for what role she might fill on the air, I think that has to be limited."

I said my piece straightforwardly. Roone's reply made it clear there would be no protracted argument:

"Well, that's your opinion."

I also had an opinion about what I considered a blatant conflict of interest.

While she was on the ABC Sports' payroll, Donna de Varona was involved as a member of the executive board of the United States Olympic Committee (USOC). It was my belief that since ABC was engaged in business activities with the USOC she should have held one position or the other. The conflict of interest became most clear when Donna lobbied for the candidacy of Anchorage, Alaska, to be the United States' designated city for the 1992 Winter Olympic Games. Senator Ted Stevens of Alaska was a major supporter of women in sports and, consequently, Donna, who had been active in the women's movement and served a term as president of the Women's Sports Foundation, developed a relationship with him. It was natural, then, for her to support the Anchorage candidacy.

Several cities were competing for that designation, among them Lake Placid, where ABC had been so successful in televising the 1980 Winter Games. And here we had Donna de Varona, an employee of ABC Sports—indeed, the assistant to the *president* of

ABC News and Sports—actively urging the naming of one city over another.

Donna's dual role was a violation of ABC company policy and should never have been allowed to happen. I don't blame Donna. As I eventually learned, her contract recognized her USOC position.

My assignment, to weave her into the fabric of ABC Sports and somehow involve her in the department's day-to-day operation, was impossible to carry out. And, as nicely as I could, I told Donna just that when I met with her in Korea in April of 1984. We had gone there to meet with the International Olympic Committee and the Seoul Organizing Committee about the Olympic Games in 1988, and she came to my room to discuss her future. I explained that I knew what Roone wanted to accomplish, but that I didn't think it could be done. At the very least, it was a most clumsy conversation. I explained that ABC Sports' management team was set and that I was opposed to pushing somone aside to make room for her. Arledge had made promises that we just couldn't keep. It was painful to tell Donna that, and I tried to soften the message by telling her I would do what I could for her. She raised no fuss, and in fact handled the conversation with grace and style. But I know she was confused and hurt.

We put Donna to work in three areas of the telecasts of the 1984 Summer Olympic Games from Los Angeles. She was the expert commentator on swimming, and did well at that. She also did some interviews that were quite good. But when we put her in the studio with Jim Lampley as cohost of our late night show, she was—well, like a swimmer out of water.

Donna, who has made a considerable contribution in her areas of expertise, deserves a lot of credit for her longevity, having been on the major network scene for over two decades.

Almost as awkward as the Donna de Varona situation was the hiring of Anne Simon. John Martin, programming vice president at the time, was mainly responsible for bringing her to us. Anne had been working at a local station in New Orleans, and Chuck Howard agreed with Martin that she should be signed to a contract. Her main assignment was sideline work on NCAA football telecasts, for which she was paid in the neighborhood of ninety thousand dollars a year.

Anne was pretty, but when you've said that you've just about said it all. She did some decent interviews, but most of the time it was obvious she was straining, and credibility with the viewers became a factor. Anne had to be led by the hand on most of her pieces, with Howard, who produced the telecasts on which she appeared, having to feed her questions through her earpiece. Much of the time, he was literally telling her what questions to ask. One Saturday afternoon, for instance, she asked Bear Bryant something he didn't like and he jumped all over her. (Later he wrote her a letter of apology.)

John Martin had resigned by the fall of 1983, but had promised Anne she would work the 1984 Olympic Games. When Roone and I discussed her contribution, or lack of it, we agreed not to renew her contract, but since John had made a verbal commitment to her for the Olympics, I prevailed upon Roone to give her a limited role. She did a few interviews on the gymnastics coverage, but that was it. We told her we would not sign her to another deal. Her agent, Art Kaminsky, asked if we'd keep her on the payroll for a couple of additional months while she looked for other work, and I agreed, despite strong objections from some of our people. She should never have been hired in the first place, and she knew she had no future with us, but I'm sure she appreciated the extra couple of months we gave her while she looked around.

One woman who might have made a real impact in sports is Kathleen Sullivan. She was making some headway at ABC News, and Arledge, who was extremely fond of her, determined she should be on the Olympic telecasts, where he placed her alongside Frank Gifford as daytime cohost in Los Angeles. They were an attractive team and Kathleen was quite good, coming across as articulate and picking up quickly on what we were trying to accomplish. But she was tough and demanding off-camera, and it was clear that she had her mind set on a career in news.

Another woman who had a brief fling at ABC Sports is Andrea Kirby, and there is little doubt she had more real knowledge of sports than perhaps any other woman ever on network television. Andrea had paid some dues as a sports broadcaster in Florida and Baltimore, and she kept sending tapes to Chuck Howard and bugging him for an interview. She was relentless, and eventually, continuing to want a woman sportscaster if we could find one good enough, we paid her sixty-five thousand dollars a year and started her out with Dave Diles on the college football scoreboard show. She hung in for a couple of years, and eventually was making eighty-five thousand dollars before we decided not to sign her to another contract.

Andrea wanted desperately to be a star. She was acutely aware of how much time she spent on camera, and how many stories were assigned to her, compared with anyone sharing the stage with her. She insisted on having a wardrobe mistress in the studio to help her prepare her clothes. Had she possessed the talent to back up her high image of herself, she might, indeed, have become a star. But Andrea did too many dumb things on the air, largely because she was too loose, too sure of herself. For example, one day on the football score show she decided to go braless. A woman of fine proportions, she wore too sheer a blouse and we weren't even off the air before the ABC switchboard lit up with viewer calls about Andrea's see-through attire. As much as the nation might be crying out for equal rights, ABC's viewers were not yet ready for something that up-close-and-personal. But I'll say this for Andrea—she *was* bold.

Eleanor Riger became the most prominent off-camera woman in television sports, as a producer at ABC for a number of years. She played an important role in the women's movement. Ellie handled assignments a notch or two below the major ones, but she was extremely loyal and a valuable member of the team.

The coordinating director of "Wide World of Sports," and also a producer, is Carol Lehti, who, along with Linda Jonsson, former coordinating producer of NBC's "SportsWorld," was also a pioneer for women in television sports. Carol has devoted her life to ABC

Sports, and her proficiency in the postproduction area has been of inestimable value.

In recent years, a young woman who worked for me has blossomed into perhaps the most creative woman in the industry. She is now a producer at ABC Sports and also associate coordinating producer of "Wide World of Sports." Her name is Amy Sacks. Given to excesses at times, she nevertheless has demonstrated considerable ability, and her innovative ideas are much needed in a business where so many are doing so much of the same thing.

Not long ago, ABC Sports hired a new female announcer, Becky Dixon, who had been doing local television in Tulsa. She comes across as unnatural and ill at ease on the tube. Maybe it's nervousness about being in the big time, and perhaps in time she'll relax and get better. But, in the meantime, it seems to me to be the same old story—hiring someone before that person is ready for the major leagues and using the network as a training ground.

On the other hand, NBC's hiring of Gayle Gardner, a very competent studio performer for ESPN, is an example of a more natural transition—from a national cable network to a major broadcast network.

Keith Jackson once had a valid suggestion about the hiring of women and ex-athletes as broadcasters:

"Some good people can, and have, come out of the ranks of the professional athletes. The networks simply have to be more careful in the selection," said Keith. "I always thought maybe ABC would do something about that. I was on an airplane one time and happened to be seated next to Leonard Goldenson. I tried to sell him on the idea of developing a farm system within the affiliate stations. You could reach out annually and take ten sportscasters, and bring them into the network environment for a couple of weeks and let them observe the daily operation. Let them sit in the production truck at sports events. Let them sit in the control room with producers and directors. Then you could follow their work with the affiliate stations, and I guarantee you there'd be a greater development of talent, whether the person had a jock background or not. You could do the same thing with some of these women who obviously are hired because they're pretty faces.''

There's no denying that regardless of how far we have come as a society we're still lagging socially behind our technology. It bothers me to confess that it still exists, but there remains a stigma that says that a sports audience will not be as quick to accept a female television performer as a male. And we can't deny that to some extent it exists also in the executive suite. An example:

Charlie Stanford was vice president of legal and business affairs at ABC Sports and reported to me. He needed a second-in-command, and we had decided that he would do all the preliminary interviewing, then when he'd narrowed the list to three or four, would bring me in to interview them. The process took a considerable amount of time, and I queried Charlie about whether he was making headway. Finally, he told me he had interviewed a hundred people, but that he now had the list down to three men. I interviewed each of them, but none jumped out of the pack as a stick-out sort of candidate. Most of the time in situations like that, one person will put a head above the crowd and you just know that's the one. Not this time. When I completed my interviews, Charlie asked me what I thought. I told him the candidates seemed equally impressive, but that none seemed overly impressive.

"There is one other person,'' Charlie ventured.

"Who's that?''

"Well, it's a problem.''

I wondered what kind of problem he was alluding to.

"Well, it just wouldn't work. You see, she's a female and I just don't think she would fit.''

I told him I didn't see that as a problem and that I wanted to interview her.

The long and short of it is that we wound up interviewing a bright, poised woman named Chris Hikawa. My only concern was whether she would be strong enough to deal in the male-oriented—and, yes, male-dominated—arena of network television sports. After just a few minutes of the interview, it was obvious that Chris was both talented enough and strong enough. She was immediately hired.

So now the women's liberation groups around the country will be able to say: "Isn't that just wonderful? These guys crow about hiring one woman over a hundred men, when she obviously is the most talented candidate, but care not one whit about Anne Simon and Phyllis George." And I understand and sympathize with them.

Today there is much discussion at the networks about wanting to hire capable, talented women and have them blossom into major performers at every level of sports broadcasting, but it's mostly empty talk; however, NBC Sports should be given credit for hiring Gayle Gardner and then assigning Gayle Sierens in December 1987 to be the first woman play-by-play announcer on an NFL telecast.

And I believe more women will occupy prominent roles in television sports, including major-event play-by-play assignments.

12

DIRTY DEALING

*The Unsavory Story
of How ABC Lost NBA
Basketball to CBS*

"Get me Bob Cousy," the man ordered one of his aides.

"But Roone—"

"You heard me, get Bob Cousy."

"But, Roone, there's something you ought to know. You see—"

"For the last time, get me Bob Cousy. And that's final."

And so, Bob Cousy came to Roone Arledge's office, stuck out his hand to greet his new boss, and uttered these never-to-be-forgotten words: "Hello, Woone."

Bob Cousy turned out to be a class act, whose slight speech impediment did not affect his broadcasting ability, so thankfully there were no regrets about hiring the former Boston Celtic star as a basketball commentator for ABC Sports.

ABC televised National Basketball Association (NBA) games for nine seasons, from 1964–65 through the 1972–73 season. While it is true that the NBA has never enjoyed the ratings success at CBS that it did at ABC, it nonetheless is a major-league package, and one that ABC should never have lost. It's been a real money-maker for CBS: In fact, CBS's average rating of 15.9 for the 1987 Celtics-Lakers final series was an all-time high for any NBA series, with game six the highest-rated daytime basketball—college or pro—in television history at 17.3.

Those early years of their marriage represented an outstanding period of growth for both ABC Sports and the NBA. The major markets—New York, Los Angeles, Chicago—had good teams, and naturally Red Auerbach's Boston Celtics were outstanding (some things never change). The ratings were consistently in double figures and the pro game became a great hit, both artistically and commercially.

ABC's contract with the NBA wound down with the season championship in 1972–73, which was the year the New York Knicks won their second world championship in the showdown series against the Lakers. Walter Kennedy was NBA commissioner then, and, while personally a nice man, Walter let himself be controlled and manipulated by the owners who made the most noise, like Jack Kent Cooke, then the owner of the Lakers and now owner of the Washington Redskins, and Ned Irish, then the head man of the Knicks. When it came time to talk about a new contract, we found we had two major areas of conflict: blacking out local viewers on home games, and televising the NBA in the fourth quarter of the year from October through December, the beginning of the season, which we did not want to do.

In leading the way on the home blackout issue, Cooke and Irish were looking at the long-range picture, where they could see the coming proliferation of cable television. I recall Cooke ranting, "How can we give the fans free television of our home games now, and then when we're faced with the widespread use of cable, expect them to pay for seeing those games on cable?" Irish echoed every word said about blackouts, as did Alan Rothenberg, then the attorney for the Lakers and an alternate governor of the club, in league conclaves. (Rothenberg is now president of the Los Angeles Clippers.)

Franklin Mieuli, then the owner of the San Francisco (now Golden State) Warriors, was equally hung up about the need to televise NBA games in the October–December time frame. "How can we begin a season in October," he wondered, "and let three months of the season go by before we show our faces on network television? We need to build public interest in professional basketball. We need network exposure during the football season in order to sell tickets. Waiting until the football season is over simply destroys momentum."

Mieuli had a point, but for us the ramifications of his concept were onerous. First, I questioned the wisdom of starting the NBA season on television at a time when the nation's collective head is turned to college and pro football. The NBA wanted ABC to air the basketball games on weekend afternoons. Putting them on Sundays against the NFL would have been suicidal; CBS and NBC would have eaten us alive in the numbers game. As for Saturdays, we were committed to college football.

So the meetings went back and forth between ABC Sports and Commissioner Kennedy, and there seemed to be no way to come to an agreement as neither side would budge on these critical issues. There was a provision in the existing agreement that required the league to present us with a final offer, after which we had a certain number of days to say yea or nay.

And here, once again, arose the specter of Barry Frank. He and Al Michaels' late father, a nice man named Jay Michaels, were agents for the league. When it came time to put together the final proposal to ABC, the NBA's power triumvirate of Cooke, Irish, and Mieuli wanted to reverse the line from the old tired joke: Instead of making us an offer we could not refuse, they wanted to tender one the network simply could not accept. And the trio of owners wanted Barry Frank to tell them what they could insert in the contract that would force ABC to say no. Barry, as always, came up trumps: "For one thing, you can insist that the network start the telecast of a Saturday pro basketball game between two and three o'clock in the afternoon, New York time, from October to December." This, of course, was the very time we were committed to televise NCAA college football.

To add to the pain, the NBA included another sticky little clause calling for ABC to pay the league $9 million dollars a year if, for any reason, we couldn't live up to the precise details of the deal. Nine million just happened to be the amount of monies the NBA wanted for television rights each year.

We obviously had no option but to reject the proposal, thereby freeing the NBA to go over and make a deal with CBS, where it has been ever since. We did file a lawsuit against the NBA, but lost the case. It was the first time in the distinguished career of Clarence Fried, of the prominent firm of Hawkins, Delafield & Wood, that he'd ever lost one for ABC. Clarence never fully understood the NBA or the case, and consequently did not build a good foundation in court. He'd sometimes refer to the NCAA as the "NBAA" and, in all, poorly presented our case. Despite that, I still believe we should have won. The league meeting that tied ABC in knots occurred on February 21, 1973. Consider this testimony about that meeting from Barry Frank when our attorney was attempting to establish that the league was structuring a contract we could not sign:

FRIED: Will you state as nearly as you can recollect the conversation that took place on that day? [A conversation involving Frank, Irish, Mieuli, and Rothenberg at the Barbizon Plaza Hotel on Central Park South in New York.]

FRANK: The genesis of the conversation was an attempt on the part of the four people at the meeting to construct the final terms and conditions that would be offered to ABC pursuant to its existing agreement with the NBA. That was the nature of the meeting.

FRIED: Did anyone at that meeting say we have to draft this in such a way so that ABC cannot accept it?

FRANK: Yes, sir.

FRIED: Who was it that said that?

FRANK: I believe it was Mr. Rothenberg who made that statement.

FRIED: Do you recall what Mr. Rothenberg said in that connection?

FRANK: Well, Mr. Rothenberg and the other members of that committee had intended to draft an agreement that would be as difficult as possible—I believe what they said was that we have got to draft an agreement that is as difficult as possible, or, if possible, impossible for ABC to accept. . . . The basic suggestion made for the most binding limitation on ABC's ability to accept was the inclusion of a clause that provided that some games are to be telecast in the fourth quarter of the year, fourth quarter of the calendar year, which are to be specifically required to be broadcast on Saturday afternoons . . . and, further, specifically that the starting time period of those games be specified as between two and three P.M. That was one of the numerous factors that were included as part of the overall offering to ABC.

Frank later told how the league had compiled a "laundry list" of other stumbling blocks to the successful execution of a contract. The league wanted the right to dictate the schedule, approval of announcers, and approval of the pregame and halftime formats.

More testimony:

FRIED: Mr. Frank, in the course of that meeting, did Mr. Rothenberg say, "Let's think of as many things as we can that will, in effect, screw ABC"? [After several objections, the overruling of those objections, and back and forth conversation involving attorneys for both sides and the judge, Frank was ordered to respond.]

FRANK: He said what I have just testified to; that let's find, in effect, as many ways as we can to screw ABC. He used the euphemism. A common euphemism for the word. . . .

FRIED: Well, what was the exact word that he used?

FRANK [TO THE JUDGE]:   Am I required to answer that, Your Honor?

THE COURT: Yes, we're all men. Any women here? Listen, they go to the movies, they hear that.

FRANK: I believe he said, "Let's find as many ways that we can that we can fuck ABC."

Despite testimony that was overwhelming by the league's own agent, ABC lost the case. The judge, Hyman Korn, never fully grasped the conspiracy undertaken by the NBA.

It was brought out that the league had been engaged in pretty conclusive discussions with CBS long before our deal expired. And, no question about it, the NBA felt it could exert much more control over the people then running CBS Sports, headed by Bill MacPhail, than it ever could over those in charge at ABC Sports.

During one meeting with the NBA owners, Arledge had felt the brunt of Mieuli's assault. "Just who the hell do you think you are, anyway?" he yelled at Roone. "What makes you an expert? You think you know what games to put on the air and when? We know a hell of a lot more about our sport than you do, and we know what should and should not be done!"

Except for a pasting from Walter Byers in Phoenix one year and the time prior to the Los Angeles Olympics when Peter Ueberroth tangled with Roone and ended up cussing at him, it was as severe a chastising as I've ever seen Arledge receive.

We had also had a flare-up with the owners when we discussed the ratings for the 1971–72 season. It was during that season that the Lakers ran off thirty-three straight victories before losing to the Bucks in Milwaukee. We televised that game nationally on a Sunday afternoon and had a tremendous audience as Kareem Abdul-Jabbar scored thirty-nine points and had twenty rebounds to lead the Bucks over the Lakers of Wilt Chamberlain and Jerry West, 120–104. When we compiled our ratings figure to present to the league to show pro basketball's acceptance level with the public, we omitted that telecast because it would have distorted the true picture; it was one of those things you put an asterisk on because it would have created an inaccurate reflection of the overall numbers. Mieuli was furious with us for that, accusing ABC of a putdown plot.

Once the lawsuit was behind us and the NBA and CBS began their relationship, there were flirtations involving the league and ABC. And, wouldn't you know it, the principal architects in the attempt at a reconciliation were Jack Kent Cooke and Alan Rothenberg!

One day Cooke called me and spoke as if I were his best friend in the whole world: "My dear Jim, what a horrible mistake we made. We should never have left ABC Sports. It was just a horrible error. I believe the NBA and ABC Sports should be remarried. And I sincerely hope we can reestablish our relationship. Why don't you and I see what we can do about this?"

We did try: twice with a certain degree of conviction, and once without corporate support.

When the first contract with CBS was winding down, Cooke sent a man back to ABC for a meeting with Arledge. Roone had asked me to sit in on it, and when I left my office to go next door to his, lo and behold, there sat Alan Rothenberg, waiting outside the door. I thought, what odd turns this world takes! One of the architects of the defection scheme—although he was working for Cooke and doing what he was told—was now waiting to see if he could resurrect a deal out of the ashes he and his pals had created. It didn't happen, and one of the reasons it didn't was because of our lingering bitterness and resentment. Too, the NBA replacement programming, ABC's "Superstars" and the Sunday "Wide World of Sports" series, were doing very well.

When the league came back to us to try a second time, the issues were money and weekday evening television. ABC by then was going great guns in prime time, but the league wanted to telecast its finals in those time periods. It also wanted more rights money than ABC was willing to pay.

Through it all, we had at least established relationships with the commissioners who came after Kennedy. We had dialogue with Commissioner Larry O'Brien and his deputy, David Stern, and later with Stern when he took over from O'Brien. Indeed, with Stern we came close to getting back the television rights to NBA games, and I think we would have if Roone Arledge had been less concerned about butting heads with the new ownership and Capital Cities had not been quite so queasy. Here's the story:

When the latest NBA-CBS contract expired at the end of the 1985–86 season, the league had an obligation to negotiate first with CBS, which it did but without reaching an agreement. (CBS by then had two suitors, and of course divided loyalties, in that it was doing business with both the NBA and the NCAA.) That's when Stern and I began to talk seriously about the NBA coming back to ABC. We had no basketball then, and so could have given the NBA great continuity in terms of both scheduling and promotion. By December 1985, we were heavily involved in a series of discussions with the NBA, but because nine months earlier Cap Cities had closed the $3.5-billion deal to take control of ABC, the negotiating was more complicated than usual.

After talking with Stern, I'd take the issues to Fred Pierce and Mark Cohen, executive vice president of the ABC Broadcast Group. All they kept telling me was that Cap Cities was not at all receptive to doing a deal for pro basketball. Our new owners were concerned in principle about the ever-escalating television-rights monies for sports, and a National Basketball Association deal would have meant a 100 percent increase in the budget for the NBA right off the bat. There was also concern expressed about the upcoming National Football League negotiations. If we gave such an increase to the NBA, it was wondered, what would the NFL expect?

Cap Cities was also fearful that since the increased dollars would go to the players, this would lead—staggering thought!— to a proliferation of drug use in the NBA. The new bosses had circulated a letter saying it was instituting a double-tough drug policy at ABC, and indicated that the use of dogs to sniff out drugs among employees was not out of the question. In the summer of 1987, a drug-testing program was announced for all new Capital Cities employees. Drugs are a problem for the whole of society, not just the sports world, and I'm as sensitive as anyone to the problem, but it shouldn't be the responsibility of a television network to police drug use among athletes. Besides, the NBA had by then been much more up front and aggressive in addressing its players' drug problems than any other major sports organization.

Despite this somewhat paranoid posture about the evils of drug use, I believed the deal could still be made, even though the NBA had an obligation to return to CBS should ABC not meet the terms and conditions last offered to and rejected by CBS. Stern had set a deadline for concluding a television deal with some- one, and so I pressed Pierce and Cohen for us to make him an offer. Similarly, I urged Arledge to become more involved in the negotiating process, feeling, as I still do, that if he had shown a really strong interest and a belief in the NBA, he could have swayed the Capital Cities brass over to our way of thinking. But Roone knew we were waging an uphill battle, and he obviously decided that this was not the issue on which to push the new owners.

The commissioner kept pressing me for a reply, one way or another, and I kept stalling for more time, until finally Stern extended the announced deadline by twenty-four hours. I was frantically trying to reach Arledge to get him to make a last-minute pitch to the Cap Cities people, and finally did so from a bar at the Hilton Hotel, just across the street from ABC's corporate offices. Although he agreed with me on the value of the NBA package, he was lukewarm, and I knew when we hung up that he would not press the case. The following day, I called David Stern and told him, much to my chagrin, that we could not make a proposal. The new deadline arrived and the NBA and CBS were remarried. CBS laid out $173 million for the deal, a jump of almost 100 percent, but it was a very good deal for them even at that figure. CBS is still making good money with professional basketball, at a time when ABC Sports is urgently looking for profitable programming.

It would have made for an interesting two-network battle had ABC become a serious player in that poker game. The league wanted to return to ABC, if for no other reason than that at CBS the NBA has to contend with college basketball climaxing just at the time the pro division races are being decided. Our deal would have put the NBA on national television every Sunday afternoon at 3:30 P.M. Eastern Time, and we could have built a solid foundation up through the playoffs, delivering not only large audiences but consistent promotion and continuity of programming. This is the point I kept emphasizing to the NBA people: that their games would be special to us, and not in conflict with other basketball programming. The package discussed was for 160 games at 40 games a year for four years. We projected a profit of more than $20 million over the life of the contract, but Cap Cities apparently did not think that was a healthy enough return on such an investment. I dare say ABC Sports will not realize similar profits from the programming it airs versus NBA basketball. CBS Sports, I am assured, will realize considerably more than a $20 million profit by the time the current contract expires.

Maybe back at Cap Cities/ABC headquarters there lingered a bit of the old-world thinking about basketball being largely a black man's game, and, because of that, maybe it was perceived as not the greatest deal in the world for either viewers or advertisers. I know some of that thinking existed when ABC got out of the pro basketball picture in 1973. No one wants to admit it, nor publicly talk about it, but discussions have gone on for years at the networks about how many blacks the sports audience will tolerate. For instance: How many blacks could you tolerate on a pro football team? Could you tolerate a higher percentage in basketball because there are only five guys on the court for each team? Do you risk losing the allegiance of a largely white audience? Sure, it's racism and, sure, there is still plenty of it left in all aspects of American society.

In contrast, I was involved as a fan in a wonderful human experience during the early seventies. I've been a New York Knicks' follower for as long as I can remember, and it's a bit painful that I haven't had much to cheer about for so many years. But the team that had Walt Frazier and Dick Barnett, then later Earl Monroe, in the back court, and Bill (now Senator) Bradley and Dave DeBusschere and the captain, Willis Reed, up front was just that—a team—and they were five guys who went out and got the job done without having any overpowering people. I don't think anyone on the court or in the stands counted heads to see who was black and who was white. And that happened a lot of years ago and we've grown as a society since then. I perceive a very positive change in recent times in viewer reaction to the proliferation of blacks in basketball.

I don't think advertisers are concerned what color the players are. The fans and the advertisers are just like the players: They think mainly about winning—and, in the case of the advertisers, about ratings!

I'd like to end this chapter with a couple of happier recollections of our NBA days.

ABC Sports used an assortment of announcers in the years from 1964 through 1973, with Keith Jackson and Chris Schenkel doing the play-by-play. After Bob Cousy and Jack Twyman and others, including Lenny Wilkens and Jerry West, we settled on Bill Russell as the expert analyst. Russell became one of our major hits. He was refreshingly candid, his humor had a bite to it, his laugh was infectious, he had a good personal image, he knew the game inside out, and most important of all, he knew it was only a game. Bill meshed very well with Jackson: In fact, the Jackson-Russell team may well have been the best combination ever to work NBA basketball telecasts.

Here is Keith Jackson on Bill Russell:

"He just may be one of the more learned men of our country. Not many people know this, but when Bill quit playing basketball he bought himself a motorcycle and put a bedroll on the back of this huge machine, and he rode it all over this land. He went to all the places he had heard and read about—to Monument Valley and the Pecos River and the Black Hills and God-knows-where-all, just everywhere he'd always wanted to visit. And he camped out and milled about and met people from every-where, people from every walk of life. Then he went on a college lecture tour and for about three years that's all he did, night after night, going around and rapping with young people. He talked with college kids, privileged ones and deprived ones. He talked with the happy ones and the angry ones, sensing the fabric and feeling of the people. He still has some of his anger and insecurities, but, then, so do we all. I tremendously enjoyed the time I had with him, doing the basketball broadcasts. He's a man with a personality, and we got along well because I appreciate him as a man as well as for his considerable basketball skills.

"I remember one broadcast in particular—the Milwaukee Bucks were playing the Los Angeles Lakers, and Kareem Abdul-Jabbar was just a kid playing for the Bucks and they were doing a pretty good number on the Lakers. Inside, they were working on Wilt Chamberlain and doing a dandy job of it, and I made the comment that I didn't know if I'd want to get Wilt Chamberlain mad at me. And instantly Russell asked, 'And why not?' Well, I broke up right there. And that told me why Russell had played so well all those years when his Celtics went up against Wilt. He'd get Wilt mad, and then Russell would be in control of the situation.''

Finally, one of my favorite stories from an old NBA coverage:

After one particular nationwide telecast, Chet Forte, the former all-American who was involved with our coverage from the very start as a producer and director, shared his limousine on the way to the airport with the then color commentator, Jack Twyman, the former NBA all-star. No sooner had they gotten comfortable in the car than Twyman began a postmortem on the game—and here I'll make up some names because I really don't recall which teams were involved:

"You see, Boggs matched up well against Nelson. Powell has that bulk and so he was able to keep Hartinger from getting the ball down low. They double-teamed Frederick and forced him to work extra hard, and as a result he was pooped out down the stretch and they were able to take advantage of his fatigue. And, of course, Childs has always played well against Wolfe, dating all the way back to when they played against each other in college. And that Simon—check the records and you'll find out he always plays a big game against these guys. For as long as I can remember, they've somehow matched up well against those guys, and even though they have a lousy record, they either beat 'em or give 'em one hell of a game.''

Forte was livid.

"You *asshole!*'' He screamed at Twyman. "Didn't it ever occur to you that this is exactly what ABC Sports is paying you for, to tell this sort of thing to the viewer? Why in God's name didn't you tell it to the audience? I'll be goddamned if it does me or the audience any good to hear this tremendous analysis on the way to the airport!''

Jack didn't confine all his analysis to a limousine, however, for he was a valuable performer on ABC's NBA telecasts.

13

DECISIONS I STILL CAN'T BELIEVE

*Why ABC Doesn't Televise
the Two Top Tennis Championships,
and Other Mishaps*

In the sixteenth century, before anyone heard of Howard Cosell or Roone Arledge—or ABC Sports, for that matter—Margaret of Austria wrote in a letter, "I am prepared and at rest with my conscience; I have no regrets."

My conscience and I are doing very well, thank you, but I do have some regrets.

There are four major events that ABC let slip through its corporate fingers, and I used to cringe when I saw them being televised on other networks. They are the Daytona 500 stock-car race, the Orange Bowl football game, the U.S. Open Tennis Championships, and the All England Tennis Championships at Wimbledon. I accept the proposition that one network can't have all the goodies, but we had these four and we lost them. Sometimes it was our fault; sometimes it wasn't.

I suppose, by the standards set by the good old boys who drive those awful-sounding cars with sponsors' names plastered all over them, I was right out of the eastern establishment. But this Ivy Leaguer was a strong supporter of stock-car racing, despite the argument most frequently put forth that it was only a regional sport. If you want to look on a map at the places where the races are held, you could still argue that proposition, because there are none in the New York or Chicago areas, and so far as I know no one in Boston is clamoring for something they might call the Paul Revere 500.

Yet the sport is so immense in places like Daytona Beach and Darlington, Atlanta and Charlotte, Richmond and Talladega, that it has forced the advertising world to sit up and pay attention, even though it may be muffling a few snickers about the way Richard Petty talks. But I can say this about stock-car-racing people: They never pretended to be anything they weren't. Sure, they were a little defensive, because they knew "those slickers from New York" made snide remarks about them. When we started televising stock-car racing in the early sixties, they knew they were perceived as hard-drinking hell-raisers who probably learned to drive with such reckless abandon while running moonshine over the South's back roads, and who wouldn't get behind the wheel of one of those machines if they had a lick of sense.

Perhaps the attitude of a gofer we hired to work on one of our stock-car telecasts epitomizes the attitude of both fans and participants alike. He was a gangling and wonderfully laid-back country lad, with an air about him that suggested he could handle any crisis, including World War III. When he was told at the end of a long Saturday under a broiling sun that he'd better get a good night's sleep, since Sunday's race day schedule was certain to be a grueling one, this is what he drawled:

"Well, I'll tell ya what I'm gonna do. I'm gonna stop off and git me a pint of bourbon and a six-pack of cold ones, go home, kick off my boots, lean back and put a couple of David Houston albums on my stereo, and jes' sit there and enjoy the hell out of Saturday night. That way, I'll be in damn fine shape for to-morrow."

No ulcer would dare invade that boy's body!

There are races almost every weekend, all over the place, both stock-car and championship-car racing, but the two big ones are the Indianapolis 500 and the Daytona 500. Completing negotiations with the promoters of those races to let ABC do them live on network television is one of the legacies of which I'm most proud.

For a lot of years, I had a wonderful relationship with Bill

France, the boss at Daytona International Speedway and at the time the most powerful voice in the National Association for Stock Car Auto Racing (NASCAR), and with his son, Bill junior. We had gotten involved with the Daytona 500 race at a time when the other networks were still timid about the sport, and there was never any reason to think the relationship and our arrangement would ever be in jeopardy. We persuaded the France family to let us do Daytona live in 1976 by finally agreeing to black out five states—Florida, Georgia, Alabama, North and South Carolina—assuaging the Frances' concerns about the effect of a live telecast on their attendance. Both the race telecast and the crowd were overwhelming successes, which made what followed even more painful.

In more than a quarter century in television sports, I've never had a closer business relationship with any man than I enjoyed with Bill junior, which is why it hurt so much when he took the race away from ABC Sports. After televising Daytona for three years, at an annual rights fee of four hundred thousand dollars, our contract came up for renegotiation. We had offered four hundred fifty thousand dollars for the television rights for the 1979 race. Bill made it ever so plain that he wanted to remain with ABC, but he made it just as plain that he wanted more dollars (six hundred thousand–six hundred fifty thousand) if there was any way he could get them. In our last session, we left it like this: Shop around, see what offers you can get from either CBS or NBC, or both, then get back to us. The understanding was for him to merely test the waters before checking back with me.

A few evenings after that meeting with France, the National Football League gave a farewell party for Bob Cochran, who was retiring as its broadcast coordinator. It was a nice gathering at Rockefeller Plaza, and as I wandered about saying hello and greeting old friends—and in some cases, old adversaries—it occurred to me that I didn't see any of the top people from CBS Sports. That was more than strange; it was eerie. Here was a party for a man who had worked hand-in-glove with CBS more than any other network, and none of the CBS brass was there to salute him. Then, as I walked back to my office, the puzzle began to come together. Of course! The CBS brass was in Daytona Beach, talking about the Daytona 500 rights! But I quickly dismissed any concern because of my solid relationship with Bill France, Jr., and our agreement that he would get back to me before anything was finalized.

CBS was in Daytona Beach, all right, where it was stealing the Daytona 500 right out from under our noses. Would you like to make a wild guess as to the architect of that deal? It was my old buddy, Barry Frank, who had left ABC Sports as a vice president a number of years earlier but was at that time in charge of CBS Sports. Whether there or at Trans World International, where he's served two separate terms, Frank has been instrumental in several deals that have caused ABC a lot of what could be called the agony of defeat; however in representing sports organizers, Barney also brought us a lot of positive programming over the years.

The minute I got wind of what was going on, I hopped the next flight to Florida in an eleventh-hour effort to turn things around. It was too late. Bill France the elder met me at the airport, we went to a restaurant for dinner, and there I was told that the deal was already closed. There was no way out of it. The Frances had given their word. I argued that they had given their word to me, too, and a whole lot earlier, promising that they would not finalize a deal until after getting back to me.

"Jim, they just came down here and made us this huge offer, and told us they had to have our answer immediately or the offer would be withdrawn," was Bill junior's explanation. "We just knew ABC would never go for that kind of a number, with the figures we'd previously been talking about. We simply felt we *had* to take the CBS deal."

I countered, "Bill, you know that one telephone call was all I asked. Just one phone call. You may have been right. Maybe we wouldn't have gone for that big a number. But you owed me the call. That was the deal we had. You had given me your word."

There was nothing else to say. The Frances had signed a $5 million five-year deal with CBS starting in 1979. The rest of the dinner was very quiet. It was a very sad moment in my career.

When ABC coughed up the television rights to the Orange Bowl, there was no betrayal. Our crystal ball was just a little cloudy.

ABC Sports had done the Orange Bowl for three years, 1962–64, had been faced with three lousy games and some pretty poor ratings, as the contract came up for renewal. Tom Moore, then president of the ABC Television Network, wanted to continue the deal, but for the only time in the history of ABC Sports, the ABC board of directors failed to approve a deal. So the Orange Bowl people took their proposal to Tom Gallery, who was head of NBC Sports at that time, and the meeting there followed the same script as ours, preventing the consummation of a deal.

Later, the Orange Bowl executive director, Earnie Seiler, who ran the event with such an iron hand for so long, was at a cocktail party with Gallery and asked "Would your opinion of our game change if we agree to play at night?" Gallery, who had never been one to miss a beat, had another meeting with Seiler and closed a deal.

So the Orange Bowl went to NBC in 1965, where it became a nighttime extravaganza and a massive hit. In the years that followed, Roone Arledge would claim that it was his idea to put the Orange Bowl in prime time, but I guess at the time he neglected to mention that to the Orange Bowl representatives or the ABC board.

Daytona was difficult to swallow, the Orange Bowl just happened, but ABC can't blame anyone else for blowing its right to televise Wimbledon and the U.S. Open Tennis Championships. We actually had captured lightning in a jar with these events and simply didn't realize it. Indeed, if I spend another twenty-five years in television, I will still believe that the loss of those two tennis classics stemmed from the most stupid corporate thinking in the history of sports broadcasting.

Admittedly, at the time the decisions were made, tennis was going through its most difficult period, with the dispute over professional versus amateur tennis plus the growing power struggle over control of the sport. The U.S. Open back then wasn't open at all, but was called the USLTA (U.S. Lawn Tennis Association) National Tennis Championships, and in televising it in 1967 we incurred a loss of forty thousand dollars. The ABC corporate brass determined that was too much of a financial beating, and we backed off this event, which was held annually at Forest Hills in New York City. Contrast our loss with CBS' current five-year U.S. Open contract—an average payment of over $15 million per year, including cable rights. (Ironically, I produced ABC's last telecast of this event.)

Thankfully, we didn't back off another New York City event many years later. In 1981 I was the primary advocate of ABC's telecast of the New York City Marathon, a magnificent human experience involving more than twenty-two thousand participants and 2 million spectators in 1987.

We lost Wimbledon for five thousand dollars less than the U.S. Open loss. The rights and the basic coverage provided by the British Broadcasting Corporation would have cost us thirty-five thousand dollars in 1969. Too steep, we said, no doubt overinfluenced by the fact that some of the better players were at the time boycotting the event and the field didn't look too scintillating. Thirty-five thousand dollars for Wimbledon! NBC today averages approximately thirteen million a year, including cable rights.

Oddly, we built a reputation as long-range thinkers who made long-range decisions, ofttimes on events hardly anyone had heard of before. But with those two tennis tournaments, the biggest events of their kind in the world, we made decisions based solely on what was happening at the moment instead of intelligently trying to look a little way into the future.

We could have taken the hundred thousand dollars we paid Billie Jean King *not* to work, invested it in the rights to Wimbledon and the U.S. Open, and had twenty-five thousand dollars left over. And Billie Jean wouldn't have been upset with us!

The FCC would not have been upset either if CBS had not billed a tennis competition as "the Heavyweight Championship of Tennis" and led viewers to believe that the winners would rake in all the money. In fact, all of the participants were guaranteed a sum of money irrespective of how they finished in the competitions.

In the first match, on February 2, 1975, Jimmy Connors defeated Rod Laver. Connors won the second match, on April 26,

1975, over John Newcombe, then on the last day of February in 1976 he beat Manuel Orantes. Finally, Conners whipped Ilie Nastase on March 5, 1977. The first three matches were staged at Caesar's Palace in Las Vegas, with the last one held at the Cerromar Beach Hotel in Puerto Rico. The advertising and the promotion for the first three matches described the events as "winner-take-all."

Now take a guess as to the identity of the man who represented the promoter, Bill Riordan, in selling the first event to CBS? The answer is our old chum Barry Frank. He had left ABC Sports in 1970 to become vice president of Trans World International, but by the time the final match was to appear on CBS, Frank had joined CBS Sports.

During the final telecast, announcer Pat Summerall described the duel between Connors and Nastase as winner-take-all, when in truth Connors had been guaranteed $500,000 and Nastase $160,000. Summerall's comment was, "This is two hundred fifty thousand dollars, winner-take-all." Prior to airtime, Frank notified both the CBS press and sales departments that the match was not winner-take-all, and, from the Houston area, he called the CBS producer to instruct him to advise the CBS announcers not to refer to it that way.

The FCC doesn't like it when what you see and hear isn't really what you get. Congress held a hearing and wondered why CBS couldn't have called the matches "funsies." One congressman called the matches "almost a fraud." CBS later apologized on the air and admitted that viewers were deceived.

Clearly, CBS should not have aired the misinformation and, having done so, should immediately have corrected the error. However, I can empathize with CBS Sports having been involved with the U.S. Boxing Championships, which will be dealt with later. Frank would say that the incident led to his being dismissed by CBS but, of course, not before he engineered the Daytona 500 deal.

Losing Daytona, passing on Wimbledon and the U.S. Open, and seeing the Orange Bowl blossom into such a major happening made getting the Kentucky Derby away from CBS all the sweeter.

14

STEALING THE ROSES

*How the Kentucky Derby
Switched to ABC After
27 Years on CBS*

There is nothing in the world quite like Derby Day at Churchill Downs in Louisville, Kentucky. The enormous infield crowd, the celebrities, the attractive spectators in their luxury boxes, the owners, the trainers, the brave jockeys and the beautiful yet fragile horses make "The Run for the Roses" a unique sports spectacular.

The national anthem precedes the playing and singing of "My Old Kentucky Home" as the horses and their riders parade to the post, and you have to be an emotional neuter not to experience a great torrent of feeling at that special moment. Even people who care not a whit about horse racing on any other day of the year become totally involved and caught up in the excitement of Derby Day. One person who does care a whit about horse racing is my wife Lynn, who has always considered the Derby her favorite sports event.

Our acquisition of television rights to the Kentucky Derby was a tremendous coup for ABC Sports. There's no event that had been on one network before switching to another as long as the Derby had been on CBS—twenty-seven years—dating from 1948. Their laxity and our groundwork enabled us to snatch it away from them.

Chris Schenkel was the man who opened the door for us to

Churchill Downs. Chris was familiar with the people there, and had gotten Roone Arledge introduced to Wathen Knebelkamp, for many years the Derby's kingpin, on one of their visits there simply for the enjoyment of the occasion. That's how the flirtation between ABC Sports and the Derby had begun, but as I look back on the things that led to our acquisition of the television rights, two other factors also stick out. The first was Lynn Stone taking over as president of Churchill Downs and being willing and having the courage to break with tradition. Stone looked at ABC as an organization that would do things differently, and in the process breathe new life into the presentation of the Derby on television. I'm surely not suggesting that CBS treated the Derby as just another horse race, but as the years had passed, there had been less and less effort to turn it into a happening. The second factor was CBS's carelessness and complacency.

CBS took its long relationship with the Kentucky Derby people for granted. You might say that they forgot to send flowers once in a while to the folks who present the roses. Additionally, there had been some turmoil in their front office, a changing of the guard with Bill MacPhail leaving and Bob Wussler taking over, and they just neglected to do their homework. Lynn Stone left Churchill Downs in 1984. Tom Meeker, an aggressive and self-assured lawyer, took over as president and has overseen many changes at the track, including construction of the very impressive Kentucky Derby Museum, which opened in 1985.

When the CBS contract was up, their network officials assumed that the deal would be extended, as it had always been in the past, but we came in with a heavy financial package that was way out in front of what CBS had been paying, offering $3,750,000 for a five-year contract. Those figures may not look too impressive now, but they were staggering back in the mid-seventies. We also agreed to air the Wood Memorial from New York, and another three-year-old race from Florida, to help build the excitement for Derby Day in Louisville on the first Saturday in May.

Once that day arrived, in 1975, ABC made the Kentucky Derby a happening rather than a horse race. Nothing I've worked on in my time in broadcasting has given me as much satisfaction as bringing the Derby to the network that gave me my start.

And wouldn't you know it, we stumbled a bit in our first Derby telecast!

We hired announcer Chic Anderson to call the Derby. Regarded as one of the finest thoroughbred-racing announcers in the world, Chic had been calling races since 1959 and had called the Derby for CBS for six years. As the field of fifteen headed into the stretch, Foolish Pleasure, the eventual winner, seized the lead. But Anderson told the national television audience, and a crowd of more than a hundred thousand, "Here comes Prince Thou Art taking the lead!" Prince Thou Art never was in the lead and eventually finished sixth. Chic caught his mistake just before the end of the race.

When Chic Anderson died in March 1979, the *Louisville Courier-Journal* included these words about the 1975 Derby in his obituary:

"But even though the mistake stirred up a storm of commentary, nearly all of it was sympathetic toward Anderson and complimentary to his exciting descriptive abilities and long record for professionalism and accuracy. Anderson's composure during the brouhaha also served him well. He gave a calm, accurate call of the first six finishers as soon as he realized his mistake. Two weeks later, at Pimlico, he gave a flawless call of the Preakness Stakes that included a blow-by-blow description of an exciting stretch duel between Foolish Pleasure and Master Derby."

In the days after the Derby telecast, CBS issued news releases criticizing ABC for what it called our failure to acknowledge the mistake on the air. We believed there was no need to call further attention to it. After all, Chic had corrected his own mistake, and to say anything further would have served only to embarrass him. Later he did flawless work for ABC on other Derby telecasts.

Anderson's faux pas brought to mind a tale told years ago about two of the legends of early broadcasting, Bill Stern and Clem McCarthy. It seems McCarthy, too, flubbed the call in an important race, and Stern, best known for his football broadcasts, rode him unmercifully about the mistake. The colorful McCarthy fired back, "Well, Bill, you just can't lateral a horse," referencing Stern's custom of saying there had been a lateral when he had the wrong man carrying the football.

ABC's initial Kentucky Derby telecast produced some furious infighting involving the wives of our lead announcers. We had assigned both Jim McKay and Howard Cosell to the telecast, and while Jim was to be the host of the program, anyone with an ounce of sense knew that Cosell would try to see to it that he was the focal point of any show with which he was involved. He just wouldn't have it any other way.

Preparations had hardly begun when Chuck Howard, who was producing the telecast, began to feel pressure. Some of it came from Cosell, very little came from McKay, and a lot came from their wives, Margaret McKay and Emmy Cosell. Anyone who has been privy to the inner workings at ABC can tell you that Margaret McKay has always stood tall for Jim. Emmy Cosell never got into Margaret's league, but as we did our own Derby preparation, she made it clear she didn't want to see Howard relegated to any kind of supporting-player role in the telecast.

"Just how much time is Howard going to have on the air?" she asked Chuck Howard. And: "Obviously, Jim is going to be on camera for the opening of the show. I assume Howard will be on camera just as much?"

And this from Margaret McKay: "Now, Chuck, Jim's not going to be embarrassed, is he? Just how is this thing going to work? After all, Jim *is* the host of the show!"

Chuck Howard was in a quandary for days. He told me before the telecast, "Jim, I can't both produce and referee." And he had to keep everything inside him since Chet Forte, who was directing the show, and Cosell were linked at the navel. Had anything erupted and become a public issue, Forte most assuredly would have sided with Cosell, and then there'd have been more hell to pay. Whatever resentment Jim might have felt, he kept it pretty much under control. He and Cosell were never chummy, but I think they have always had respect for each other as professionals. They never squabbled openly, even though I know Cosell always felt McKay was rather bland, while McKay had considerable difficulty tolerating Howard's overpowering ego.

During that first Derby experience, McKay got into a rehearsal and was working on his "tease"—the beginning of the show in which the audience is told what's in store and induced to stay tuned—when Cosell emitted a mild protest that everyone but McKay thought was funny: "Tell me, will we have time for anything else on this telecast after McKay gets through with his tease?" McKay was more subtle, and would get in his digs with a gesture or by shaking his head.

That first telecast, despite the bobble on the stretch call, was very successful, both aesthetically and economically, and we knew we had made a sound deal. But once it was over and Chuck Howard got back to New York, he immediately told Roone what he had told me—that he could referee the battles between the wives, or he could produce, but that he couldn't do both. To Roone's credit, he spoke with both Howard and Jim and told them they'd have to put an end to the backbiting. In subsequent years, while there may have been concerns on the part of the women and their husbands, they were kept under wraps.

Cosell loved the Kentucky Derby telecasts. It was a new venue, a new crowd to work, and the atmosphere at Churchill Downs was forever festive. ABC Sports and the sales force at ABC went all out to insure that the sponsors enjoyed themselves, and no matter how much he liked to complain about the demands on his time and the lack of privacy, Cosell reveled in the attention the Derby gave him.

Eddie Arcaro was a big help early on as an expert commentator. He had won five Kentucky Derbies, and he knew everyone and so could give us great access to jockeys and trainers and owners. Later, when wanting more candid commentary, we hired Bill Hartack. Jack Whitaker always had a prominent role in our Derby telecasts after he moved over from CBS in 1982, and rightly so in that he's a consummate pro who could conduct insightful interviews with owners, trainers, and jockeys. Jack is also highly respected for his sports essays and he has contributed some poignant ones on horse racing.

I'll always have a special fondness for the Derby and appreciation for my relationship with Lynn Stone. Lynn was in my New York office one time when Cosell happened by. Howard immediately launched into one of his routines, and soon had us both in stitches. Before he left, he invited Lynn to accompany him to his apartment on the East Side to have cocktails with him and Emmy. Lynn agreed, and they met later in the lobby of ABC headquarters and adjourned to Cosell's apartment. When they arrived at the lobby of Cosell's apartment building, the elevator operator looked at Cosell: "Excuse me, sir. What floor?"

Howard stared at the elevator operator with disdain and reluctantly stated his floor number. When they got off on his floor, and the elevator door had closed behind them, Howard said to Stone, "New man."

I guess the thing I miss most about the Derby is the special get-togethers the track hosts for a limited number of invited guests. It has become a part of the rich Kentucky Derby tradition, this coming together after the telecast, after the award presentation, and after most of the people have started the long trek home.

The governor of Kentucky toasts—with a mint julep, naturally—the winning owner. Normally, the winning trainer and victorious jockey are also present. There, one could feel the history, the sense of tradition, and the charm and the class of the Old South. We had just witnessed the most important sports event in the world on that day, and I always reflected on how fortunate I was to spend Derby Day at Churchill Downs.

The Preakness Stakes came to ABC in 1977, and although we worked very hard to get this second jewel of the Triple Crown, we again were helped by CBS's complacency. After we'd closed our deal, Bob Wussler indicated strongly in the media that CBS didn't place tremendous emphasis on the event, a statement which appeared to be in the sour grapes genre and failed to endear him to the Preakness people. We had pursued the Preakness via Lee Meyers, agent for the Maryland Jockey Club, a wonderful old vaudevillian who had worked with Billy Rose and Jackie

Gleason, although Nathan Cohen, a low-key, astute executive who had been vice president of the Maryland Jockey Club, was the individual who made the decision in our favor. We signed the deal in the fall of 1975, so that when CBS televised the 1976 race, it was a lame-duck year for them. The Preakness usually features the Derby winner. In 1985, however, Robert Brennan of Garden State Park stole the Derby winner away for the Jersey Derby. Later, Brennan became the catalyst in bringing together the three Triple Crown tracks to form the $5 million Triple Crown Challenge.

The Belmont Stakes, the third leg of the Triple Crown, came to ABC in 1986 almost by default. Neither CBS nor NBC was much interested in doing the race since ABC had both the Derby and the Preakness. In fact, ABC got the Belmont for a measly $250,000, after CBS had been paying $3 million dollars to televise it. The New York Racing Association and its president Gerry McKeon are a bit more pleased with their Belmont deal these days, but the figures still don't approach the numbers CBS paid.

Thus, for the first time in over a decade, one network televised all of the Triple Crown events.

15

EXCELLENCE AND EGO

Major League Baseball,
Al Michaels and
Captain Courageous

People on the inside at ABC, and those peering critically through the windows from the outside, will debate for years the wisdom of the network getting involved with major-league baseball television broadcasts, starting with the 1976 season.

ABC had last televised baseball in 1965, while the NBC network had televised major-league baseball seemingly since the beginning of recorded history—having first televised the World Series in 1947. The NBC executives got a little cocky and a bit careless, just as CBS had done with the Kentucky Derby rights. NBC misread the importance the then commissioner, Bowie Kuhn, and the owners placed on having baseball telecast in prime time. The network wanted either to drop entirely, or substantially reduce, its prime-time involvement, and once word of that reached Kuhn, he made a beeline for ABC and asked if we had any interest. We did, although there were some differences of opinion within our camp.

One argument was that live sports events in the summer would be better than reruns, and that, besides, making a deal for regular season games would give us the opportunity to acquire rights to the World Series, the American and National League Championship Series, and the All-Star Game. The counter contention was that the network had a large movie inventory and would do much better from a financial standpoint rerunning movies than by involving itself in the expense of live sports programming that had an uncertain ratings potential.

In regard to the latter, when you're looking at a 162-game schedule stretching from early April to October, no single game has enough meaning for it to draw a large prime-time audience. Additionally, viewers all around the nation have available to them huge amounts of local baseball coverage. Pile onto that already bulging heap the vast hordes who watch games on the so-called superstations out of Atlanta, New York, and Chicago, and you have further seriously diluted your potential market. The question in the end, then, was, Was it worth living with less-than-gangbuster ratings during the regular season to be a part of All-Star, playoff, and World Series coverage? In the end, ABC answered yes.

The critical meeting took place in the office of then ABC Television president Fred Pierce, who had summoned Marty Starger, then president of ABC Entertainment, to confer with us. Pierce laid out the pros and cons, then asked Starger's opinion.

"You say we'll have the World Series every other year?" Starger asked.

"That's right," said Pierce, "and we'll alternate with NBC on the playoffs and the All-Star game."

"Then there is no choice, Fred," Starger blurted. "You have to go for it."

I think to this day Fred Pierce remains a bit surprised at how quickly and positively Marty favored the baseball package. It was no mere assent, but a ringing endorsement, and I've often since wondered what Pierce's decision would have been had Starger been even a little bit tepid. As it turned out, a deal was struck for $92 million to be divided between ABC and NBC from 1976 to 1979. The next four-year deal was for approximately $185 million, and the contract that runs from 1984 to 1989 is costing the two networks more than half a billion dollars each. And, of course, that's for rights only! That's before you roll out even one camera and haul it to the ballpark. The bottom-line losses at ABC have been *very* substantial, about which we'll have something to say at the end of the book.

Beyond the ratings and profit and loss factors, baseball was a bothersome project for ABC from the very start. In 1976, our first season, the network's attention was focused on televising the Summer Olympic Games in Montreal. There's pressure enough in doing any Olympic telecast, but the 1976 Games, being on North American soil, would have great impact because of the emphasis on live programming. There was neither the time nor the manpower to focus as heavily as we needed to on baseball.

Chuck Howard, for many years vice president of program production and the man in charge of setting up ABC's baseball coverage: "Baseball got stuck in the corner. It was almost incidental because of the weight of our Olympic Games responsibilities. In every aspect—what announcers to hire, the production of the games, the engineering side, the aesthetics of the shows—everybody's thoughts were subjugated until the Olympics were behind us. It was only when we went into the playoffs that our thoughts and energies got fully into baseball. It's unfortunate, and perhaps it was to a great degree unavoidable, but that's the way it was."

ABC's first, and most forgettable, baseball broadcast team consisted of the late Bob Prince, Warner Wolf, and Bob Uecker. Al Michaels, who was doing local play-by-play for the San Francisco Giants, was announcing our secondary games that first season.

Prince was a star in Pittsburgh; Wolf was a major hit in Washington, D.C. Both were busts on the network. As the long-time voice of the Pittsburgh Pirates, Prince was "kinfolk" to Pirate fans, who had come up with the saga of the "terrible towels." When it became apparent a batted ball would clear the fence, Prince's familiar thundering cry of "You can kiss it good-bye," stirred the heart of every fan afflicted with Pirate-mania. He was a thoroughly capable baseball announcer, and a fine man, who devoted a lot of time and energy to ABC Sports to try and make "Monday Night Baseball" a hit. But it takes time for an announcer's idiosyncrasies to catch on with the national television audience. One of television's hard truths is that the lower the rating, the less time you can afford to dilly-dally waiting for something or someone to catch fire.

Ratings brought Warner Wolf to network sports. Warner was a colorful character on the CBS-affiliated station in Washington, D.C., and research indicated that, as the hottest local star in the nation's capital, hotter even than Willard Scott, the daffy weatherman who went from Washington to NBC's "Today" show, he was a major reason the ABC station there was doing so poorly in the local numbers game. Tom Cookerly, who was then running the ABC affiliate in Washington, and who was well connected with the network, wanted Warner out of town in order to help his own news ratings, and asked us to make a network deal with Warner so he would no longer be on the air in Washington on the CBS station. Warner's agent quickly got involved in negotiations with both ABC and CBS.

We won Wolf, and brought him aboard with great fanfare. Roone Arledge hosted a press conference at the famed "21" and introduced Warner Wolf to the media as "the next Howard Cosell." It was too big a buildup, one that could never be equaled by performance. Warner was just not compatible with network television, but to his credit he stuck it out in local television in New York, winning a fine following and eventually making more than three times his top salary at ABC Sports.

Bob Uecker had a lot less experience than Prince and a lot more than Warner. We hired him partly because he knew the game, but mainly because of his sense of humor. You know, prime time, "a happening," "more than a game." . . . Bob had a following because of his self-deprecating humor, and especially the way he talked about his own mediocrity as a player. He'd made a number of appearances with Johnny Carson on the "Tonight Show," but this was eons before he had his own sitcom on network television, and a long time before he figured his seat must be "in the front row." As we put the package together, you could make a case for the chemistry, albeit mostly an untried experiment in the lab. Prince, a character in his own right, doing the bulk of the play-by-play; Uecker, adding spice and humor; and Wolf, the hopefully budding star being introduced to a national audience.

Chuck Howard sensed trouble right from the start. The three men had gotten together for a few practice telecasts during spring training, and Chuck returned to New York and reported to Arledge that he saw problems. "They just don't mesh," he ventured. But with the efforts being concentrated on the Olympic Games, there was no time for fine tuning, and we stayed with the lineup.

Prince wanted to be a major contributor, was very loyal to ABC, and was "okay." Uecker is a funny man, but when you are asked to summon that humor all the time, over the long haul whether you're Bob Uecker or Dandy Don Meredith, it has a tendency to wear thin. Wolf just never fit in.

After the 1976 baseball season, Warner repeatedly tried to reach Arledge to determine his future with ABC Sports. Roone, of course, never responded to his calls, nor his correspondence. In frustration, Wolf decided to come to ABC's headquarters and confront Arledge face-to-face. When he got to Roone's office, the door was closed, and Roone's secretary, Jeannette Hektoen, said her boss was on the telephone. Warner said he'd wait. He waited and he waited, and then he waited some more. From time to time, Jeannette made Roone aware that Warner was still camped outside the door. Finally, near the end of the business day—perhaps because nature was calling so urgently—Roone stormed out of his office and did indeed confront Warner, barking at him, "You can't keep me a prisoner in my own office!"

For any member of a television production team to defy a direct order from a producer while on the air is a sin so heinous as to be almost unthinkable, but once Warner did just that.

He and former St. Louis Cardinals pitcher Bob Gibson had been assigned to do a game between the Philadelphia Phillies and the Atlanta Braves. During the production meeting preceding the telecast, producer Terry O'Neil announced that he had acquired some footage of the yacht *Courageous* winning the America's Cup, and since Ted Turner, the owner of the Braves, also was the skipper of the *Courageous*, he wanted to work in some of the sailing during the baseball telecast. O'Neil said that this probably would happen during the last third of the telecast, more than likely during a pitching change. He asked Warner to write a script for the piece, which was to run about fifty seconds.

O'Neil rose rapidly in the ranks at ABC Sports until finally he was assigned to produce "Monday Night Football." Terry is talented, but alienated people with his arrogance, and was relieved of those duties before the regular season telecasts began. Later he became executive producer of NFL football for CBS, before leaving CBS to become an independent producer. He'll always remember his confrontation with Warner Wolf:

"Warner told me straight out that he would not write the script. So I told him we'd write it for him. Then he said, 'You don't understand. What I'm telling you is that I will not say *anything* on the air about Ted Turner.' And he refused to give me a reason at that time. I saw no sense in having a major flare-up in the production meeting in front of a lot of people, so I just told him I planned to run the videotape on Turner, and when it ran, I'd expect him to have something to say in the way of a voice-over description. I left it at that.

"That evening, before he went up to the announce booth to do the game, he stopped by the production truck and told me the reason he wouldn't even utter the name of Ted Turner is that he thought Turner was anti-Semitic. I was flabbergasted. I repeated what I'd told him before—that we would run the tape and that we'd expect commentary from him. Sure enough, late in the game there was a pitching change, and I told Warner through his headset that the tape was coming up. It did, and all I got from the booth was silence. Not a word. Turner's victory played, with no one telling the viewer what the hell it was and what it was doing there on a baseball telecast."

There were lots of telephone calls about that. Warner had violated not only a direct order from a producer, but a reasonable one at that. He had let his personal bias get in the way of his professionalism, which was intolerable.

Uecker lasted well beyond Prince and Wolf, and showed remarkable class over the several years he remained with the network. He accepted whatever baseball assignments he was given, whether he got the "A" game, the main telecast of the night, or the "B," or less important, game. When he was shunted aside during the playoffs or World Series to make room for heavy hitters like Reggie Jackson or Tom Seaver or Johnny Bench, and eventually Jim Palmer, he took it without whimpering, and I'll always respect him for that.

The heaviest hitter ABC ushered in was Howard Cosell, whom we introduced for playoff coverage in that first season of 1976. The regular-season ratings dictated the need for change. With so many games compared to football, and so many fewer television sets in use in the summer, which meant lower ratings, we could not make "Monday Night Baseball" a happening like "Monday Night Football." But we could try to pump in more pizzazz, and who better to do the pumping than Cosell? This is where Roone Arledge stood not only firm, but tall.

To my knowledge, no one conducted a poll at the time, but had you asked for a show of hands on how many major-league owners wanted Cosell on baseball, I'm betting there would have been fifty-two hands cemented deeply into fifty-two pockets in the twenty-six owners' pants. Bowie Kuhn was dead set against it, as well. Perhaps comments Howard had made the year before we acquired the rights to the major-league baseball package had influenced their thinking. Cosell in 1975: "Baseball is an activity whose time has passed; it is a laborious game played by tedious people and it consumes a boringly long time to play. It is, at best, a medieval game." But this was our call, not baseball's, and Roone's decision was to place Cosell in the "Monday Night Baseball" booth alongside play-by-play man Keith Jackson. The seating of Cosell there remains a watermark in the announcer-approval issue that has been so hotly debated ever since people began doing sports broadcasting.

Arledge saw the issue as so critical that it would be a deal-breaker: Either ABC had the right to assign Howard Cosell to work major-league baseball or ABC would not be doing major-league baseball. So Cosell did baseball, and he worked well enough in the booth that he and Commissioner Kuhn became fast friends, with many of the owners becoming delighted to have him involved. Howard's attitude had obviously changed regarding baseball after he joined our telecasts. Witness his comments in 1976: "It's a game I have loved since childhood, since I learned to play stickball in the streets of my neighborhood. Some of my fondest memories have to do with the times I spent at Ebbets Field and in the Polo Grounds, marveling at the deeds of Jackie, Duke, Pee Wee, Campy, Oisk, Sal the Barber, and so many, many others. It's a game like no other in the world."

Years later, although Howard still professed to love the game, he began making noises about getting off the baseball beat, and wanting to spend his summer evenings with his beloved Emmy at their home on Long Island. It was Bowie Kuhn, as much as anyone else, who talked him into staying. Bowie was a big enough man to admit that he had been wrong about Cosell. He was also to my mind a very effective commissioner, who unfortunately was vastly underestimated by a limited number of club owners who forced him out.

In the early years, it was conceded that ABC did not have a top-flight baseball announcer. Good as Keith Jackson is, and as versatile a performer as he has been for so many years, baseball is not his strongest suit. There was also the factor of the lodgelike atmosphere of baseball: You're either a member of the lodge or you're not.

Keith Jackson: "One of the things baseball people complain about a great deal is the fact that there are people like myself, or Cosell, or any number of other people from other networks, who come into their business on an infrequent basis. You're intruding into their domicile, as it were. Baseball is a game of daily nuances and subtleties and the season is merely an accumulation of those little things. When you drop in and do ten 'Monday Night Baseball' telecasts, or drop in and do the playoffs or the World Series, well, you're naturally not going to be quite as informed as the man who's been there for a hundred and sixty-two games. It's the good-old-boy syndrome. You're not in the fraternity and you're gonna find resistance."

Within the walls at ABC we acknowledged that we needed a

baseball announcer who would achieve wider acceptance, both on the air and with the baseball people. We had a stable of internationally known announcers, yet were being constantly adversely compared with NBC in regard to our coverage and calling of the game within baseball, and the advertising community, and the media. Some of the criticism was fair; other aspects of it were strictly a matter of things being repeated so often they become accepted as gospel—one such being that Harry Coyle, of NBC, was the only director who really knew what he was doing when it came to televising baseball. Coyle's abilities were undoubted, but ABC could be very proud of the job Chuck Howard, Dennis Lewin, and Chet Forte did for many years with major-league baseball. However, such criticisms, and our sensitivity to them, were factors in our bringing Al Michaels to ABC Sports on a full-time basis.

It was easier for Al than most people to get the attention of a network because his late father, Jay Michaels, had long been a successful and dynamic figure within the television industry. However, although his father's name may have gotten Al in the door, it was his own work that got him hired once he was through it. He had paid some dues and gained some valuable experience broadcasting minor-league baseball in Hawaii, and spending half a dozen seasons doing play-by-play for the Cincinnati Reds and the Giants, before we hired him.

The agent representing Al at that time, Ed Hookstratten of Los Angeles, nearly bungled our hiring of Al on a full-time basis after the 1976 season. With Al's blessing, Ed was driving a very tough bargain, and it got to the point where Arledge wanted to pass on the deal. I argued with him that Michaels could turn into a very important announcer for ABC, and that we needed younger talent, and it was through my persuasion that Michaels was signed to his first multiyear contract. He worked the "B" games in the early years, then, during his contract that ran from 1980 to 1984, he took over the lead baseball play-by-play role from Keith Jackson.

From day one, Al was very professional on the air. He disliked the suggestion that he sounded much like veteran Dodger announcer Vin Scully, and scoffed when it was hinted that, since he had grown up in the Los Angeles area listening to Dodger games, he had deliberately copied Scully's style.

By 1980, Michaels was making $315,000 a year and had enjoyed a huge increase in recognition because of his historic broadcast of the U.S. Olympic hockey team's gold-medal victory in Lake Placid, where he delivered the memorable line, "Do you believe in miracles?" After this, he resented what he deemed his inferior baseball play-by-play role and, even when he got the top billing all to himself, it still wasn't enough. He had been making noises about leaving, and, although we weren't much concerned about NBC because his first love is baseball and Vin Scully and Joe Garagiola were entrenched there, we thought he might jump to CBS for a big offer to do college football and college basketball. So, thinking highly of his talent if not his attitude, we agreed to pay him $1 million a year beginning in 1985—a very far cry indeed from the $1,750 a game we had paid him back in 1976.

Make no mistake about what I think of Al Michaels' talents: He's the best all-around play-by-play man in the business. He arrives at each assignment thoroughly prepared, very confident, and with excellent perspective. He had called hockey just once in his life prior to Lake Placid, yet he came through in glorious fashion, and particularly in handling all those difficult foreign names without a flub. He had the identification down pat, he pronounced each name correctly, and his commentary was impeccable. When he did track and field in the 1984 Summer Olympic Games in Los Angeles, he was squarely on top of that challenging situation day after day.

Having said that, here's a prediction: Al Michaels, unless he changes, will never achieve the superstar status reserved for the giants of the business, the status he yearns for, the acceptance he craves, such as, for example, Jim McKay has earned over the years. To me, he simply lacks the presence of a McKay or a Dick Enberg or a Brent Musburger. Also, although Al has the opportunity to do it all, now that he's in the lead role of ABC's "Monday Night Football," I believe he needs to display more warmth on the air, be a bit more natural. In short, he needs to give the people at home a reason to empathize with him.

Despite his enormous success, Al Michaels is still very insecure; he's excruciatingly concerned about his image, and overly sensitive to what the print media writes about him. He knew all along that he had my strong support, and was assured repeatedly that he was the play-by-play voice of the future at ABC, but he always wanted the future to begin yesterday. He reminds me of a quote I once read: "It is not he who has little who is poor; rather, he who always wants more." Al is the type of person who can never be satisfied. Consider that, even after his achievements on baseball and his Olympic successes at Lake Placid, Sarajevo, and Los Angeles, after completing his first year as the lead performer on "Monday Night Football," he told an interviewer that he had been at ABC for eleven years and that things had not moved very swiftly for him during the first ten.

I was less than thrilled when I saw that quote.

Al takes precautions against bad reviews. It has become almost a ritual for him to say something flattering on air about some sportswriter, sports columnist, or television critic, which to me is out of line for any television announcer.

Chuck Howard, who probably worked with Michaels more than any other producer, says: "Al's a most talented man. Professionally, he is thoroughly capable and easy to work with. He's very quick to pick up on things. He prepares well, and once you tell him from a producer's standpoint how you want something to be done, that's it. He's very good on the headset, takes direction well. But he has this massive ego, and it's a major problem. I've never seen a guy, not even Howard Cosell, read the newspapers more extensively to find out what people are writing about him. It's of tremendous concern to him and he is incredibly sensitive about it. Now everyone who is successful in this business has a pretty decent-sized ego, and we all like people to say nice things about us, but most of us are confident enough of our abilities that we know, when we do a telecast, whether it was good or bad or somewhere in between. We don't need to wait until the reviews come out to make that determination. And if the review is bad, it's not for most of us the end of the world. With Al, a bad review is shattering. For the last three or four years I was there, it was obvious that Al was going to great lengths on the air to extol the virtues of a great number of writers. That's a safeguard against bad reviews."

Director Andy Sidaris, who's been at ABC Sports since the very beginning: "I've said this to Al Michaels' face many, many times—he's absolutely obsessed about what is said about him in the newspapers. . . . He's a marvelously talented guy, but he has this terrible paranoia about criticism. I'm one of his biggest supporters and great admirers, because the man has real talent, but if he's not careful, he's going to let this thing about publicity ruin him. He ought to go out and do his job and forget about the rest of that garbage."

Dennis Lewin, now second in command to Dennis Swanson at ABC Sports, has been a strong Al Michaels supporter from the beginning, and he's spoken with Michaels more than once about the problem.

"How much of a star Al can be depends on him," said Lewin. "He's very sensitive about criticism. I've talked with him in the past about overreacting to newspaper criticism. He claims he's not worried about it, yet he remains extremely sensitive to it."

No one in the business has more talent than Al Michaels—only he can alter his mind-set and image.

One of the game's more powerful and colorful owners is Ted Turner. ABC Sports went to the mat with him in 1982.

The battle lines were drawn when it appeared that Turner's Atlanta Braves would make it to the League Championship Series by winning the National League's Western Division title. Turner also owns TBS, known as WTBS until 1987, the superstation in Atlanta that televises most of the Braves' games. Braves' telecasts are picked up by satellite and retransmitted to cable systems all around the nation. There was no way ABC or Major League Baseball could allow playoff games to be shown on a superstation that would be in direct and widespread competition with the network that was paying so many dollars for exclusivity.

Commissioner Kuhn alerted Turner to the problem in midsummer of 1982 and they met in New York. Baseball couldn't budge and Turner wouldn't. Turner said he informed the commissioner that the Federal Communications Commission, and the Congress, defined WTBS as a local Atlanta station. Our agreement with baseball permitted telecasts in the markets of the teams in the playoffs by the teams' local "flagship" stations. Since WTBS was the Braves' flagship station, he thus felt he had every right to carry the League Championship Series if the Braves were involved in it. And that's what he meant to do.

Baseball and ABC had no choice but to file suit in federal court in New York. The case came up at the tail end of the regular season before U.S. District Judge Mary Johnson Lowe. Turner, of course, was the key witness for the defense, and I was one of the main witnesses for the plaintiffs. The court had accommodated Turner so he could leave to fulfill a previous business commitment, and he was at his southern-gentleman best. In fact, he was almost syrupy in his gratitude to Judge Lowe, a black woman with a no-nonsense attitude. "Thank you, ma'am. You're very sweet, ma'am," he said. I watched the judge bristle as Turner spoke. Ted was being condescending, and although the case was far from over, I felt that he had committed a serious error.

During my deposition before the trial, there was discussion about "willing" superstations and "unwilling" superstations. As best I understood it, a willing superstation was one that worked with various cable systems around the country and encouraged them to pick up its signal. Conversely, an unwilling superstation wouldn't go out and hustle its signal to the cable people. Turner's WTBS certainly fell into the willing category. He later testified that 90 percent of his station's audience was scattered around other parts of the United States, with but 10 percent in Atlanta. He didn't even get his hackles up when Phil Forlenza, the attorney representing ABC, suggested that as much as 95 percent of the station's advertising revenue came from national sponsors. From the start, it was clear Turner would have an uphill struggle proving that WTBS was this little-bitty-old station down there in Atlanta just shuffling around, trying to get along, and wanting nothing more than to let the good folks in and around Atlanta see their beloved Braves in the playoffs. Just to top things off, Turner's people had been advertising the Braves as "America's Team," the Dallas Cowboys of major-league baseball.

Forlenza did a masterful job, but from the outset I didn't see any way we could lose. The judge pointed particularly to the statement I had made that it was "totally beyond comprehension" that ABC would purchase exclusive rights to Atlanta Braves' games that at the same time would be broadcast on cable to other markets around the country. Commissioner Kuhn and Sandy Hadden, baseball's general counsel and secretary-treasurer, also testified regarding baseball's right to sell ABC exclusive television rights, and to what that exclusivity meant.

On the witness stand, Turner admitted that the promotional material used by his superstation described WTBS as national in scope. Just four months before, on June 2, 1982, Turner had testified in front of a U.S. House of Representatives subcommittee:

> As you know, Turner Broadcasting operates three different television networks that provide sports, entertainment and news programming to the public over cable. Twenty-one million cable homes now receive movies and the home games of the Atlanta Braves and the Atlanta Hawks [another Turner property] over WTBS, Atlanta, the Superstation.

When those remarks were read into the record in the New York trial, Turner quickly pointed out that the opening remarks before that congressional subcommittee had been prepared "by our Washington lobbyist."

And what about the promotional material that described Turner's operations as "Cable's Most Popular Network"? Ted parried, "It might be stretching it a little."

During the late stages of Turner's testimony, he and Forlenza got into a verbal tug-of-war that I found amusing. But the judge didn't laugh. On the one hand, Turner was crowing about the superstation's importance and its national scope, about how many homes it reached and how far-reaching was its influence, but for the purposes of this case all he wanted was for WTBS to be recognized as one station, the flagship of the Atlanta Braves.

FORLENZA: Do you consider Turner Broadcasting System and the superstation to be a national network?

TURNER: Not really. I would like for it to be someday.

FORLENZA: You believe that it is a local flagship station?

TURNER: Absolutely. It is, you know, somewhat more than that; that is why we came up with the phrase "superstation." We are kind of in a little bit of a twilight zone.

FORLENZA: I am sure you are.

ABC won that case. Turner Broadcasting System was enjoined from broadcasting the Braves' playoff games over Superstation WTBS. It was a shutout.

16

AS IGNOBLE A BUSINESS AS EVER

*The Manly Art of Self-defense
—Mine Especially!*

.

Most people with an ounce of sensitivity occasionally have a serious question or two about an activity whose purpose and intent is to render another human being unconscious.

The Marquis of Queensberry called boxing "the manly art of self-defense," and it was he who is generally credited with formulating the rules by which the endeavor is played out. The closer you get to boxing, though, the more you might think the whole scheme was devised by the Marquis de Sade.

The plain truth is that for as long as there has been boxing, right from the bare-knuckle days when fighters had to dodge the police as well as each other's punches, the sport has been constantly under attack in one way or another. And yet it survives, albeit sometimes like a punch-drunk fighter stumbling around what the old-timers called "the squared circle." It survives, I suppose, because of what it is: man-to-man combat. When the promoters and lawyers and managers and, yes, the television networks, have made their deals and the publicity drums no longer are beating, and when the trainers have given their last-minute instructions and the crowd is buzzing with anticipation and the seconds step out of the ring and the bell sounds, it then is down to the simplest and starkest of all confrontations, one man against another man. Under the hot lights of this minute portion of the arena, they come together and they go to war with only their fists and their hearts and stomachs for weapons. Perhaps it will last ten, fifteen rounds. Maybe it will last only a few seconds. There is no sport quite like it.

Boxing has not been the best of sports for me professionally. In fact, it produced two of the darker periods of my life, both times because my integrity was questioned. If asked how I would describe myself, the thing that is the most important in my life is my integrity. I strongly resent having it questioned.

Don King, the promoter with the electric hair—someone said it looked like that of a man whose execution was called off ten seconds after they pulled the switch—came to me in the summer of 1976 with the grand notion to put a boxing tournament on ABC. It would be called the U.S. Boxing Championships.

Over the years, I'd had a very good relationship with Don King. He's a character and a hustler, and you have to know how to deal with him or he'll push you farther than you should allow yourself to be pushed. I'd never let King do that, and I'd found that after he'd done as much pushing and shoving as he could, and wrung out every dollar he could extract, he stood very solidly by whatever commitment he had made. Also, if you were to ask Don King today what he thinks of me and the relationship we've had, I think he would say it was Jim Spence, working through ABC Sports, who put Don King on the map. I was the architect of ABC doing a series of prime-time boxing telecasts, and Don and I made the deal for the first-ever network million-dollar fight, Muhammad Ali versus Ron Lyle, in 1975.

When King came to me with his proposal for the U.S. Boxing Championships, we met in the ABC Sports conference room on the twenty-eighth floor. Roone Arledge did not attend that original meeting, but as soon as I had the proposal in hand, I took it to him. It appeared to be a very well-thought-out plan for a boxing tournament in the various weight divisions. *Ring Magazine* was for years regarded as the bible of the boxing industry, and the plan was to use the magazine for the records of the fighters and as the basis for the divisional rankings. The late Nat Loubet was then head of *Ring* and one of his employees, Johnny Ort, was assigned to oversee their involvement.

Over the years, boxing had been on a roller coaster, and it seemed to be in a confused state at that time. The post–Ali era was nearing, and we thought this tournament as proposed by King had the potential to create a spark in the various weight divisions and hopefully arouse new interest in boxing overall. Also, we were very aware that if we said no to him King most assuredly would take the idea to CBS and NBC. In those days there was the attitude, prevailing at each network for most of the time since ABC Sports had gotten seriously into the sports business in 1960, that "we must have *every* event! We can't afford to lose a single one to the other guys."

After a series of meetings, plus untold numbers of telephone calls involving King and Larry Gershman, who was then head of Don King Productions, we struck a deal during the fall of 1976 to pay King a little more than $2 million for the rights to televise the U.S. Boxing Championships. The series was to run for ten weeks. The project met with immediate enthusiasm from all quarters, it generally being conceded that this was an idea whose time had come, and that securing the television rights to it was at least a mild coup for ABC Sports.

The first telecast was set for January 16, 1977, and involved the heavyweights Larry Holmes and Tom Prater. In the interim, we had assigned to the project a young associate producer, Alex Wallau, who had been hired by ABC originally to turn out on-air promotion pieces but who was a boxing nut, one of those guys who follow the sport religiously, collect memorabilia, and really have intense knowledge about fighters and the sport overall. We agreed to pay Wallau thirty-five hundred dollars to work up some background information, and do research, and collect data for Howard Cosell. The idea was for Wallau to also be on hand for each telecast, to help out as and where needed.

Some weeks before the first telecast, we began to hear discomfiting rumblings about the project. We received some letters and telephone calls from boxing people, inquiring about certain fighters and wondering why they were in the tournament, and why certain others were left out. One of those left out was Marvin Hagler, who, we would later learn, was excluded because his people did not want to sign away any options for future fights. We would also subsequently ascertain that, if you signed up for the U.S. Boxing Championships, Don King automatically owned rights to your future fights.

We had no evidence of any wrongdoing at that time, but the rumors were enough for me to assign Alex Wallau to look into them, and to analyze the tournament and its fighters and give me a capsule summation. That report came to my desk on December 11, 1976. Frankly, it was much bulkier than I had anticipated, and, busy as ever, I skimmed lightly over it without paying a lot of attention to details. Like everyone else, I have 20/20 hindsight, so I now wish I had digested it much more carefully, although I cannot say if things would have developed drastically differently if I had.

I asked Wallau for a follow-up report, briefer than his initial dossier, then, when I received it, assigned Bob Greenway, then manager of program planning for ABC Sports, to study it and summarize its contents in a separate memo to me. It transpired therein that Wallau had concluded that half of the first dozen fighters who were to appear on the first program were of inferior talent and did not belong in any elimination tournament; and that twenty of the remaining forty-odd boxers also had no business in such a competition.

This was six months before Roone Arledge began dividing his time and attention between sports and news, so he and I were able to communicate constantly. Roone had seen a copy of Greenway's memo, and during one of our meetings we brought all the rumors and innuendos fully into the open in the process of making the decision whether to forge ahead or to drop the project.

It was Roone's idea to set up a meeting with King to discuss our concerns and then compel him and the other principals to sign affidavits swearing that the rankings were sound, the records legitimate, and that the fighters had gotten into the tournament on merit. This would be the first time in the history of ABC Sports that we had forced anyone we dealt with to sign an affidavit. Should the decision then be to proceed, we would have Howard

Cosell explain, on the first show, why the tournament did not include every fighter who might reasonably be expected to compete in it. Roone also had Cosell call Angelo Dundee, one of the most knowledgeable boxing men in the world, to check on the caliber of fighters who were in the tournament. At the time, we were not aware that Dundee had a vested interest in several of those boxers, but, as Cosell would later swear, Dundee was a long-time ally of his who, Howard believed, "wouldn't dare lie to me." Dundee said he thought Prater stood a chance against Holmes, and was quite positive regarding the fighters entered. Cosell himself stated that the tournament was conceptually sound and was good for boxing. There was near-unanimous agreement among the sporting press to the same effect.

The critical meeting was set up with King for December 29, 1976. Cosell and Greenway were on hand, too, when King and I met at the Dorset Hotel on Fifty-fourth Street, just a few steps from ABC headquarters. There was no point in pussyfooting around, so I went straight to the point:

"Don, is there anything wrong with this tournament?"

King acted offended. "Are you crazy? Of course there's nothing wrong with it," he quickly responded.

I told him the things we were hearing, the rumors about the false records, the rigged rankings, the inclusion of inferior fighters and the exclusion of some worthy ones, and the suspected kickbacks.

"Don, I'm telling you that this is a tremendous opportunity for you and ABC Sports to build something good for both of us, and if there is anything wrong with this tournament, you are absolutely crazy to let it occur."

Again, King assumed a look of stunned incredulity. How could I listen to such trash? Surely, I could not believe such drivel. The series was as critical to him as it was to us, and he assured us that everything was in order.

After the meeting, I took the information to Roone Arledge, and before I left his office late that afternoon, we were both leaning toward "go," which we finalized when I talked with him on the phone from New Orleans, where I had flown for our Sugar Bowl telecast.

The ratings were good—a 14.6 for the opener and an average of 10-plus for the first four shows—and there were some memorable settings for some of the fights—on the flight deck of an aircraft carrier in Pensacola, Florida; at the Naval Academy in Annapolis, Maryland; and inside the prison in Ohio where King had done time for a manslaughter conviction (for which he later received a pardon from the governor of Ohio)—before the series was yanked off the air four weeks before the end of its scheduled 10-week run.

The rumors had intensified, as we kept hearing more about phony rankings and phony records, to the point where we had no option but to do our own investigation. Alex Wallau, working alongside Jeff Ruhe, then assistant to Roone Arledge, made an exhaustive search and came up with some alarming discrepancies between the real records and what we had been told by *Ring Magazine*. Suddenly, the tournament that conceptually was so sound, and so well accepted, was in shambles.

The word "scandal" is not too strong, because that's exactly what it was as the event lost all legitimacy. The new *Ring Record Book* came off the press, proving beyond any doubt that there had been severe tampering with the records.

I called King and told him it was critical for him to come immediately to Arledge's office. When he arrived, we told him what we had learned and that we had decided to abort the series. He was very upset, protested that his integrity was at stake, and insisted he knew nothing of any chicanery. What we knew was enough, though. We had been shown a red flag months before, and had not looked stringently enough beyond it. I was too busy, too inattentive, and I'm not proud of what evolved. ABC Sports took a ton of heat from critics, and we had it coming.

The only positive thing to come out of it all are the more stringent safeguards now used by all three major networks in terms of fighters and their records and the competitiveness of matches. There is a greater sense of responsibility as a result of ABC Sports having been dragged through the mud. While I am opposed to federal control of boxing, I am in favor of a national organization, created through congressional legislation, but operating independently of the government, to oversee the sport.

There were fast and far-reaching investigations. Phil Forlenza, attorney from Hawkins, Delafield & Wood—one of ABC's outside law firms—got an independent counselor to do an in-house investigation. The lawyer assigned to the task, Michael Armstrong, concluded that there was no actual wrongdoing at ABC Sports, but that we were negligent in not taking stronger precautionary measures before allowing the tournament to go on the air. Then I was interviewed by the Federal Communications Commission, and Arledge, Cosell, Wallau, and I were invited to appear before a congressional subcommittee in Washington. It was an invitation, rather than a subpoena, but when the FCC starts breathing down your neck and a bunch of congressmen want to hear from you, it gets your attention!

The official name of the congressional group was the Subcommittee on Communications of the Committee on Interstate and Foreign Commerce, and the hearing was called "Network Sports Practices." It took place on November 2, 1977, in Room 2118 of the Rayburn House Office Building. The room was packed with media people and spectators and the setting was electric. Cosell is always a lightning rod, and his presence inevitably created a bigger hum than would ordinarily have been the case. Members of the subcommittee were U.S. Representatives Marty Russo of Illinois; Louis Frey, Jr., of Florida; Edward Markey of Massachusetts; Marc Marks of Pennsylvania; Henson Moore of Louisiana; and Lionel Van Deerlin of California, chairman. The counsel for the subcommittee were Harry Shooshan III and Philip Hochberg. We had Everett Erlick, general counsel for ABC, Inc., with us, and he also testified.

Perhaps I should have been intimidated by it all, but I wasn't. I had not been involved in any wrongdoing, and although I had made some errors of judgment, I knew I would tell the truth, and I didn't foresee any skeletons coming tumbling out of my closet. However, some of the questions did get a little testy:

Congressman Russo asked, "Is it your policy to request of an employee of yours to prepare a memorandum and then not read it?"

I told him it wasn't, then added: "I think in this particular instance, in part the preoccupation with other activities—and I'm not trying to cop out—obviously I made a mistake in not reading the portions that I didn't read, but I think the preoccupation with other activities, one of which was the Moscow Olympic Games, was one factor leading to why I didn't read the remaining portions. We had some concerns in the period about the quality of the fighters. What I intended to receive [from Alex Wallau] was a less detailed, less involved [report] than the document that he gave me. . . ."

I then pointed out: "Mr. Wallau was a relatively new employee of ABC Sports and in all candor his credibility was untested; his opinion was one man's opinion and it was obviously a subjective judgment. I did ask him for the analysis so I obviously expected his opinions, but it was one man's opinion."

Before each telecast, networks conduct what are called production meetings in order to explain to announcers and others involved the precise plans and goals for the show and how they are to be attained. It was brought out during those congressional hearings that Wallau had offended certain people during the production meeting for the very first show, and that consequently there were fears for his safety and well-being. As far as I have been able to learn, there were no specific threats, nothing you could pin down.

For all his expertise, Wallau could be abrasive at times; he not only knew a great deal about boxing, but was quick to tell you how much. In that first production meeting, he made it plain what he thought of some of the matchups, and didn't hide his disappointment over some of the rankings. People involved in putting the promotion together were in that meeting, just as National Football League representatives, for example, are involved in production meetings that precede pro football telecasts. Alex had been just as outspoken whenever the subject of the boxing championships arose previously, so this wasn't the first time the King people were displeased with him.

The series producer, Chet Forte, brought the threats to the attention of Arledge and me. Chet told me about them in a telephone call late one night to my apartment in New York, saying that he, Forte, was concerned for Alex's safety. I pressed Chet for more details. He had none, he said, save for the suggestion that someone had made—that Wallau keep his mouth shut or someone might shut it for him. Forte then told the same story to Roone in a meeting in his office.

When Arledge appeared before the subcommittee, under questioning by attorney Hochberg, he responded this way when asked what he thought Chet Forte meant when he said he feared for Alex Wallau's safety: "Mr. Forte, I think, was half serious about it, but he's normally given to very volatile behavior, and what he said was something to the effect that 'this guy is gonna get himself killed if he is not careful. This is a rough crowd we're dealing with.' "

When Erlick, the ABC counsel, was testifying, he told of learning, first through a telephone call and then through a signed affidavit, that a fighter "had been promised a ranking by a certain individual if he would give up a certain portion of his fee to get in the tournament."

Earlier, I said I went into those hearings with a pretty definite mind-set of thinking nothing would surprise me. I was wrong.

During one of the pauses in the hearing, amid some strong questioning directed at me, Arledge leaned over and whispered to me: "You'd better tell them what *you* did or they're going to crucify you."

Suddenly, I felt very alone in that jam-packed hearing room. It was like the Lone Ranger and Tonto being surrounded by hostile Indians, and the Lone Ranger saying, "We're in trouble," and Tonto answering, "Where do you get that *we* crap, white man?"

What *I* did? Was that a cue for me to throw up my hands and surrender? Was I to confess that I was the architect of this whole scheme? That I knew all along about the shabby record-keeping by *Ring Magazine*? That I was aware of the phony records and the sham rankings, yet continued to plunge ahead with the tournament? That he, Arledge, was kept in the dark and not involved with every major decision concerning the series, right from its embryonic stages? Was I to prostrate myself on the railroad tracks to save my boss from the onrushing train? Or would simply throwing myself on the mercy of this august body suffice?

Either way, it wasn't going to happen. Although we thought we had acted properly at the time, clearly we—I—should have

238

been more diligent before we went on the air. I'd had a hard enough time handling my own embarrassment about that, but had done so without stretching a truth or coloring a fact. I would take only my own lumps.

Moments later, there was a recess in the proceedings, and without speaking further with Arledge about the previous testimony, or responding to his suggestion, I made my way to the hallway and asked directions to the men's room. I was about to leave there and was washing my hands when Cosell came in with another man. As they stood side by side at adjoining urinals, Cosell commented, "Arledge is letting them hang Spence."

It was brought to our attention that another boxer had gotten into the championships by whipping an opponent who had lost something like fifteen straight encounters, including twelve by knockout—a fighter known as "the King of the Stiffs." But his manager was well connected in the Baltimore area, and a friend of Don King. The subcommittee had a lot of that kind of data, too.

Congressman Markey seemed to be trying to take a chunk out of me when, assuming a posture of piety and self-righteousness and glaring at me, he said: "It boggles the mind to think that a top staffer who put together a memo, and, just among interoffice chatter, he [Alex Wallau] wouldn't perhaps have mentioned to two or three people that the tournament included someone whose reputation is beating 'the King of the Stiffs,' and knowing kickbacks were possibly being alleged in your operation, would not in one way or another have reached you. I find that to be unbelievable, just plain unbelievable."

I glared right back and said, "I think it is the truth, sir."

Markey responded merely with, "Boy!"

I never went to the gallows. There were no reprimands at ABC. We knew where the system had failed. We would not make that same kind of mistake again.

We turned over all the evidence we had collected and gave it to the United States attorneys in New York and Maryland, but nothing ever came of it. No one was indicted, and as far as I know, no one was ever punished in any way, nor even reprimanded, by any boxing commission or any other authority.

The day we pulled the plug on the tournament—when King was in Arledge's office—Roone stated that we should back out of a prior arrangement we had with King for a Roberto Duran–Edwin Viruet fight that was not part of the U.S. Boxing Championships.

I protested that one had nothing to do with the other, and that we had made a commitment and should honor it, and Arledge finally went along with that, and Don King never forgot my standing up for him that day. However, when he was later indicted—and subsequently absolved—on income-tax charges, we refused to do business with him while his case was pending. ABC was referenced in the indictment; we had paid King fifty thousand dollars to settle a dispute involving his representation of George Foreman, and the Internal Revenue Service was claiming that he had failed to report this money. Don was upset that I told the *New York Times* that we had suspended our business relationship, particularly as CBS and NBC initially continued to do business with King, and I know that to this day he feels I let him down. To even things out, I feel the same way about the U.S. Boxing Championships.

ABC's relationship with George Foreman was curious. He first made headlines by striding around the ring at the Olympic Games in Mexico City, carrying the American flag after some other black athletes had showed clenched fists and bowed their heads when the National Anthem was played. He then went on to win the world heavyweight championship in January 1973 by knocking out Joe Frazier, then lost it the following year to Muhammad Ali. We signed him to a contract that called for a first negotiation/first refusal on his upcoming fights, and for him to do some commentary for us.

Foreman was whipped by Jimmy Young in 1977 and, although only twenty-eight, quit boxing that year, partly, he claimed, out of love for his mother, but mainly because of his religious beliefs.

Instead of showing up at a scheduled news conference to announce his retirement, he sent the following wire:

AS IGNOBLE A BUSINESS AS EVER

TO THE AUDIENCE AND PEOPLE PRESENT PARDON MY NOT BEING
THERE AND PARDON MY PRESENCE IN BOXING PERIOD THERE HAS
NEVER BEEN BUT ONE CHAMP AND THAT IS THE SON OF ALMIGHTY
GOD JESUS CHRIST I CAN NO LONGER CLAP MY HANDS AND SING
PRAISES TO ANYONE BUT HIM GOD BLESS YOU ALL

GEORGE FOREMAN

(Ten years later, nearing forty, Foreman came out of retirement and won his comeback fight in Sacramento, California. Like many others before him, Foreman called on skills that had been diminished by time.)

With the congressional hearing behind us, I went back out on the boxing limb when we were offered the Earnie Shavers/Larry Holmes fight for "Wide World of Sports." Until that time, Holmes was best known as one of Muhammad Ali's sparring partners, so no one gave him much of a chance against Shavers. Nevertheless, I decided to go ahead with the fight, even though I was alone at ABC Sports in thinking it had some merit, and the result was that Holmes whipped Shavers and earned the right to go against Ken Norton for the heavyweight championship in June of 1978. That one went on ABC in prime time, and boxing fans will long remember the final round as one of the most stirring in the history of the heavyweight division. The telecast got ABC a 40 share, a very impressive showing in the ratings.

By the fall of 1979, the stage was set for a rematch between Holmes and Shavers, to be held in Las Vegas. By then, Alex Wallau was intimately involved with all of ABC's boxing productions, but his judgment having been upheld in the final showdown of the U.S. Boxing Championships, he was even more headstrong and cocky and full of himself. In a bar at Caesar's Palace one night, he got chatting with Richie Giachetti, who had been involved as a trainer with Holmes, and was in and out of Don King's doghouse over the years, and who also had had a scrape with the law. Giachetti was loose-tongued with liquor that evening as he and Wallau got around to talking about ABC's relationship with King and the storm over the U.S. Championships, and suddenly he blurted out: "You know, don't you, that King is taking care of Spence?"

241

Wallau was stunned. "What do you mean by that?" he asked Giachetti.

"Just trust me. King is taking care of Spence. I know."

Alex Wallau now had a tiger by the tail, but knew not where to turn with it and said nothing to anyone until after the Holmes-Shavers rematch, when, sitting at poolside with Bob MacDonnell, a lawyer with the Hawkins, Delafield & Wood firm, he related what he had heard. Now MacDonnell had to ask himself, "What in hell do I do with this piece of information?" He decided to pass it along to Phil Forlenza, his superior in the law firm, who passed it on to ABC counsel Ev Erlick, who in turn passed it to Arledge and Fred Pierce. By this time, the rumor had also reached me, and I was enraged by it. On October 19, 1979, I wrote a "personal and confidential" memo to Arledge and sent copies to Pierce and Wallau. It read:

> I understand that you have been made aware of an allegation, related to outside counsel by Alex Wallau, that Don King is "taking care of me." For the record, this incredulous allegation is totally false. Based on Alex's conversation with outside counsel, which conversation should have taken place first within ABC, and included statements relating to my integrity, I suggest immediate disciplinary action be taken against Alex Wallau.

It turned out that Wallau had told MacDonnell that he felt my relationship with King was a very close one, and that, consequently, ABC Sports was buying fights we should not have been purchasing.

Erlick and Pierce decided I should undergo a microscopic investigation by Forlenza, the attorney, in which I would have to produce all my bank records, brokerage-account statements, and other financial documents! After having given ABC nearly twenty years of faithful service, it troubled me to be subjected to that kind of scrutiny, yet on the other hand, because of the major boxing scandal just two years before, I could understand how jittery the top executives were.

When Forlenza and I began our session in the conference room on the fortieth floor at ABC, I read into the tape recorder my memo to Arledge about Wallau, then made the following statement:

> I would also like to say, for the record, that I have never, in all my tenure at ABC, dating from 1960 to the present, taken any improper payment or remuneration from anyone. I also am prepared to make available to the appropriate parties my financial records, upon request. I am ready and willing to answer all queries concerning the allegation in question, including television rights agreements related thereto. I do not feel a responsibility, however, to answer questions involving my business judgment.

Two months later, Forlenza came back with the only report he could have produced: Jim Spence has done nothing in any way, shape, or form to sacrifice one ounce of personal integrity. However, even at this distance, I think Arledge should have gotten the investigation killed, and that Alex Wallau should have been disciplined.

Nevertheless, I saw to it that some years later Wallau got the chance to go on network television as a boxing analyst.

From among our established play-by-play people we thought we could adequately cover the blow-by-blow part of our boxing shows, but that we needed a second voice, another presence. Ferdie Pacheco, the so-called "Fight Doctor," did commentary for NBC, was articulate and knowledgeable, and built himself a good following, as had Gil Clancy at CBS. We needed a comparable expert. We briefly considered using Sugar Ray Leonard, but finally decided his commentary was too shallow. Next we considered Jimmy Jacobs, now the comanager of Mike Tyson, who won the world heavyweight championship in 1986, but he was so involved in managing fighters that it would have been a conflict of interest. However, he gave Wallau a strong recommendation, telling us that "he's the best guy you could possibly hire."

This strong recommendation made us take a second look at Alex and at an audition tape we had already done with Wallau. Except for his lack of on-air experience and the fact that he wasn't known outside the boxing fraternity, there were few minuses. I made a strong pitch to Roone to go with Wallau, but at first he voted that down, just as he had my suggestion to discipline Alex earlier. I argued some more, reminding Roone that we had sent Alex to Seoul, Korea, for World Cup boxing, and had been pleased with his presence and with what he had to say, despite his nervousness. Finally, I prevailed upon Arledge to use Wallau, and we set about the business of signing him to a contract.

We wanted Alex to make his debut on an amateur card in December of 1985, but he said he'd be more comfortable breaking in on a pro card, so we set it up for him to work a Mark Breland fight in Lancaster, Pennsylvania, in late January. He was making over $125,000 at the time, but he and his agent wanted another $50,000 for him to become an on-air talent. On the eve of the fight, Wallau was already in Pennsylvania, but his contract had not been signed. Irwin Weiner and Bob Apter, our director of administration and financial controls, were negotiating for ABC Sports, and they asked for my opinion and I gave it: If the deal is not set, Wallau does not go on the air.

It wasn't, and he didn't. My thinking then, as now, was that as Wallau became good, the money would flow, so he should worry at this point only about getting the new phase of his career off the ground. We couldn't buy a pig in a poke, and, if he failed, he could revert to his old job as our off-the-air boxing expert. Alex and his agent were just as firm, so Chris Schenkel did the show by himself. The deal was later consummated, and I continue to hold to my original opinion that Alex Wallau can develop into the best boxing expert in television. (I was distressed to learn in the fall of 1987 that Alex was undergoing treatment for cancer.)

Since Alex and Howard Cosell tangled more than once (Howard always thought Wallau was encroaching on his territory), I'll bet Alex chuckled when Cosell got caught "predicting" winners of fights the results of which he already knew. Cosell has given boxing some nasty punches, but this time it was Howard who wound up with a black eye.

ABC was televising the Olympic box-offs, live from Las Vegas, in July of 1984, which fights would determine the makeup of the United States Olympic team that would compete later in the Summer Olympics in Los Angeles. One of Cosell's goofs came during the fight between Pernell Whitaker and Joey Belinc, a very close scrap in the 132-pound weight class. At the end of the third and final round, we went to a commercial break; then, as he came back on the air live, Cosell said: "This fight should be closely scored . . . [but], no question, I would give it to Whitaker."

Just then, ring announcer Chuck Hull called Whitaker as the winner. It was not a popular decision with the crowd, but a casual television observer would have had to concede that Howard Cosell really knew what he was talking about. In this case, he definitely did, because he'd had the result in his hand before the ring announcer made the call.

Here's how it happened this time, as it happened with some regularity at others:

Our system called for Bob Yalen, a respected boxing aficionado who began working with Alex Wallau and whom we later hired full-time, to receive the scoring of the bouts over a phone line at ringside, then write it out for Cosell so that he could go over the scoring and tell the audience the round-by-round results. Clearly, this gave Howard all the information before it got to the hands of the public-address announcer, but he should not have used it as he did. What Howard should have said was, "Ladies and gentlemen, I've just been handed the results and Whitaker won the fight, three to two." Better still, he could have remained silent and let the ring announcer do his job. Instead, he used privileged information and made it sound like it was his own expert opinion, then compounded the problem later by denying the whole thing. The pity of it was that he really didn't need the results, because his opinions were very accurate most of the time. Thereafter, we established a policy that announcers would not be given round-by-round results and scoring until *after* it was announced to the public.

Here's the transcript of what happened (note the part that's tagged VOICE OFF-CAMERA):

COSELL: It has been a hard-fought battle. Belinc trying to score in this third and final round [bell sounds]. That's it, that's it. And the crowd stands and cheers for Joe Belinc. Well, let's see if the crowd enthusiasm is correct. Belinc goes back to his corner; his cornerman tells him he has won without question. Manny Steward doesn't think so. We'll be back. [Commercial.] All right, we are back live—we await the decision. The crowd clearly for Belinc, but to me that's highly questionable. They don't have the decision yet.

VOICE OFF-CAMERA: Whitaker three to two.

COSELL: However, this fight should be closely scored. No question, I'd give it—I would give it to Whitaker." [Announcement: Whitaker Wins]

COSELL: There it is—it was a three-to-two decision for Pernell Whitaker, and the crowd boos, but amateur boxing scoring, and these men know the scoring systems in amateur boxing. I would have given it to Whitaker, too, as I indicated. So Pernell Whitaker will go to Los Angeles, but he finally met a man worthy of being a great opponent, Joe Belinc."

The *New York Post* lambasted Cosell three days later, the headline blaring the news: COSELL SNAGGED IN OLYMPIC FIGHT SHAM. The paper quoted veteran manager and trainer Lou Duva, who now is involved with several former Olympic champions: "Cosell calls us vultures on TV because we're out there watching over kids we've trained since they were puppies, then he goes on the air to give his opinions on the fight and he already knows who won and by how much. So who's the vulture? Hell, every result was known in advance. We're sitting there waiting for a result, and the guy gives us a wink before the ring announcer's even ready. Then you've got Cosell on the air acting like he's a genius."

Yalen confirmed that Cosell "sometimes knew" the results ahead of time. At the same time the *Post* published the article, Cosell was in San Francisco to cover baseball's All-Star Game and could not be reached—or didn't want to be reached—to comment on the article. Later he issued the following statement:

This story is part and parcel of a documented long-term vendetta against me by certain writers of the *New York Post*. It uses as its source a professional boxing manager, trainer and promoter whose record of conduct in that sleazy and discredited business speaks for itself—in a state where the conduct of professional boxing is under close scrutiny by the FBI and various state agencies. While under the system used in the Olympic boxoffs, ABC's statistician did have a line which provided him with the results just prior to the formal announcement. The record will show that my opinions as to the winner and loser were stated before those results were known to me. Indeed, during the course of the two-day event, I expressed opinions freely while the bouts were in progress and on the first day, for example, did so before the bout in which Craig Payne beat Tyrell Biggs. My record of journalistic integrity stands—I don't believe that of the *New York Post* does.

Just a suggestion: Don't invite anyone from the *New York Post* to any party you are thinking of throwing for Howard Cosell.

Most of those champions from the 1984 Los Angeles Olympic Games wound up signing contracts with ABC Sports. Whether any would become a fighter people still buzzed about twenty or thirty years down the road, like they did about Joe Louis and Sugar Ray Robinson, wasn't to us the issue, which was: Were they good enough fighters and were they marketable for television? I decided that they were both, so after discussing the deal with Roone Arledge I authorized Bob Iger, who was director of program planning at the time, and now vice president, programming, to sign them to a contract right after the Games, and he worked out a deal with five of them—Mark Breland, Tyrell Biggs, Evander Holyfield, Pernell Whitaker, and Meldrick Taylor—who were being handled by the promoter Dan Duva and the manager Shelly Finkel. They made their professional debuts at Madison Square Garden in New York, in prime time on ABC on November 15, 1984.

It surfaced right after the signing that Biggs had a drug

problem, one that predated the Olympic Games, causing both Duva and Finkel to want him taken off the telecast. Iger and Charlie Lavery of our office wholeheartedly agreed, and were vociferous in their belief that it would be unwise to become involved with an athlete we knew had used cocaine. Biggs, the Olympic superheavyweight champion, deserved an opportunity to prove himself. He was just a kid and I decided to take a chance on him. My decision was that we would establish a deadline of November 1—two weeks before the fight—and have him tested for drugs. If he tested positive, he'd be out, but if we got it in writing that he was drug-free, he would have the opportunity to fight. After all, we might save more than just a career; we might save a life.

Biggs passed the test and appeared on the card and, despite some booing that accompanied his uninspired performance, won his first fight as a pro. He later told Phil Berger of the *New York Times* that he went back to his cocaine habit after that fight, blew thirty thousand dollars, and had a scary experience in which his heartbeat was so accelerated that he thought he was going to die. He then said he checked himself into a drug clinic for professional help. Biggs told reporters in 1987 that he had been "clean" since the beginning of 1985.

My hope is that these young men save their money. Boxing gives to hungry, talented young men the opportunity to make a lot of money very fast, and too often they find ways to spend it even faster. It is a craft with a mysterious allure that can make you rich in the ring, and then kill you outside it.

Boxing never killed me, but it did take a couple of mighty swings that inflicted some severe pain.

17

SPORT'S BIGGEST ONE-DAY SPECTACLE

ABC and the Indianapolis 500

Spectacle: 1 a: Something exhibited to view as unusual, notable, or entertaining; *esp:* an eye-catching or dramatic public display [from *Webster's Ninth New Collegiate Dictionary*].

For as long as I can remember, the slogan, or byword, of the Indianapolis 500 has been "the greatest *spectacle* in racing." You cannot lump the Indy 500 in a group with the Olympic Games, the World Series, the NBA Finals or the NCAA Basketball Championship because they are multiday events, but for sheer excitement in a single-day event and as a piece of Americana, I rate the race alongside the Super Bowl, the Kentucky Derby, and the Rose Bowl.

The 500 is so much more than just a race; like the Derby, it attracts people who don't watch another race all year long. Because of the drama and pageantry and the unbelievable massive crowds and the lightning speeds, the Indy 500 takes on special meaning. First run in 1911, it is an event you have to believe will endure forever—the largest single-day happening in all of sports.

Since Speedway officials jealously guard attendance figures, outsiders never know officially how many people jam into the Indianapolis Motor Speedway, a two-and-a-half-mile racing oval with the infield so spacious that a nine-hole golf course inside the track goes almost unnoticed.

What other event has the lure of the Indy 500—the parade of celebrities, the bands, the playing of "Back Home Again in Indiana," the release of the colorful balloons, and then what may be the single most exciting moment in sports—the start of the great race.

ABC's relationship with the Indianapolis Motor Speedway began in 1961 with our telecast of Time Trials that year, and in 1965 we first televised the race. Music Corporation of America did the race live on closed-circuit theater television in the sixties, before which an Indianpolis station, WFBM-TV, televised the 500 live but only locally.

The ABC-Indy romance started the same way the ABC-Kentucky Derby romance did—with Indiana-born Chris Schenkel opening the doors for us. Chris had a long friendship with the people at the Speedway, most notably the owner, the late Tony Hulman. Interestingly, Tony, a true gentleman in every sense of the word, carried a small card containing those famous words "Gentlemen, start your engines"—I suppose to guard against the unlikely event that his memory would fail him amid all the noise and confusion.

In the early years, the race would be recorded on film, edited down to acceptable time limits, then aired on "ABC's Wide World of Sports" a week later. A major breakthrough came on May 29, 1971, when we did our first quick "turnaround"—in other words, videotaped the race and played it back on the network the same night, in prime time. With the awesome sound and breakneck speed of thirty-three racing machines, simply recording the event is a hazardous and grueling exercise. Add to that the postproduction work required after a 2:15 P.M. finish— or later, depending on accidents and the weather—and problems in getting a three-hour show ready for air at 8 P.M. Indianapolis time are truly gigantic. Indeed, the Indy 500 same-day delayed telecast was the most difficult single-day task in television sports, approached only by covering all eighteen holes of the United States Open Golf Championship.

That very first prime-time program was in 1971, the year the pace car plowed into the photographers' stand. Incredibly, there were no fatalities, but people were running in every direction as the pace car slammed into the stand, and I wasn't far from the accident when it happened, standing, as was my custom, near a big tree at the first turn to watch the start of the race. Eldon Palmer was driving the pace car that year, with the astronaut and later U.S. Senator John Glenn in the front seat, and Speedway owner Tony Hulman in the backseat alongside Chris Schenkel, who was describing the start of the race for our telecast later on. It's a wonder all of them weren't killed.

After the crash, most people blamed Eldon Palmer, but Schenkel disagrees: "Eldon Palmer saved our lives; he was an expert driver. They had a braking flag at a certain point in the pits and that flag was to be Eldon's signal to begin braking at that spot. The last time I looked, we were doing a hundred thirty-five miles per hour up pit row, and then all of a sudden the braking flag we practiced with so many times was nowhere to be seen. The crowd in the pits surged out and covered up the braking flag so Eldon hit the brakes and we started sliding. I knew we were going to hit the stand. Miraculously, only one person was seriously injured."

I feared the worst as I ran back toward the crash site, but was greatly relieved to see that Chris was not seriously injured. Later, he would tell me that being able to recognize me made him realize that he was all right. That evening Jackie Stewart, three-time world driving champion and our expert commentator, insisted that Chris return to the Speedway to help release any fear he might have. Although still pretty dizzy, Chris went on the air very briefly that night.

The late Jim Clark won the race the first year ABC televised it, and there had been so much controversy stirred up ahead of time with real or manufactured animosity between United States and European drivers that his victory served only to add to the tension. Some of the members of the world road-racing fraternity had roundly criticized Indy, saying there wasn't a lot to driving there because, after all, all one really had to do was to go fast and keep turning left.

When another foreigner, the late Graham Hill of England, won the following year, his achievement was cheapened by some American drivers who claimed he laid back in second place and just waited until trouble overtook the leader. The suggestion was that Hill was a cautious and conservative chauffeur who'd be content to accept second place, or worse, unless victory was dumped in his lap.

In 1967, the trophy was back where it properly belonged, the patriots figured, when A. J. Foyt won his third 500, and they were happy, too, when Bobby Unser followed him to victory in 1968. The Americans then quickly claimed Mario Andretti as one of their own when he won in 1969, even though Mario was born in Italy and was every bit as much at home on the more sophisticated grand prix racing circuit as on the oval tracks. Back-to-back triumphs by Al Unser in 1970 and 1971 (who would get a record-tying fourth victory in 1987) and Mark Donohue's victory in 1972 set the stage for the blackest month in the history of the event.

In May 1973, the Great God of Rain spent practically the entire month in Indiana, to the point where one radio announcer finally claimed that the only way they'd ever determine an Indy winner would be to place all thirty-three cars out on the track, then declare the first one to rust out the champion.

The average speed of the field that year would be 192.32 mph, some eight and a half miles an hour faster than in 1972. Everyone attributed the increase to the "wings" on the rear of the cars, which had been roundly blamed when Art Pollard, a veteran driver with much experience at Indianapolis, for no obvious reason lost control on a practice run in turn one and hurtled headlong into the wall and was killed. Critics said the cars now were too fast, that they "took off" like airplanes. Arguments had also raged about the car's fuel tanks, so placed that the drivers were practically sitting on top of them. As if that weren't enough, veteran drivers were also cursing United States Auto Club and track officials, saying they were too lenient in driver testing, that they were allowing too many greenhorns onto the track for this, not only the most important of American races, but surely the most dangerous as well.

The race was to have been contested on Monday, May 28. The rains came, then went, the storm clouds teasing officials, spectators, and competitors all morning long, causing a delay of four hours. Then, just nine seconds into the race, there was a horrifying crash as Salt Walther, never regarded as one of the abler drivers, lost control and hit the wall. Flames—invisible since the fuel they use at Indy burns white instead of orange or red or blue—spread all over Walther and his car and splashed into the stands and onto a dozen spectators who had been on their feet, wide-eyed. Ten minutes later, the rain came again in torrents, as Walther and the injured spectators were on their way to the hospital.

The rains stayed through Tuesday and by nightfall, with the infield a lake, most of the more than four hundred thousand people who had crowded inside the huge oval—some of them actually to watch the race!—had gone home. They missed the worst part of it all.

By the time they got the track dry enough to race, midway through the day on Wednesday, everyone was unbelievably uptight. I don't know what the psychologists would have come up with had they been able to examine the psyche of the drivers at that moment, but if they had not been severely jarred by all that had transpired, they were either tougher than I imagine anyone could be or more insensitive than any human has a right to be. Somehow, they got the race started safely, and essentially it stayed that way for more than one-fourth of the scheduled 500-mile distance.

Swede Savage, a twenty-six-year-old Californian who had narrowly escaped death in a home-state crash two years before, led early on, but when he pitted for fuel on the fifty-ninth lap, Al Unser took over from him. Savage meant to get back in command, but as he went into turn four, he lost control in a groove that was saturated with oil, the car going every which way, down across a strip of the infield and back across the race track, and then headlong into the wall, where it erupted into a sea of white flames. Savage was conscious then, but had difficulty getting unhooked from his safety harness and was severely burned. He would die of his injuries more than a month later.

A fire truck took off from the pits, but raced the wrong way up pit row, where it struck Armando Teran, a twenty-two-year-old pit crewman for the STP team. He was tossed thirty feet into the air, like a rag doll, and died later that day.

The race was stopped for almost ninety minutes, then went seventy-four more laps before it was mercifully concluded as the rains arrived once more. Gordon Johncock, who had taken the lead on the seventy-third lap, was declared the winner. It was, in 1973, the Indy 332½.

Jim Murray, the gifted syndicated columnist of the *Los Angeles Times*, wrote: "The attrition rate was about that of World War II U-boats. Gordon Johncock didn't so much win the race, he just happened to be the one standing there when they decided to end it. The Speedway officials just sort of handed it to him and said 'Here, you take this home with you. We're getting out of here!' And they wouldn't take no for an answer."

At the end of it all, we weren't sure if we could adequately tell the whole sad saga on television that night, but in one of the severest tests ever of our production people, they came through in magnificent style.

A number of changes have been made at the Speedway over the years. The foils, or "wings," were greatly modified, restrictions were imposed regarding on-board fuel, and the location of the fuel tanks was changed to get them out from under the driver's seat.

The Speedway itself has also undergone modifications to make the track safer for drivers and spectators alike; however, there is one area of concern I have discussed with two different Speedway presidents, John Cooper and Joe Cloutier.

There are thirty-three cars in every Indy 500 field, and in the pit area, each car has a tank containing 250 gallons of fuel sitting in the open, separated from the track by a narrow grassy area and a wall only a few feet high. It hasn't happened yet, but the odds are that one day a car could leap across that wall and explode one of those fuel tanks. There are literally thousands of fans pressed up against the fence behind the pits and seated in the stands just a step away. This is to my mind presently the greatest single danger at the Indianapolis Motor Speedway.

The 1974 race was relatively trouble-free as Tom Binford replaced long time chief steward Harlan Fengler. Candidly, Tom's leadership has resulted in cleaner, safer races and there have been no driver fatalities in the 500 since he took over. Johnny Rutherford won in 1974 as he did in 1976 after Bobby Unser had taken his second Indy in the intervening year. Foyt then won for the fourth time in 1977 and Al Unser for the third in 1978 (his 1987 success tied him with Foyt for most victories). Rick Mears got the checkered flag in 1979 and Rutherford was victorious for a third time in 1980. The following year, Bobby Unser's much disputed victory distinguished him as the only driver to win the 500 in three different decades—the huge argument being about whether he had illegally passed Mario Andretti while the yellow caution flag was out.

We taped that entire race, of course, and Jackie Stewart did the commentary on all but the opening laps that evening, as the show actually aired, giving us the advantage of hindsight and enabling Jackie to point out exactly where the illegal passing took place. Unfortunately, Unser took Stewart's comment of "Look, look, right there you can see that Bobby Unser is passing Mario Andretti on the yellow" as a direct slap and got steaming mad about it. However, the owner of his car, Roger Penske, filed an appeal, and some months after they had dropped the checkered flag, Unser was declared once and for all officially the winner.

Gordon Johncock won the race again in 1982 in the closest finish in 500 history—sixteen-hundredths of a second. Rick Mears made a lengthy pit stop and was a bit over twelve seconds behind Johncock with about a dozen laps to go, then picked up a second a lap and caught Gordy as the white flag came out. Johncock beat Mears into the first turn of the final lap and still held the lead as they approached turn four. With four hundred thousand people watching and cheering, Mears tried unsuccessfully to sling-shot Johncock coming off the fourth turn as they raced to the thrilling finish in the Indianapolis 500 with the first $2 million purse.

The following year, Tom Sneva, who had been the first Indy driver to qualify at a speed in excess of 200 mph was successful for the first time. It was a richly deserved achievement for Sneva, a former schoolteacher who had proven years before that he was a capable driver, but who had been dogged by bad luck.

That also was the year ABC Sports and the management of the Indianapolis Motor Speedway clashed openly about comments made by Jackie Stewart. The "Wee Scot" had been doing our race commentary for years, during which he had always been extremely safety-conscious and very outspoken about things he believed could and should be done to make life easier and safer for both drivers and spectators. As a result, he had had periodic flare-ups with the Speedway brass, and it was no secret that he was not their favorite commentator. It was also no secret that certain officials, along with some of the veteran American drivers, harbored resentment against Jackie, not only for his candor but also for his foreignness and his worldwide reputation. You know: Who does this little pipsqueak with that funny accent and high-pitched voice think he is, coming over here and telling us how to run our race?

Jackie's troubles eventually reached the boiling point in May of 1983. He had done yet another feature about safety, and word of the piece reached track officials—indeed, no doubt some of them had watched him working on the videotaping. Joe Cloutier called me in my hotel room in downtown Indianapolis, and the moment I picked up the phone, I could tell the Speedway president was upset. He strongly expressed his concerns, then asked that we not air the piece. I told him I hadn't seen it, and thus couldn't comment on the specifics of it, but promised to look at it and get back to him. I then called our producer, Chuck Howard, who assured me it was a solid piece of journalism. However, although from our conversation the piece seemed to be sound, I asked that we put Jackie back on camera to refer to the steps the Speedway had taken through the years to improve safety, thus ensuring that the piece had ample journalistic balance. Then I called Roone Arledge in New York to fill him in on the matter, because it was obviously going to be a most sensitive one. My recommendation to Roone was that we go ahead and air the piece.

Joe Cloutier and I had known each other for many years, and it was unlike him to make the kind of request that he had. There was now of course the gamble that the issue could affect future negotiations for Indy television rights. However, Arledge agreed that once we made certain the piece was journalistically balanced, it should air. By then, the controversy had become known in media circles, so that had we backed off we would have stood to be accused of letting the Speedway dictate what we should and should not put on our television network. But it was still a tough call. When television purchases the rights to an event from the event's promoter, it in effect creates a partnership with that promoter, so there is always the question of how objective it can be in covering the event when the challenge is to keep the promoter happy while at the same time maintaining journalistic integrity; and make no mistake about it, it is a most difficult tightrope to walk when, as in this case, the partnership involves one of the most important events in sports.

However, sometimes you just have to put that relationship in jeopardy, and that's what we did when we made the decision to go ahead with Jackie Stewart's controversial feature on track and driver safety. We had made our decision literally on the eve of the race, and since it was my custom to spend a little time with Cloutier on the morning of the event, I decided to give him the bad news the next day. I told Joe at the same time that I had screened the Jackie Stewart piece, that it had been updated, and that in our opinion it had a very fair balance.

This was what Jackie said that made the Speedway officials so mad:

"Here at the Indianapolis Motor Speedway in years gone by, I have been more than generous with my praise for the safety precautions taken here, for the personnel and equipment that deal with emergencies when they do occur. However, motor racing will never be safe, and here at the Indianapolis Motor Speedway where the speeds are so high, accidents such as this [we showed an accident] can occur. In 1975, Tom Sneva came in contact with another car close to turn two. Pay attention to how high the race car goes [Sneva's car went very high]. The engine and transmission went for more than two hundred yards. They could easily have reached the crowd, without a debris fence. And then, another accident, this time with Johnny Rutherford in 1981 at Phoenix. Incidentally, neither of the drivers in those accidents was seriously injured. But, again, pay attention to what happens in the accident—how high the race car goes.

"If an accident were to occur, such as you've just seen, on this main stretch at Indy, where speeds of two hundred miles an hour plus [speeds on the straightaway reach 220 mph] are achieved, it's easy to recognize that a wall of this height—here—would simply not be enough to retain such an accident. Keep in mind, on race day, the hundreds of pit crew, and just beyond them fuel tanks, and behind them an enormous number of spectators— thousands of them. In my opinion, what we require here is a debris fence, right up here, similar to what you would see on the outside of the racetrack. Only then do I feel the sort of accident that can surely occur could be properly retained.

"Another area for my concern is pit lane. I'm now standing at the entrance of pit lane, and the cars will be coming off turn four at about, oh, a hundred fifty to a hundred sixty miles an hour at this spot here. Now it's not exactly a billiard-table surface, as can be seen by the scores in the road here, caused by these cars at that speed. The cars can get, as you can see, quite unstable [the video then showed a race car bobbling as it came out of turn four and ran over the notches, or grooves in the racing surface]. Now pit lane itself is less than fifty feet wide. If a car were to come into this situation and have a coming together with another car, as occurred last year with Rick Mears, who knows that the cars could not get into the air and really do some great damage? Because, remember, those race cars can be almost classified as aircraft accidents when something goes wrong. They're holding fuel, and of course the hazards that I spoke of earlier are all there. I suppose ideally what I would want is more space between the pit inside wall and this fence protecting the spectators. Then I would want this fence here to be much higher, actually a debris fence, because if something big were to occur you would have to protect those spectators.

"Now the Indianapolis Motor Speedway has an enormously good record for safety, and above all, for the protection of spectators. But it would be wrong, as I said at the beginning of this piece, to bury our heads in the sand. What we have to do is have preventive medicine; before an accident takes place, we should look after what should be done. It's no good closing the gate after the cows have gone out."

Cloutier was grim-faced when I gave him the news, and it didn't take a genius to figure out what he meant when he told me, "Well, Jim, it's your business what you put on your network. I can't control what you put on the air, but don't forget, *I* control the television rights to the Indianapolis 500."

Joe has always been a straight-shooter with me, and his point was that he had sold ABC the rights to come in there and televise the race, not to criticize the plant nor the way it operated. Joe's feeling was that if, during the race, an accident occurred, we had a perfect right to tell factually why it happened, or even why we conjectured it happened. Then it didn't matter who told the story or did the speculating, be it Jackie Stewart or Jim McKay, or one of the reporters in the pits.

My point was that our first responsibility was to cover the event, to approach it as a news story, and because of the hazards of the sport, that meant focusing exceptionally heavily on the safety factors involved, including even, if we found them, what we regarded as safety shortcomings.

Instead of having him call the race alongside Jim McKay, as he had for years past, we made Jackie the host of the prime-time telecast in 1982. It was a role he neither sought nor relished, and he felt he was being punished—or at least "hidden" to a degree. It probably won't do any good to explain yet again that Jackie's protests about safety had nothing to do with our decision not to use him any longer as an expert commentator, because it certainly didn't help at the time. The move was made simply because Sam Posey, a former Indy driver and an articulate man, had worked our Indy telecasts since 1974 and had provided incisive commentary, and we thought it was time to make a change.

Later, Jackie asked that we reinstate him as our expert commentator in the booth. He thought then, and he thinks now, that the Indianapolis Motor Speedway dictated his removal from that role. I told him we were in his debt for all he had brought to the telecasts for so long, that his reputation had added a lot of credibility to our telecasts, and that Posey brought us more in-depth commentary. And that's the truth: At no time did the Speedway people make any suggestions about leaving Jackie off the telecasts, nor threaten ABC with the loss of the contract if we kept him on.

Jackie's concerns about safety remained, and so he did another piece on the subject for the May 27, 1984, telecast. This is what he said then:

"What you have just seen is not a racing-car accident; it's like an aircraft accident. The total destruction of a car at that speed is incredible. As I speak to you now, we have had no report on Patrick Bedard's condition. But really, in my opinion, it's a synonymous accident with these very high speeds that I spoke of at the opening. In my opinion, they are excessively high. Only last night, I spoke to the great Parnelli Jones and I spoke to A. J. Foyt, and I spoke to the man who's fastest around this speedway, Tom Sneva. They all said that they were all going too fast, because if something did go wrong, it was difficult to see life expectancy being in the correct conditions. It's this type of accident that I think should convince us that we do have to go slower on this track and lots of others."

It was not a statement designed to win back the affection of Indy officials. Again, they figured, Stewart was meddling. And, as it turned out, that was Jackie Stewart's last Indy 500 telecast for ABC Sports, because after that he decided not to continue in the host role.

Jackie Stewart: "I thought the safety pieces I did were very fair, honest pieces. For as long as I was at the Speedway, from the days of Tony Hulman through the days of John Cooper to the days of Joe Cloutier, I told them all what I thought of the situation with regard to the pit wall and the risk of an accident, one of such proportions that it could jeopardize automobile racing not only at Indianapolis but around the world as well. . . .

"Over the years, I had been nothing but flattering to the Speedway. I had done technical pieces and safety features every year, and had expressly pointed out all that they had done right.

I've had every compliment for them. I have never been difficult or biased. But I'll always believe that the pressure from the Speedway caused ABC to get rid of me. I believe it was a matter of getting rid of Jackie Stewart to ensure there wouldn't be any stumbling blocks in the way of getting a new contract signed to do the telecasts."

Before the problems involving Jackie ever surfaced, I had done much arguing for live television coverage of the race. My position was that here we had one of the great single-day events in the history of sports, whose reputation was being tarnished by delayed telecasts, with the resulting declining television ratings and negative criticism from the media. Unfortunately, the Speedway was very much against it.

The ratings had been in single digits in 1981, and they declined again in 1982. Then they went to 14.1 in 1983, slid back to a 12.9 in 1984 when Rick Mears won for the second time, and plunged to a 9.7 and a very modest 18 share when Danny Sullivan won in 1985. From 1984 to 1985, there was the loss of 7 more share points. It was a trend I saw no way to reverse, other than by switching to a live telecast.

The embarrassing 1985 rating, plus the mention of a magical dollar figure, finally persuaded Indy to break with tradition and sign a contract to go live with the race starting in 1986. The magic number was $4 million. We had paid $1.5 million for the tape-delayed telecast in prime time in 1985.

In my final negotiations with Joe Cloutier, I told him I believed that together we could change the image of the Indy 500. "This is a great American classic," I said, "and if we stop doing delayed telecasts, we can give the race an entirely new, important, and positive thrust."

Cloutier's major concern was what live television would do to attendance. He referred to the more than 260,000 seats he had to fill with paying customers. "Going live may do severe damage to the gate," he told me. "My concern, Jim, is that if live television does not work for us, how can we get this thing back to where it was?"

There were concerns at ABC, too. The advantages to a delayed prime-time telecast are that you are able to edit out the duller moments of the race, thus creating a smoother presentation, plus having a much bigger potential audience at night. But the telecast was not thriving in prime time, and although by going live we would alienate some soap opera fans for a while, we would be able to revert to entertainment programming at night. My feeling going into the deal was that we'd have a pretty fair curiosity audience for the first live telecast, then might slip a bit for a year or two, but that eventually the live Indianapolis 500 would become part of the tradition of sports television in the United States.

Joe and I debated back and forth, but when I proposed the $4 million figure for the first live telecast, Joe grinned and said, "You just hit the magic figure." It was clear what he'd had in mind, and we shook hands on the deal. And then, of course—and wouldn't you just know it—the rains came and flooded the track for days, spoiling the 1986 debut of live Indy coverage. In all, there were three delays, and when the thirty-three-car field finally heard the call, "Gentlemen, start your engines," Tom Sneva's car wouldn't start.

Bobby Rahal won that first live race. The national rating was an 8.8, less than that for the last prime-time show, but not at all bad considering that the event finally was held a week after the Memorial Day holiday.

The story line in 1987 was a dramatic one, with Al Unser getting an unexpected ride and winning for the fourth time. The rating was up, to a 10.1, so in just two years the live telecast rating surpassed the performance of the final prime-time delayed show.

There are always great stories unfolding at Indy, and the race will always stand out for me as one of America's greatest sporting spectacles.

18

"A GAME TO BE PLAYED, NOT WATCHED"

High Jinks On and Off the Golf Course

The Masters is the first leg of golf's modern "Grand Slam," which is completed by the U.S. Open in June, the British Open in July, and the PGA Championship in August. ABC has televised the last three of those events since 1966, 1962, and 1965 respectively, and naturally has long coveted and made numerous attempts to obtain rights to the Masters, which, although seemingly "owned" by CBS, has actually always been aired by them on just a year-to-year contractual basis since 1956.

Why have those efforts failed?

Here's a quote from Hord Hardin, one-time United States Golf Association president who became chairman of the Augusta National Golf Club and the Masters in April of 1980, and who runs the event with the same kind of iron hand as his legendary long-time predecessor, Clifford Roberts: "ABC will never get the Masters as long as Roone Arledge is there. He's kooky! He went Hollywood with those funny suits and that dyed hair."

When Hardin was the key figure at the USGA, he had been instrumental in moving the U.S. Open from NBC to ABC, and had unhappy memories of his dealings with Arledge at that time. "He was my best friend in the world when he wanted something, but once that was history, I couldn't even get him to return a telephone call."

It was also Hardin's feeling—and I'm sure a feeling shared by other ultraconservative traditionalists, albeit erroneously—that ABC dictated the terms and conditions of its golf coverage, or at least tried to. No such thing would happen with the Masters, at least as long as Hardin was running the show. Throughout its tenure at Augusta National, CBS has been instructed rather than consulted on many elements of the telecast, from the reduced number of commercials to the style and language of its announcers. ABC Sports has always had some requirements imposed on its telecasts of the U.S. Open by the USGA, but they are nowhere near as stringent as those governing CBS's coverage of the Masters. At Augusta National, all involved with the telecast have to tiptoe around as though making their way through a field of eggs, lest they upset some cherished tradition or blot the tournament's image of noncommercialism. And of course it is mainly tradition and noncommercialism that make the Masters the Masters.

ABC never made any secret of its desire to acquire the Masters, not only because it would give the network the four Grand Slam tournaments, but because of the sheer joy of televising such a prestigious event, and after the death of Roberts I thought we had a chance at it. Roberts' designated successor was Bill Lane, a relatively young and modern-minded businessman from Houston. In order to help it call the shots, the Masters had never gone for top dollar from CBS, and when I met with Lane, I got the feeling that a significant jump in rights fees might have turned the tide for ABC. However, Lane soon became seriously ill and died without having had the opportunity to make much impact on the tournament. Since then, no other network has had a chance at it, and probably won't unless CBS pulls a monumental blunder. And of course, the Masters traditional one-year-only contract for the television rights is a strong safeguard against that.

For many years, ABC was the most prominent network in televising the tournaments of the PGA Tour, with a long history of covering the Bing Crosby National Pro-Am (now known as the AT&T Pebble Beach National Pro-Am), the Hawaiian Open, the

Los Angeles Open, and many others, including the prestigious Tournament Players' Championship and the Tournament of Champions. Despite the fact that its golf ratings have never been big by comparison with those of the major team sports, like the other networks, ABC made money from golf due to the strong support the game attracts from advertisers seeking the attention of high-earning middle-aged men, who constitute the major part of just about every golf tournament's television audience.

But for the miscalculation of the present Tour commissioner, Deane Beman, ABC would still be very prominently involved. Beman's predecessor, Joe Dey, one of the most respected people in golf, had been executive director of the USGA and was well versed in all aspects of golf, particularly in his understanding of the problems television faced in covering the sport. When he left and Beman took over in 1974, Joe asked me to spend time with the new commissioner so that he might come to better understand the mutual concerns and difficulties we faced.

I was happy to do so, and I did my best to explain to Deane about ratings, sales, time periods, production costs, and the like. Beman got fixed in his mind the idea that the PGA Tour should be on one network, in that it would thereby gain impact from continuity of coverage style, plus powerful on-air and print-media promotion. When he brought that idea to ABC Sports, he was talking about our televising twenty-five events a year, or more than half the schedule.

Our answers were that, first, we simply could not accommodate that many events in the hours available to the network for sports, relative to our commitments to other sports; and, second, that we believed golf could not stand that much exposure. But Beman was adamant, even though he got essentially the same response when he took his proposal to NBC. However, at CBS he was met with more enthusiasm, even though CBS also thought twenty-five events was too many. Deane then came back to us, in what he obviously assumed was a stronger bargaining position, and put on the table a proposal for giving eighteen events to CBS while retaining "an ABC affiliation" via the Hawaiian Open, the Glen Campbell-Los Angeles Open, the Tournament of Champions, and the Byron Nelson Golf Classic. The proviso was that the Crosby, the most prominent tour event ABC had been televising, move to CBS.

It wasn't a deal I relished, but it seemed to me better than giving up the PGA Tour altogether, so I suggested to Roone Arledge that we agree to it, provided we got a price break on the four events we retained. Roone balked. He felt strongly that if we lost our best event, the Crosby, to CBS, then we should let the others go as well. I argued that Hawaii, Los Angeles, the T of C, and the Nelson surely were a cut above the average Tour stop, and that by retaining them we'd keep a foot in the door. As it turned out, Beman escalated the rights fees for those four events to such a level that the whole thing became exorbitant in our view, and we passed.

I later learned that Beman and Steve Reid, who was handling the negotiations for the PGA Tour, calculated that our interest in keeping the four events was so great that we'd readily agree to the big boost in rights prices, and were very surprised at our decision. They then became upset when we issued a press release in late 1977 stating that 1978 would be ABC's last year on the PGA Tour, Beman arguing that our announcement damaged his bargaining position with NBC.

In the intervening years, there has been off-and-on dialogue about ABC getting involved, but for a variety of reasons it did not happen until recently when the network became involved once again.

ABC's involvement illustrates how the business of network television golf has come full circle. Back in 1953, the "World Championship of Golf," sponsored by George May, was played at the May-owned Tam O'Shanter Country Club in Chicago. ABC charged May a fee of thirty-two thousand dollars that year for the first national telecast in the United States of a golf tournament, won by Lew Worsham with an eagle on the final hole.

Until relatively recently, the networks paid substantial rights fees for golf tournaments and bore the financial burden of recovering their costs via sales to advertisers. Based on current golf audience levels, however, the networks can't generate from certain events enough advertiser revenue to cover television rights payments, production, and other costs plus a profit. Golf production is extremely expensive, ranging as high as two million dollars for eighteen-hole coverage of the U.S. Open. (ABC first provided eighteen-hole coverage of the U.S. Open at Southern Hills in Tulsa in 1977.)

The networks are once again requiring guaranteed sponsor support for many of the events on national television. This sponsorship revenue, flowing to the networks via the PGA Tour, including the Seniors, and the Ladies Professional Golfers' Association, covers network expenses, enabling them to achieve at least no worse than a break-even financial position. The sponsor is included in the title of the event and receives a specified number of commercial units during the network telecasts. In some instances, the organizing group, with a sponsor on board, will purchase air time from the networks, thus guaranteeing the networks a profit, and are then entitled to all the commercial units in the telecasts in order to cover its financial outlay.

Another trend is evolving—the utilization of outside production companies to provide engineering facilities and manpower more cheaply than the networks, due primarily to the retention of nonunion personnel.

The networks, then, have shifted the financial risks from themselves to the golf organizers, who are charged with developing the vitally important tournament sponsors. This appears to be the wave of the future except for the "majors."

All the networks endure relatively poor ratings for golf, and each has tried a different approach to covering the game in trying to improve them. So far, none has enjoyed any real success.

ABC long ago decided on a more personal type of coverage, doing its commentary essentially in blocks featuring Jim McKay, Jack Whitaker, and Peter Alliss, and concentrating mostly on the golfers in or near the lead. CBS noisily argues that it does golf better than anyone else, but there is nothing particularly distinctive about its coverage, and it is frequently criticized for jumping randomly from player to player without trying to build any kind of theme or coherence into the shows. NBC sends a couple of commentators— "foot soldiers," they have been called—onto the golf course to walk close to the competitors and to get occasional comments from them during regular PGA Tour events. ABC has also assigned commentators, led by former PGA champion Bob Rosburg, to follow play on the ground but not to converse with players during their rounds. I think talking with players during action is intrusive and agree with the organizers of the major championships who do not permit it.

Not the least of the many and unique challenges in televising golf is getting the commentary right—both the personalities and the content—and in that regard ABC was specially blessed for many years by the presence of the late Henry Longhurst. We loved him for his dry English wit and the many hilarious moments he gave us after hours, but he was also—and much more by instinct than training—a great professional. For instance, I'll always remember his three cardinal rules of golf commentary.

The first of these was never to describe anything for the viewer at home unless he or she could see what you were talking about. The second was never to talk during the playing of a shot. The third was, when you don't have anything intelligent to say, don't say anything—just allow for "a few brilliant flashes of silence."

I'm a little at variance with Henry on his first rule, because, when something important is occurring that the camera simply cannot depict, I think an announcer has an obligation to tell his audience about it. However, I'm in total agreement with Henry on the other two rules, and I think his third is an absolute classic.

I first ran across those Longhurstian principles in a piece Alistair Cooke did for *TV Guide* when I was flying to the U.S. Open at Inverness in Toledo, Ohio, in 1979. Jim McKay was seated in front of me, and I tapped him on the shoulder and handed him the article to read. He did so, then handed it back to me without saying a word. I hoped that indicated he had gotten Henry's message.

In 1985, just before our U.S. Open coverage at Oakland Hills in Michigan, I called our announcers together and again reminded them of the sage advice of their late colleague. I had long been concerned about not only the quality but the quantity of conversation during our golf telecasts. In order to have maximum impact, I told the group, we really had to guard more carefully against excessive chatter. Tell the story by saying only what needed to be said, then hush—that was the essence of my pleading. In other words, be selective and restrictive, and cut the idle chatter. It was one of my more interesting sessions with announcers, perhaps most notable for the number of silent stares I got.

Some American viewers don't agree, but I think the inclusion of a British commentator on golf telecasts—as remains the case today at CBS with Ben Wright and ABC with the prescient Peter Alliss—enhances the program. After all, the game evolved in Scotland, and there's a certain quality of insight and feeling in those familiar with its earliest forms that we simply cannot match over here. That's largely why we hired Henry Longhurst. He had done golf commentary for the British Broadcasting Corporation, and proved to be a charming man with an idiosyncratic perspective on the game—and on life—and a brilliant command of the Queen's English. Everyone loved his phraseology, and particularly the curious way (to Americans) he perceived and described things. For example, instead of saying that a putt went in through the back door, Henry would invariably say the ball came in "through the tradesman's entrance." He brought a special flavor and a new dimension to our golf telecasts, even though some viewers found him a trifle stodgy and sometimes difficult to comprehend. The latter problem tended to arise late in the telecasts, since Henry was prone to keep a bottle of rather powerful refreshment with him on the tower, to ward off evil spirits and perhaps the chill of the late afternoons.

Someone once asked comedian George Gobel if he took a little nip before going onstage, and George snapped, "I certainly do! You don't think I'm going out there alone, do you?" It could fairly be said of Henry that he never went into a telecast alone, and everybody involved with the golf shows knew about it. Why was it tolerated? Well, that was simply part of the freight you accepted with this marvelous character, and it really had no adverse effect on the shows—indeed, Henry just "warmed" to the task of telecasting as the day wore on. However, we were wrong to accept Henry's *modus operandi*.

I always tried to attend the major golf championships that we televised, for three reasons. First, I thought it was important to make an appearance in terms of our relationships with the organizing groups—the United States Golf Association, the Royal and Ancient Golf Club of St. Andrews, Scotland, and the Professional Golfers' Association of America. Second, these were significant events in the life of ABC Sports and I believed it was important for me to show the colors with the crew during such times. And then, of course—and perhaps I should have made this the number-one reason—I love the game so much that I probably couldn't have stayed away if I'd had reason to.

It was on such a trip—at the U.S. Open at Hazeltine National Golf Club in Chaska, Minnesota, in 1970—that I first met Henry Longhurst.

As soon as I arrived at the hotel from the airport, I went to my room and freshened up, then headed for the hotel dining room, figuring that's where I'd find the producer, Chuck Howard, and the rest of the ABC people. As I walked across the dining room to join them, my eyes fell on Henry, face down and apparently asleep in a plate of mashed potatoes and assorted other dinner leftovers. It was a scene right out of *Where's Poppa?* in which the late Ruth Gordon, playing George Segal's mother, pulled the same dido. It appeared he had "warmed up" a little too much that evening.

During our coverage of one British Open, Bob Goodrich's assignment one morning was that of—well, let's call it babysitting Henry. ABC was doing the championship on videotape back then, and the plan was to shoot a scene set—to establish our presence at the site of the championship—before recording play during the afternoon, then take the reels back to London for final editing. The completed package would finally be flown to New York, from where it would be aired at the appropriate time.

This is how Goodrich remembers the day:

"My orders were simple: 'Make certain Henry doesn't have any gin before the scene set.' We were to do the piece about noontime, so I kept close to him and he was fine. However, he did slip away from me once, at about eleven, saying he needed a bit of soup, or tea, or something. When I found him with a glass of gin, I thought, 'Oh, shit!' So I told him that John Martin, who was in charge of things, didn't want him to have anything to drink before we taped the scene set. Henry assured me he was just having one little nip, and that's all he had. Everything went 'swimmingly,' as Henry might say, as we did the piece, then off Henry went to Edinburgh Airport for his return to London.

"We kept shooting until maybe five or six o'clock that evening, then jumped in a car and went tearing off to the same airport for our flight to London. When we checked in, we were informed the flight was running fifteen minutes late, so John and I decided to treat ourselves to a cocktail. And, of course, who should be sitting at the bar but Henry Longhurst! And it was then seven o'clock at night! He looked up and said, 'Gentlemen, it's about time for my flight. I'm on the two o'clock, you know.' I'll be damned if he hadn't sat there at that bar and missed the two o'clock, the three, the four, the five, and the six. By the time we got there, he was using two hands to get the glass to his mouth. We managed to get him onto our plane and we all trooped off to London together. I was just a kid, but for as long as I live, I'll treasure my memories of Henry Longhurst. What a wonderful man he was."

One of the truly legendary stories of Henry's "warming" goes back to the U.S. Open of 1969 in Houston, when he and the other members of the team, along with the corporate bigwigs, were staying at the Warwick, a European-style hotel with an abundance of paneling and fancy brass. After dinner one evening, during which Henry had consumed his share of what some people like to refer to as "see-throughs"—that clear balm with the trade name of Tanqueray—he announced to one and all that he was going to retire for the night and, in a somewhat uncertain manner, left the table to repair to his room.

Maybe half an hour later, the other members of the group decided it was time they headed to bed, too, and duly filed out of the dining room on the way to the elevators. Near them was a telephone booth, and in it they spied the rumpled form of their English colleague, slumped down and soundly in the arms of Morpheus. One of the group gently nudged the great man awake, whereupon Henry lifted his head and with a growling sort of harrumph proclaimed, "The lift doesn't seem to be working."

He had missed the elevator by a chip shot.

The most amusing commentators today on American golf telecasts are NBC's Lee Trevino and the former PGA champion and long-time ABC analyst, Dave Marr. Like the rest of us who worked with Henry, Dave had a special fondness for the crusty Englishman. They had met several times before, but Dave wasn't sure Henry remembered him, so during one of the early telecasts they did together in the British Isles, David approached Henry, stuck out his hand and said, "Hi, Henry, I'm Dave Marr." All Henry said was, "Of course you are."

Despite many Longhurstisms of that caliber on the air as well as off, I still think Dave Marr came up with the best one-liner ever during one of our Hawaiian Open telecasts. Raymond Floyd was in the lead, but had pulled his tee shots to the left on both the fifteenth and sixteenth holes. The seventeenth was a treacherous hole with the Pacific Ocean licking the shore from tee to green, and as Floyd stood on the tee needing to protect a one-shot lead, Jim McKay observed:

"Well, David, he's going to have to be careful not to put it to the left on *this* hole." Quick as a cat, Marr shot back, "Yeah, the next drop area is Guam."

Almost as good was Dave's line when Johnny Miller was putting together that fabulous string of victories at the very outset of the winter tour in the early seventies, and McKay observed that Miller had "been hot." "Yeah," Marr cracked, "you might say he birdied January and February."

The PGA Championship victory in 1965 was Marr's crowning achievement in golf, and his memories of it capture the essence of the man's insightfulness and warm sense of humor:

"The final day, I was playing in a threesome with Jack Nicklaus and Gardner Dickinson. I had a two-shot lead going to the eighteenth hole, but it's a long par four and I'd made six on it the day before and I was choking like a dog. I mean, when you're chewing gum and you can't make just one little ball of spit, that tells you you're choking. I put my tee shot into the left-hand fairway bunker, and there's a big lake down there in front of the green, and I just couldn't take a chance, so I decided to lay up short. Billy Casper had made a pretty good run that day but he was already finished, and I knew I could make a bogey and beat him.

"But here I was, getting very, very nervous. It suddenly occurred to me, 'David, you can win the PGA.' I mean, this is no rinky-dink tournament, you understand, this was my chance. You begin to think all sorts of things, and I was just a lit-tle bit scared.

"I had won tournaments before, so I knew where the winner's circle was. I remember winning the Greenbrier Open in 1960, my first victory on the PGA Tour, by seven shots, with 67-67-67, then a closing 63. That's not what you'd call stumbling in, you know. I remembered the feeling I had then, and also how Sam Snead walked right by me and never said a word. I mean, not *one* word. Here we were at his home course, and he passed me like a freight train passing a hobo and never said, 'Nice going, kid,' or 'How's your mother?' or anything. Just kept right on walking.

"But this one, the PGA, was altogether different. I can't say I was even aware of the presence of television cameras. I felt like I had Vaseline on my hands, but somehow I pulled myself together, swallowed real hard a few times, and took out the nine-iron and hit what I thought was an all right shot. And then I heard the roar of the crowd. When I looked up, I saw someone— I guess it was Byron Nelson—on the television tower with his hands held about three or four feet apart. And I said to myself, 'Oh, my God, I've knocked it stiff.' And indeed I had. It was about four feet from the flag.

"The gallery had been walking where Nicklaus hit his second shot and he had a terrible place to chip from, and chipping has never been Jack's long suit. I was figuring that, even if he got down in two, which I doubted he could do from that lie, all I'd have to do was two-putt for the title. Well, let me tell you, Nicklaus hit the most beautiful chip shot you ever saw. He pitched down that hill and I swear to God I thought it was going in the hole. My eyes blew up like a frog's. But about four feet from the hole, Jack's ball straightened out and went over the hole and stopped about one foot away. My nerves were just about shot, but I managed to make my putt and win the PGA by two. And the first guy over to shake my hand was Jack Nicklaus. He said, 'I'm so happy for you, Dave, that's great.' That was my only major, but it gave me some memories I'll never forget."

Dave Marr didn't even get interviewed on ABC that day because we were right up against deadline and had to go off the air before Chris Schenkel or Byron Nelson had a chance to talk to him. However, he's been on ABC cameras hundreds of times since. Dave was first used as a fairway reporter in 1970, then was promoted to the top analyst's spot when Roone Arledge decided not to renew the contract of the legendary Byron Nelson.

Marr took some flak when that happened, and here's how he remembers it:

"I went to Fort Worth to see Byron, and told him I was catching hell from some nice people who thought I somehow had something to do with his not being on ABC's golf telecasts any more. Nothing could have been further from the truth. Byron has always been my idol. We're fellow Texans, God never put a nicer man on this earth, and the last thing I'd ever do would be to hurt him.

"He just smiled that warm smile of his and told me not to worry, that he had made a mistake. He said he had written a letter to Arledge, telling him he'd prefer to do just the major tournaments. Byron told me he had been going to more funerals than he wanted to, saying farewells to old pals, and that he wanted to enjoy life more and to cut back on his traveling, so he had told Roone he didn't want to do any of the lesser telecasts. But he had never heard one word back from the man. Byron just never got another contract, and that was it, and I know it hurt his feelings very badly. But at least he knows I wasn't a part of easing him out."

Marr is right about the way that happened, and also absolutely correct in his appraisal of Byron Nelson as one of the most decent and likable men ever to grace the game of golf. He added a great deal of prestige and insight to our telecasts over the years but did have his own peculiar manner of speaking at times. Once, when

Byron was working the tournament named in his honor—the Byron Nelson Golf Classic at the Preston Trail Golf Club in Dallas—Chris Schenkel pointed out that Byron had to be very proud of the tournament, and particularly the volunteers who gave so generously of their time to help make the event a success.

"That's right, Chris," said Byron. "I sure am proud. Do you know that we have six hundred men volunteers working on the tournament? And that's not counting the women."

ABC also once fired Dave Marr, albeit only temporarily. It happened during the U.S. Women's Open at Winged Foot in 1972.

From the beginning, it's been a rule at ABC Sports that announcers are to show up at least one day prior to any telecast in which they are involved, and on major telecasts much earlier. When Friday arrived, Dave Marr didn't. It turned out that the producer of the telecast—a man who left ABC not long after that—neglected to inform Marr that his presence would be required. When we finally tracked him down, Dave was in San Francisco doing a personal appearance, totally unaware that he was supposed to be at Winged Foot. Not to worry, he assured us, he'd catch the next "red-eye" east, grab a quick nap, and tear out to the golf course, which he did. However, the telecast wasn't a good one, and when we asked why, the producer offered a variety of excuses, including the late arrival of Mr. Marr.

Chuck Howard called Marr that night and, on Roone's orders, fired him off the telecast.

Dave remembers:

"My wife Tally and I were to leave Monday morning for the British Open. I was going to play in it anyway, and assumed I would still be doing the telecast at Muirfield. I figured that while I was over there I'd see Arledge and tell him what happened, and he was practically the first person I ran into when I arrived. So I said, 'Roone, I have to talk with you. There's something I have to explain to you.' He was very cordial, and said, 'Anytime—just anytime you want. Be glad to talk with you.' I ended up doing the British Open telecast. A year and a half later, after many, many telephone calls and many, many messages [to Arledge], all of them unanswered, my wife and I were in New York and somehow arranged to have dinner with the Arledges. Just the four of us, after which we went back to their apartment and watched 'Monday Night Football.'

"After the game was over, Roone turned to me and said, 'Now tell me the story of what happened there at the Women's Open,' so I did. When I got through, he said, 'Damn, I wish you'd told me that before.' Tally and I just looked at each other in absolute astonishment.

"Another time, I was playing in the Crosby and Frank Gifford came out to help with the telecast, and was out on the Pebble Beach course to follow me around. When we finished, we looked up and saw Roone on the balcony of a corner suite overlooking Carmel Bay, watching the action. Gifford suggested that we go up and see him. I wasn't too fond of the idea since I didn't know Roone all that well—still don't, as a matter of fact—but Frank said it would be a good move. So as soon as I signed my scorecard, we headed up to Arledge's room.

"We knocked on the door to his suite, but nothing happened. So Frank knocked a little louder, but still nothing. We heard the telephone ringing, but no one picked it up. It was cold that day and Frank had his ski gloves with him, and as he put them on, I thought he was going to beat the door down. Unbelievable. Still nothing. And we'd just *seen* him there! Finally, we gave up.

"Later that night, ABC was having a reception for sponsors at the lodge at Pebble Beach, and when we got there, Gifford headed straight for Arledge with me following along, and immediately told him the story of what happened, and how frustrated we were at not getting an answer at the door when we'd just seen him there moments before. Pipe in hand, Arledge shrugged, and with a look of great puzzlement on his countenance said, 'I wonder where I went? Beats the hell out of me.' Frank and I just looked at each other, then walked away. I guess there was nothing else to say."

Dave Marr is a friend of both Chuck Howard, ABC's top golf producer for many years, and of the man who shoved Chuck into the dolphins' lagoon at the Kahala Hilton Hotel in Honolulu, Steve Reid, a former touring pro who later became television coordinator for the PGA Tour. The two by then had had more than one run-in, it being Chuck's feeling that Reid—whether he was speaking for Commissioner Deane Beman or himself—was meddling too heavily in ABC's golf production.

Marr recalls the final resolution:

"I like both of them, but each has a volatile personality, and you simply cannot put Mr. Nitro and Mr. Glycerine together. We had just finished the windup show of the Hawaiian Open and there had been some unhappiness with it. Chuck Howard and Jim Jennett had just come out of a meeting when they ran into Reid.

"Chuck quickly warned Steve not to bother telling him anything about the telecast, and of course with that Steve felt absolutely compelled to tell Chuck a thing or two. They were screaming at each other. Before you could count to ten, Reid had pushed Chuck into the lagoon full of dolphins. Chuck came up sputtering, and all he could talk about afterward was what the dunking might have done to his expensive wristwatch. It was a wild, funny scene."

Dave Marr is the man who told Roone Arledge, when the then president of ABC Sports once wondered why golf didn't attract a bigger television audience, "Roone, golf is a game to be played—not watched."

I guess the ratings are the proof of that, but nevertheless ABC's golf coverage from the outset was full of glorious highlights, rich in great personalities and characters, and filled with fun—especially for someone who loves the grand old game as much as I do. And here's perhaps my favorite single story from a vault of indelibly happy memories of our televising of the game.

In one of our earlier years of doing the Walker Cup golf match, the competition was held in Sandwich, England. Joe Aceti, now a successful director at CBS, was then a production assistant on the ABC team. The seaside course in Sandwich had no trees, but when Joe got back to New York and submitted his expense account, one item read: "$100—Tree trimming around the course for better camera coverage."

Stan Frankle, who was in charge of our financial affairs at that time, couldn't wait to call Aceti on the carpet, and as soon as he had him seated in his office, shoved the expense form in his face.

"It was absolutely clear from the telecast that there is not a single tree on that golf course," said Frankle, sternly. "And you have a one-hundred-dollar item here for tree trimming. Just how do you explain that?"

The mark of a good director is his ability to quickly handle problems that crop up. That day, Joe Aceti showed great qualifications when, without batting an eye, he told Frankle, "My guy did one hell of a job, didn't he?"

19

AN UNLIKELY
SMASH HIT

*Bowling Us Over
with Ratings and Dollars
Year After Year*

For a number of years now, Nelson—everyone calls him Bo—Burton, Jr., and Billy Packer have had this running argument about the relative popularity of bowling and college basketball. Burton, the long-time color commentator for ABC on the "Professional Bowlers Tour," claims that bowling is considerably more popular than regular-season college basketball among the television viewing audience, and he's willing to bet serious money on it. Determination of the bet would be for Burton and Packer, the CBS college basketball analyst, to walk through an airport and count how many people recognize each of them.

My advice to Billy Packer is, keep your money in your pocket. The truth is, bowling on ABC on Saturday afternoon outdraws college basketball telecasts on CBS and NBC, and just about anything else the other networks throw against it. For instance, should someone offer to wager you that the Masters golf tournament on CBS on a Saturday afternoon in April, with the dogwood and azalea in perfect bloom and the stars of the game stumbling through "Amen Corner," will rate higher than the "Pro Bowlers Tour" event on ABC, call me and I'll take half your action. The bowlers will beat the golfers hands down almost every time.

Why is bowling such a hit on television? There are three

reasons. First, the format, created by former ABC producer Ned Steckel, is an excellent one: five finalists, a one-game knockout, and if you keep winning, you keep advancing. Second, the tournaments are televised in the first quarter of the year when more sets are in use. Third, people who bowl—and there are more than 60 million of them—love to watch the professionals, in part because they recognize that the pros are much like the fellow next door: solid, down-to-earth people who had to work hard for what they have achieved.

Believe me, I have some ambivalent feelings about the fact that bowling kicks golf in the ratings battle. Golf is one of my great passions in life. I like to watch it and I love to play it. One of the most gratifying things I accomplished in my final year at ABC Sports was laying the groundwork for the deal that brought Jack Nicklaus aboard as part of the network's golf team. But the hard fact is that in 1986, when Nicklaus so dramatically won the Masters for the sixth time at the age of forty-six, the tournament achieved only a 7+ rating on CBS.

Unlike its experiences in golf, there has never been any question about ABC's involvement in bowling. It began in 1962, and I have a special feeling about the series—other than "Wide World of Sports," college football, and the NFL, which began its run the same year, the longest continuing sports series on network television—because I was a production assistant the first season the "Pro Bowlers Tour" was on ABC. It's not just pure luck that all the problems we have faced with the series can be counted on one hand, and were minor ones at that. The main reason for this is Eddie Elias, who founded the Professional Bowlers Association and through the years has kept a hand in it and seen to it that the image of the sport and its participants have remained outstanding. Eddie has been particularly good at comprehending the problems of television, rather than always one-sidedly favoring his own group, as often happens with sports administrators. Also espousing that philosophy is the PBA commissioner, Joe Antenora, and Frank Esposito, the PBA television coordinator for over twenty-five years.

Another reason is the personalities of the bowlers themselves. The Don Carters, Dick Webers, and Earl Anthonys of the world are a joy to deal with, decent and honest people who remain grateful to be involved however successful they become. In an era of spoiled athletes, the professional bowlers still think in terms of "we" and still care most about what's good for the sport overall. A special member of that fraternity was Billy Welu, who performed so effectively as expert commentator on our PBT telecasts until his untimely death.

Through the years, the bowling show is one we've been able to use for the baptism of our young producers and directors, in that the program is well established, with a rigid format that limits both innovation and opportunities to make mistakes. The action is concentrated on two lanes that we used to call "the TV pair," but which now are called "the championship pair." That came about in part because of my feeling that the first term suggested the sport was being subjugated to television. Young producers and directors can get their feet wet here before graduating to more difficult shows—or they can flop under the pressure of being on live network television for ninety minutes. Helpful to them is the feeling of "family" on the tour, embracing not only the bowlers but the television crew as well.

Don Ohlmeyer was one of the bright young producer-directors who paid his dues on the show:

"I was scared shitless when I first went out there. The technical director on the series then was a wonderful guy named Walt Kubilus, who had been doing the show for years and years. The way he treated me showed the spirit that existed at ABC in those days—and I'm not talking just about inside the sports division but in engineering and everywhere else, you name it. I'd say, 'Take three,' but Walt knew better, so he'd just punch up camera two, which was the shot we should have had on the air. I mean, the man would just not *allow* me to make a mistake. This went on for the first four weeks. I'd be calling for one camera, and he'd just punch up another one, and invariably the one he chose was the right one. Finally, when he figured I was ready to do it on my own, he let me go and I was calling the shots and really being the director of the show. Most of the time after that, I guess, I managed to call for the correct shots.

"It was unbelievable, the spirit and the sense of family that

UP CLOSE AND PERSONAL

existed. It was real fellowship. You know, crews can kill you if they want to, and Walt Kubilus could have killed me. It's staggering to think of the number of young producers and directors who have come through that bowling series and won their spurs. It was a great experience."

Chris Schenkel has been the perfect host for the Professional Bowlers Tour since the beginning. He is knowledgeable about the sport, but, more importantly, Chris is a warm and friendly person and one people implicitly trust. Like the bowlers, he's unspoiled, and the viewers recognize that and like him because of it.

Viewers have also liked the Professional Bowlers Tour, helping to make it one of the greatest success stories in the history of television sports.

20

OLYMPIC SHENANIGANS

*Unscheduled Fun and Games
Behind the Scenes*

ABC's televising of the 1988 Winter Olympics from Calgary—the extravaganza purchased for the unholy price of $309 million—marked the tenth time it has covered an Olympiad, a number unapproached by the other two networks combined. I was involved in one way or another in all ten of those telecasts, and they have left me with some of the most indelible memories of my more than a quarter of a century in sports television.

For instance, who could ever forget Bob Beamon's 1968 leap of twenty-nine feet two and one-half inches in the long jump, a stunning accomplishment that is still the record. Beamon himself couldn't believe it then, saying to everyone around him, "Tell me I'm not dreaming!" And believe it or not, ABC almost missed it! Beamon was to make his attempt in the early morning hours before a practically empty stadium in Mexico City. We simply were not prepared, and had just barely gotten our cameras and tape machines ready as the American jumper took off.

Centuries ago, the Olympics were suspended because they had become a political forum. No matter how lofty the goals and how exalted the principles on which they were built, they have been increasingly politically tainted in recent years, and seem to be getting worse and worse in that regard as time passes. In 1968, some of the significance of Beamon's achievement was lost because of the black-power salutes exhibited by American sprinters Tommie Smith and John Carlos when they stood to receive their gold and silver medals after the 200-meter dash. The architect of that protest was the sociologist Dr. Harry Edwards, who some twenty years later was hired by commissioner Peter Ueberroth to try to work more blacks into the fabric of major league baseball, including both front office and managerial positions.

I was the producer when Howard Cosell interviewed Tommie Smith after the clenched-fist incident. In the middle of the interview, I suggested to Howard through his earpiece that he ask Smith if he were proud to be an American. Smith hedged, allowing that he was proud of his citizenship but citing the imperfections of his native land.

The 1968 Winter Games were held in Grenoble, France, where Jean Claude Killy and Peggy Fleming made Olympic history. Killy swept all three alpine skiing gold medals before his countrymen, and Fleming continued in the tradition of Tenley Albright and Carol Heiss by winning the gold medal in ladies' figure skating.

The 1964 Olympics brought us Terry McDermott, the Michigan barber with the flying skates, a man of great humility and talent and one of the unlikeliest heroes in my Olympic memories. That was the same year that Billy Kidd and Jimmy Heuga distinguished themselves—and American skiing—at Innsbruck, Kidd winning the silver and Heuga the bronze in the slalom.

Not until 1984 would an American garner the gold in the downhill, and Bill Johnson not only did it, but brazenly predicted his victory ahead of time! In that same Olympiad, twins Phil and Steve Mahre captured the gold and the silver in the slalom, and diminutive Scott Hamilton, who makes even Jim McKay look tall, took the gold in figure-skating.

Four years before, the U.S. hockey team's "miracle on ice," along with Eric Heiden's five golds in speed-skating, had won a permanent place in my personal Olympic scrapbook.

The 1972 Summer Olympics in Munich had treble portions of charm and chaos. There was miler Jim Ryun, an almost mystical figure who held the world stage in three Olympiads, yet never won a gold, tripping and falling in a heat and thus unable to qualify for the 1500-meter finals. In stark contrast to our image of Russians, a seventeen-year-old bundle of brightness named Olga Korbut smiled brilliantly all the way to three gold medals in gymnastics. Swimmer Mark Spitz won a phenomenal seven medals, and I'll always remember the skinny kid in the floppy fatigue cap, Dave Wottle, of Bowling Green, Ohio, coming from behind to win the gold at 800 meters.

These were the Games when ABC's long-time alpine skiing expert and jack-of-all-trades Bob Beattie called a volleyball game involving Poland and East Germany. He impeccably identified players on both teams. After we went off the air, everyone in the control room complimented Bob and asked how he was able to identify the players so easily. Bob quickly responded: "It was easy. I made up the names." (The story has become part of ABC Olympic lore, although Beattie claims he was only kidding.)

Geoff Mason, appointed executive producer of ABC Sports in 1988, was working on our Munich telecasts and left a wake-up call with the hotel operator for 7:30 A.M. Just to make sure he got up on time, in case he fell asleep again, he asked the young lady to also call him at 8:00 A.M. She replied, "I understand, sir, but which call do you want first?"

Then came the nightmare of eleven members of the Israeli team being gunned down in cold blood by Arab terrorists, a memory that must never go away. That tragedy made the rest of the world realize what all of us at ABC already knew, that Jim McKay was uniquely talented, with a marvelous capacity for capturing the essence of a story or a person and relating it in a thorough and professional manner. Before the massacre of the Israeli team members, Chris Schenkel was anchoring the telecasts, but it was Roone's opinion that McKay was more suited for the role once events unfolded as they did. And more than any other factor, it was his work in Munich that catapulted McKay to real prominence.

Jim McKay agrees that the Munich tragedy changed his career: "No question, that was a major turning point. It's a shame it took that terrible tragedy to do it. I'd done 'Wide World of Sports' for eleven years up to that point, and had already won an Emmy or two, but the major attention was not there. After that, there was a huge difference in the way people recognized me. To this day, maybe ten or twelve times a year someone will come up to me in an airport and comment on Munich and say something nice about the way I handled the story.

"Actually, I don't think I've ever changed the way I approach or handle a story. In Munich, it never occurred to me to change gears, nor to say to myself that I was going to cover it in some different way. Basically, reporting is reporting, whether the stories are exciting, or funny, or terrible, as was the case at Munich. It's an event I'll never forget, and one that just happened to have a major influence on my career."

Four years later, when ABC was preparing for the Olympics in Montreal, we decided to put together as a preview show a two-hour special called "Tragedy and Triumph—The Olympic Experience," with McKay as host. About two-thirds of it was devoted to the normal previewing of the athletes and such, with the other third devoted to the massacre at Munich. Don Ohlmeyer, who put it together, called it his most important memory in sports television:

"It gave me the best feeling I've ever had in my life. The show really was a tribute to the people who had lost their lives. I became so wrapped up in it, I couldn't think of anything else for months. The show wound up winning an Emmy in the same category as the Olympics themselves.

"One morning when we were in Montreal, we got a call from one of the Israeli coaches, who asked that his group be permitted to look at the segment. We arranged for a screening, and they came over, maybe half a dozen, one morning about seven o'clock, including a girl whose coach had been murdered. At the end of the piece, which was about forty minutes long, everyone in the screening room was crying. That, to me, is what this business is all about—or at least what it can be about at times. It's the best feeling this business has ever given me."

At those Montreal games, gold medal winners Sugar Ray Leonard, and the Spinks brothers, Leon and Michael, were launched to fame and eventual world professional titles, with

Leonard's astounding upset victory in 1987 over Marvelous Marvin Hagler climaxing his brilliant career. Bruce Jenner of the United States won the decathlon, as American Bill Toomey had done in heroic fashion eight years before, and the fourteen-year-old tot from Rumania, Nadia Comaneci, brought back memories of Olga Korbut, recording seven perfect scores in winning three gold medals. Those two little girls from the Iron Curtain countries and their teammates lit such a spark for gymnastics in America that eight years later in Los Angeles a bouncy West Virginia girl named Mary Lou Retton would win the gold, an achievement that most would have regarded as impossible in the Korbut-Comaneci days.

These were the games in which Carl Lewis won four gold medals in track, tying the legendary Jesse Owens; in which American Greg Louganis won both golds in diving; in which Mary Decker Slaney collided with Zola Budd and saw her hopes for a gold at 3,000 meters go a glimmering; in which some of us were persuaded to take a more critical look at ourselves, and determined, if just for a while, not to complain so much about our lot because of the indomitable spirit and courage of Jeff Blatnick who won the gold in Greco-Roman wrestling despite the fact he was suffering from Hodgkin's disease.

When the Winter Olympic Games returned to Innsbruck, Austria, in 1976, Dorothy Hamill so captured the hearts of everyone that millions of women around the world immediately aspired to a similar hairstyle. But surely the most stirring achievement of those games was Franz Klammer's frantic downhill tear to a gold medal. He had to defeat Bernhard Russi of Switzerland, and did so by one-third of a second!

Long-time ABC director Andy Sidaris: "No question about it, that for me was the single most exciting event in the history of sports television. It was just absolutely breathtaking. Chuck Howard was producing and I was directing, and when Klammer got ready to start his run, I said to the guys in the truck, 'Now, you assholes, you better pay attention, because this could be the goddamnedest thing you'll ever see in your whole life. This guy is either gonna get the gold or he's gonna kill himself, so be on your toes and give me the best effort you have.' Well, there isn't a person who saw that run who could ever forget it. I'll never see the likes of it again as long as I live."

The 1976 Innsbruck Winter Olympics were extremely significant for ABC. This was the first time that the Winter Games would be extensively covered in prime time, with twenty-six and one-half hours devoted to the Games during evening hours in addition to our weekend daytime and late night coverage. Our prime-time rating average was a solid 21.7 and we garnered an impressive 34 share of the audience, which surprised many in the industry who had doubted that the Games would receive such viewer attention. These numbers helped propel ABC's prime-time programming to second place among the three networks during the 1975–76 season, which led to ABC becoming the number-one-rated network the following year for the first time in its history.

And just think, all those never-to-be-forgotten experiences might have gone out the window when ABC did its first Olympiad in 1964. Chet Simmons remembered a major hurdle that nearly was not cleared:

"In the end, the 1964 Olympics really helped establish ABC Sports, but they almost didn't get on the air. For some reason, the Austrians decided not to honor our credentials. Here we were, hundreds of us, over there with tons of equipment, and suddenly we were stymied. Nobody could get to the places they had to go, and the Austrians were being very stubborn about it. So some days before the Games were to open, I had no option but to go to the man in charge of accreditation, and I told him that if we did not get the kind of access we needed in order to do the show, then we would just pull out. The man stared at me a moment or two, then said, 'Mr. Simmons, then may I suggest that you just take all your people and go home.' Wow, did he call my bluff! After that we sat down and worked things out—thank God. Sometimes you think that because you're network television you have the strength of the ages, but this was one of those times when another man had a lot more clout than any television network."

There had been problems long before that. When ABC was first developing plans for coverage of those Winter Olympics, Roone Arledge set up a dinner meeting with the head of the Innsbruck Organizing Committee, a fellow named Friedl Wolfgang, at which he explained in great detail what we planned to cover and how we intended to do it. As the dinner ended, it seemed to Roone that Professor Wolfgang had grasped everything that had been talked about, although he had said very little, until, as the Austrian rose and stuck out his hand for Arledge to shake, he said, "As I leave you, I just want to say hello." The man hadn't understood one damn thing that Arledge had talked about! These were the Games where Olympic satellite coverage was born as we televised live a brief portion, about fifteen minutes, of the closing ceremonies from Austria. A longer transmission was not possible since a satellite in those days was not fixed in the sky and could only be used when it was in position to receive a television signal. Our coverage from Innsbruck aired via black and white video-tape, which was sent back to New York City by plane from Europe. We had technical facilities to feed our programs from Idlewild Airport, now John F. Kennedy International, in case the tapes didn't make it to the transmission studio on time. (Larry Kamm, now one of ABC Sports' leading directors, and I worked together in the studio as production assistant and producer, respectively, during these first ABC-televised Olympic Games.)

Four years later, we were lucky to be able to function at all in Mexico City. Our experience there, from beginning to end, had to be the worst in our history—perhaps in the history of television sports.

Most of us were staying at the Del Angel Hotel, which, we were told, had been built especially for us—although Andy Sidaris claims it was really built to give Mexico a full measure of revenge for all the border skirmishes the United States had won years before.

Having worked far into the previous night, to complete a "Wide World" show, I arrived in Mexico City dog-tired, wanting only to pile into bed and get some shut-eye. But that simply was not possible because the hotel was not completely finished. Finally, I was just about dozing off when I became aware of a shadowy form on the porch just outside my room. As I opened my eyes and sat up, the figure opened the sliding door to my room, walked in carrying a ladder, closed the sliding door, strode across the room without saying a word, and went out the door and into the hall. I never saw that character again, but it was still difficult to sleep. The telephone in the hallway rang off and on all through the night, every night. One of us would always eventually answer it, but not once did any of us get a response from the other end. Finally, one of our associate directors, Bernie Hoffman, solved the problem by yanking the phone cord out of the wall.

I had one other problem—no toilet seat!

One morning, producer Chuck Howard left a wakeup call for 7:30 A.M., never got it, but woke up anyway about 7:25. Not being able to count on accidentally waking up at the right time each day, he called the telephone operator and explained that he hadn't gotten his 7:30 wakeup call, and here it was now almost 8 A.M. "I'm sorry, Señor Howard," said the sweet voice at the other end of the line. "Please hang up and we'll call you right back. Okay?"

Announcer Bud Palmer had been in the hotel for a week when, after a particularly tedious day, he stopped at the desk and asked the clerk for his room key. He asked Bud his name. Bud told him. The clerk informed him that no such person was registered in the hotel. Bud demanded his key, and, after a long argument, ran out of patience, jumped over the desk, and pointed out his name in the hotel register. Finally convinced, the clerk gave Bud his key.

Tony Triolo, long-time *Sports Illustrated* photographer who was working for ABC at the time, told the hotel's laundress one morning that he wanted the starch taken out of the cuffs and collars of his shirts. When he got the shirts back, there was no starch in the cuffs, nor in the collars. Nor could there have been, because there were neither cuffs nor collars on the shirts. Tony was heard to say, "If you don't replace my shirts, I'm going to dynamite your laundry."

Triolo also had a problem with his suits. He wanted them dry-cleaned but the laundry washed them instead. When Tony asked to be compensated for his ruined suits, the man from the laundry said it cost him more to wash the suits than clean them and he resisted paying. Triolo said, "You have a half hour to pay me," went to his room, and, when a half hour had elapsed, threw a chair and then a television set out of his window. Then he got paid.

Late one afternoon a group of our people gathered for a cocktail, including expert commentator Parry O'Brien, the shot-putter, and his wife. Mrs. O'Brien soon decided to return to their room to change clothes for dinner, but after a while word arrived that she was trapped in an elevator. She was indeed—stuck between floors, along with two Mexican workmen who were carrying the biggest and most heavily loaded garbage cans imaginable. As everyone raced frantically to try to find someone to repair the elevator, Andy Sidaris was told that since it was Sunday and the Lord's Day the man assigned to take care of the elevators was home with his family and could not be disturbed.

Someone then located a metal rod about the size of a broomstick, enabling Parry O'Brien to take matters into his own hands. As some pushed and others pulled, O'Brien, with his great strength, pried open the doors, put his legs against the sides, ripped off a part of one of the doors, and thereby released his wife.

The toilets worked about as well as the elevators, the showers only sporadically. The floors, however, were beautifully waxed. Andy Sidaris knows:

"I'd been on the twelfth floor at a little get-together a couple of days before the Games and decided to walk a couple of floors down to my room. I'd already learned that waiting for an elevator might take a year or two. I started down the stairs, but there were no handrails to hold onto and my feet hit that fresh wax and I went ass-over-teakettle all the way to the bottom, fifteen steps in all.

"Once in bed, I couldn't sleep. There were about eight roads coming into the center of a spoke where the hotel was located. Horns were honking; tires were screeching; my left wrist was throbbing. Then at about four in the morning, I heard this god-awful screaming in the hall. I jumped up and yanked open the door, and there in the hallway was Julie Barnathan [head of engineering for ABC] standing half in and half out of the elevator. He had every piece of luggage he owned with him, including one small case that he was holding in his teeth, and he was swearing like a Marine drill instructor. I don't know that I've ever seen anyone madder.

"Julie's toilet had overflowed, water was ankle deep in his room, the hotel operator wouldn't respond to his emergency call, and he was getting the hell and gone out of his room. But I couldn't worry about him, because my wrist was absolutely killing me. Finally, at about dawn, I found a doctor, got some X rays, and found that my wrist was broken in four places. I made up my mind that if I were ever to get a decent night's sleep and function as a director on the Olympic Games telecasts, I damn well had to find another hotel.

"For weeks we'd been hearing that every hotel room was booked, but we did some checking and found out that there were rooms available at the Camino Real, a very fine joint. I had the doctor write me an excuse and I checked into the Camino Real. Roone had been hearing all the complaints about the other dump and had issued strict orders that no one was to move, with the rider that anyone who did would be shipped back to New York. I was willing to take that chance. Besides, what did Arledge know about the troubles at that fleabag? Hell, he was staying at some fancy place [the El Presidente] well away from the noisy area in a suite so big you could have played the Cotton Bowl in it, with seven thousand cut flowers, living on champagne and caviar while all his guys were living like pigs! But I really didn't think he'd send me back. After all, I had done every survey with Chuck Howard, and you were talking seven thousand camera positions!

"The Camino Real was great and I had to rub it into the other directors and producers just a little. I walked into the room where they were and told them good-bye, then I said, 'And by the way, boys, I'm really pissed. Today, the guy only left a dozen red roses in my room, and they had promised me two dozen long-stemmed yellow roses.' And out I walked. And I loved every minute of it."

The accommodations were vastly improved at Montreal in 1976, but getting there hadn't been a stroll in the park. The Montreal Games were extremely attractive in that they would be held in a terrific city on the North American continent, and much of the telecasts would be live, thus all three American networks were red-hot for the rights. Roone Arledge and I finally cemented the ABC deal in the middle of the night.

We had set up a meeting in New York with Paul Desrochers, who headed the negotiating committee for the Montreal organizing group, and were to meet him at the Quebec government house in Rockefeller Plaza. We got there on time, but there was no sign of Desrochers. After waiting twenty minutes or so, we decided that the meeting had either slipped his mind or he had been unavoidably detained, so we left a note with the security guard and took off. That foul-up led to a later meeting in Montreal with Desrochers and two other members of his committee where things went so well that at about one in the morning we came to an agreement and shook hands. I still have the notes I took that night. I wrote: "25 million dollars, November 18, 1972, 12:55 A.M."

The only snag was that Desrochers and his people wanted a confirming letter from us by eleven the next morning. There we were, in the middle of the night in a suite at the Queen Elizabeth Hotel in Montreal, with no secretary and no secretarial service available. I called the front desk and talked someone into letting us borrow a typewriter, then got some carbon paper from the hotel offices and sat down to type up the deal on hotel stationery. I had called one of ABC's lawyers, Alan Morris, and gotten him out of bed so he could help formulate the proper language for the contract. The other networks, thankfully, remained sound asleep.

Roone paced the floor nervously as I attempted to type up the agreement, but I hadn't spent much time at the keyboard since my student days working for the Dartmouth paper and it was slow going. Roone got so jittery he couldn't bear to watch me, so he went out and got us some breakfast—scrambled eggs and coffee. When I finally finished the contract, it was daylight. We read it, slept a few hours, delivered the document, and had the American television rights to the 1976 Olympic Games securely in our pockets. Then the screaming began, both from CBS and NBC and from the media and politicians in Canada. Desrochers was a member of the Liberal Party in Quebec, and someone started the ridiculous story that ABC had given the Liberal Party $5 million in cash under the table.

It was decided that Arledge would have to place his hand on a Bible and sign an affidavit swearing that there had been no hanky-panky. The only Bible they could find was written in French. Roone then jumped into the act, saying, "How do I know this is a *real* Bible?" I wondered how in the hell anyone could have located an "artificial" Bible, especially on such short notice. And wouldn't you know it, someone suggested there be another affidavit attesting to the authenticity of the Bible we finally used.

There were some real shenanigans, too, about the awarding of the television rights for the 1980 Games, the summer ones in Moscow and the winter ones in Lake Placid. Our original offer for Lake Placid was for $8 million, which was agreed to at the Innsbruck Games in 1976 where we negotiated the deal. However, concerned that the International Olympic Committee might not approve an $8 million deal, we boosted our commitment to $10 million. The IOC and the Lake Placid Organizing Committee then came back and wanted still more money, so I went to see Elton Rule, then president of ABC, and told him the deal had now gone from $10 million to $11.5 million.

Elton was suspicious, and asked me, "Now, Jim, is this going to be the end of it?"

I couldn't guarantee him that it was, because NBC and CBS were screaming that the awarding of the rights had been rigged, and, sensitive to their protests about not having had a fair chance to bid, the Olympic people set up another meeting in Paris. All three networks showed up, and we went to $15.5 million, which secured the rights.

Had it not been for the stubbornness of the Soviets, we would have coughed up $125,000 more. The start of that historic hockey final between the U.S. and the USSR was scheduled for 5:30 P.M., but we had made an agreement with the Lake Placid

Organizing Committee—Bob Allen was in charge of the hockey
—that if the two countries met in the medal round, the game would
be available to us in prime time, from 8 P.M. on. The International
Ice Hockey Federation people informed us it would require an
additional rights payment of $125,000 to accomplish that, which,
no question, was out-and-out blackmail. However, Roone and I
decided the game was important enough to fork over the extra
money. But when the matter was put to the Soviets, they had a
one-word reply: "*Nyet.*"

It seemed that moving the game would upset the Russian
television schedule, so we ended up airing that all-time classic
encounter on a delayed basis.

Like so many at ABC Sports, along with sports fans all across
America, Jim McKay regards the United States hockey team
victory at Lake Placid in 1980 as one of his most indelible work
experiences:

"I was in the studio that night as the host, and we were still on
the air close to midnight, and we had a camera on the main street
in this tiny village in upstate New York, and here were a couple
hundred Americans coming down the street singing 'God Bless
America,' and, at that time, it was hard to remember when
anything like that had last happened. My daughter Mary was at
the game, and she told me later that an older gentleman who was
seated next to her in the arena told her, 'The last time I saw this
many American flags, they were burning them.' It was amazing,
absolutely amazing."

I couldn't have been more pleased that night for our long-time
ski-jumping expert, Art Devlin, a Lake Placid resident and vice
president of the Organizing Committee.

The 1980 Summer Olympics in Moscow—the Games the United
States eventually boycotted—could have wound up on all three
American networks, which is what we wanted at ABC. We were
concerned up front that the Russians would try to make a circus
of the bidding, and to thwart that we thought it made sense to
have a three-network pool with each network getting a piece of

the action. NBC was pretty much in agreement with us, but CBS held out, figuring they had the inside track on the rights.

On the eve of the bidding session in Moscow, Deputy Premier Ignati Novikov, the head of the Moscow Olympic Organizing Committee, hosted a cocktail party and poured out the vodka for Arledge; Bob Wussler, then head of CBS Sports; and Bob Howard, leader of the NBC delegation. As I stood there watching the three American networks groveling before the Soviets, I was appalled. To me, it was degrading.

Some time later, Wussler came over to me and said, "Ask your leader to join me in the corner, won't you?"

I'd been talking with a correspondent from United Press International. I asked to be excused, then walked over to Roone and told him that Wussler was waiting to speak with him in the corner. The minute Roone joined him, Wussler announced that at long last CBS was almost certainly prepared to go for the pool broadcast arrangement.

"Goddamn, what took you guys so long?" Roone asked.

Wussler said he was waiting for a final confirmatory telephone call from New York, and would call Roone in his room as soon as he got it. As we left the party, someone informed NBC of what was afoot. Some time later, Wussler called Roone and announced, "It's a go," and the following morning most of the Americans headed back to New York, leaving the Soviets fuming. Roone said that when he told Novikov that ABC was pulling out, he could practically see the steam coming out of the Russian's ears. Then after he had cooled down a little, he offered the Games to ABC on an exclusive basis, but Arledge told him the three-network deal precluded ABC from making a unilateral deal.

The political boycott buried any chances for American television and ended up costing NBC a bundle, but before that happened, a West German named Lothar Bock made his shadowy appearance. Lothar, who was being paid by CBS, turned out to have considerable influence with the Soviets.

During the period the three networks were attempting to gain approval in Washington from the Justice Department for the pooling arrangement, it was agreed that none of us would approach the Moscow organizers, but we learned that Bock had indeed been in Moscow for a meeting with the Organizing Committee on behalf of CBS. When we confronted CBS with the information, it quickly terminated its relationship with Bock, which was a very wise move in that there was also an allegation that he was making "contributions" to at least one key Soviet official. Information came to us that Lothar had flown to the Bahamas for a private meeting with CBS chairman William Paley and tried to persuade CBS to overturn its decision. Paley turned him down.

Bock then turned to Carl Lindemann, head of NBC Sports at the time, and assured him that he could personally deliver the Moscow Olympics to NBC. Carl said later he was drinking some orange juice when Bock made his proposal, and nearly sprayed the front of the guy's clothes. Carl recovered quickly, arranged some hurried meetings with the NBC brass, flew to Moscow, and locked up the deal. Then Arledge and John Martin hastily flew back to Moscow to try and change things, but struck out. It was an $85 million deal, later to become $87 million. Insurance with Lloyds of London eased the damage, but NBC reportedly eventually lost $35 million.

A number of people mentioned to me at the time how ABC must have been chuckling over NBC's misfortune, but nothing could have been further from the truth. As professional competitors, we certainly empathized with NBC Sports, if only because the roles could so easily have been reversed: *We* could have been faced with the U.S. boycott. (Lindemann later resigned from NBC Sports when Don Ohlmeyer was hired as executive producer of the Moscow Olympics without his knowledge or blessing. NBC president Herb Schlosser and Bob Howard engaged Ohlmeyer after Carl had committed the primary Moscow production role to Dick Auerbach. Lindemann then joined CBS Sports, where he was employed until he died of cancer in 1985.)

The bidding for the 1984 Winter Olympics in Sarajevo, Yugoslavia, was a cinch. We knew the other guy's (CBS's) best bid was $90 million, and so we came in at $91.5 million and walked away with the rights.

Negotiations for the 1984 Summer Olympics in Los Angeles were done in the Beverly Hills home of the producer, David

Wolper, who was responsible for the brilliant opening and closing ceremonies that year, as well as the highly acclaimed celebration of the hundredth anniversary of the Statue of Liberty in 1986. All three networks met with David and his committee, including Peter Ueberroth, then president of the Los Angeles Organizing Committee and now commissioner of baseball. The decision was made that we should caucus, and David Wolper told us we could go downstairs to his basement for privacy. He had game machines, pinball machines, you name it, down there, and that's when we made the decision to bid $225 million. Our strategy was to go in high and blow everybody out of the tub. Arledge recommended the $225 million figure, it was okayed by Fred Pierce, it worked, and the Los Angeles Games became the most successful in television history.

But they were not without controversy. When the Soviets led the boycott of the Eastern bloc nations, a dispute arose over rights money in which ABC's contention was that if the ratings were negatively affected by the pullout of the Soviets and their pals, then we should not have to pay the $225 million. We wanted a certain number of dollars set aside until after the Games, Ueberroth wanted it settled right then and there, and on the eve of the official opening of the Olympics the argument had still not been resolved. Indeed, at one stage Ueberroth and Arledge got into a heated conversation over the telephone in which Ueberroth ended it by calling Arledge an "asshole" and slamming the phone in his ear.

I asked Roone about his conversation with Peter, and he made it plain he didn't want to discuss it. Obviously, this was a clash of two very strong wills but, in the end, I don't think it impaired their relationship, which is based on mutual respect—plus, of course, Ueberroth became a "star."

The 1984 Olympic Games reached a climax as Carl Lewis attempted to win a record-tying fourth gold medal. Chuck Howard was producing the track and field events from the Coliseum, and was keeping the studio up to date on when Lewis would be running in the 400-meter relay race in an attempt to equal Jesse Owens' gold-medal accomplishment. We were airing taped diving preliminaries at the time, albeit featuring Greg

Louganis, and Roone decided to stay with the tape. Chuck later said that he felt he should have been more forceful in urging his boss to go live to the Coliseum, but as things turned out, America saw Carl Lewis win his fourth gold medal via videotape sometime after he had actually run the anchor leg on America's victorious relay team.

It was a bad slip, and an unfortunate one for a man who had for so long been so unerringly correct in his programming decisions. But over the long haul, no one will remember that stumble measured against the weight of Roone's superb Olympic record.

The Olympics became a unifying force for ABC Sports personnel, providing not only tremendous challenges but an unequaled sense of accomplishment. We were all very proud that ABC was known as "the Network of the Olympics."

21

SPINS, JUMPS, AND
ONE HECK OF A SPILL

Escapades On and Off the Ice

Figure-skating became very good for us at ABC Sports, but not without some hiccups along the way. I remember we were going to offer twenty thousand dollars for the 1963 World Figure Skating Championships, this when Sports Programs, Inc., was responsible for sports on ABC, and after we had successfully televised the 1962 championships. For the 1962 rights, we had gone through a middleman, Dick Button, the former world and Olympic figure-skating champion, whose organization—then and now called Candid Productions—purchased the rights from the International Skating Union and resold them to us, with Button garnering a handsome profit.

Much as we liked Button's commentary on our figure-skating shows—and I believe he ranks among the finest sports television analysts of all time—we simply saw no point in dealing through him for the 1963 rights. So when the ISU set a rights meeting for Portofino, Italy, in June 1962, we informed it that we would attend and be involved as an interested party in acquiring the rights directly.

The man who went with our proposal was Jack Fitzgerald, then business manager for Sports Programs. However, finding the small town of Portofino is no easy chore, especially when you have worked all day in New York, flown all night from New York to Milan, then rented a car and set out over some very narrow, winding, and unfamiliar mountain roads.

Jack Fitzgerald: "The meeting was being held in a villa deep into the mountains. Arledge had told the ISU we'd be there, although at times during the trip I wasn't so sure. The roads were absolutely terrible, but I finally arrived and presented my card. Everyone smiled, and I sat down to wait with ABC's then Rome bureau chief, Franco Bucarelli, who had come along in case I needed help. As it would develop, we were all beyond help.

"The ISU people came out of their meeting room and informed us that the deal had been cut. It was over and done with, just like that. I couldn't understand what they were saying, but I could tell by watching Bucarelli that it was not a good piece of news. Everyone was yelling back and forth, Franco and the others, and the exchange got pretty heated. Franco told me the deal had been made with Candid Productions. Dick Button wasn't even there, but his group had cabled an offer and it had been accepted. We didn't even get the opportunity to present our case. It was obviously collusion, and we let them know that's what we thought of it, and they got all bent out of shape and demanded to know how we could question their integrity. I asked them how we could do anything else. But, anyway, Button got the rights for $12,500 when we were coming in with a bid of $20,000 and didn't even get an audience. I made it abundantly clear I thought Button had bribed the ISU."

Button then made a deal putting the 1963 and 1964 championships on CBS, which did not make for the happiest of times between ABC and Mr. Button, although my opinion of his on-air skills never changed and we later did business with him. In fact, over the years, "Wide World of Sports" covered eighteen world championships in such exciting locations as Vienna, Tokyo, and Copenhagen. American television audiences were entertained by outstanding performances from Peggy Fleming, Janet Lynn, Dorothy Hamill, Scott Hamilton, and international stars like the Protopopovs, Rodnina and Zaitsev, Don Jackson, John Curry, and Robin Cousins.

When we reacquired the championships from CBS, Button again made a healthy profit as the middleman. But, its members still sensitive over the bribery accusation made by Jack Fitzgerald, there were some tense moments with the ISU. Roone Arledge tried to placate them by telling them, "Mr. Fitzgerald isn't with us any longer," and twenty years later that became true when Jack Fitzgerald finally retired from ABC.

By the time Jack actually left, ABC was out of world figure-skating, and all because CBS had been successful in doing what we had tried and failed to do years before: pulling the rug out from under Dick Button. It came about through some slick maneuvering by Eddie Einhorn, who later would become part owner of the Chicago White Sox and who would be so intimately involved with the United States Football League. At that time, Einhorn worked for CBS, where he was in charge of the network's weekend sports anthology programs. ABC's John Martin was handling the discussions with Button, but obviously he didn't see that Button was losing control.

Einhorn beat everyone to the punch, circumventing Button and making a solid offer in behalf of CBS. The ISU was very receptive since they felt that Button had been taking advantage of them by not generating higher rights fees and, in turn, making a tidy profit for himself by securing the rights and reselling them to us at a much higher figure. Meanwhile, Button had let us know he needed more money than we had offered for the television rights, so we agreed to increase our offer. As it turned out, even as we met with Button, Einhorn had the deal made for CBS. That was in 1980 and the contract was for four years starting in 1983, but the championships are still at CBS, whose latest four-year contract was for over $10 million, not a bad increase from the $20,000 we were prepared to offer more than a couple of decades before.

Losing an event like that was a bitter pill, which upset Button so much he filed a lawsuit against the ISU, claiming that his ISU contract had been abrogated. ABC supported him in the lawsuit because of its eagerness to retain the rights to the world championships. But that incensed the ISU, so we finally prevailed on Button to drop the action, on the basis that such a move might enhance our chances of getting back into the ball game at a later date. While all this was going on, Jacques Favart, then president of the ISU, died. Some ISU representatives still contend his death was, in part, caused by the stress of the affair.

Later there was a lawsuit involving figure-skating from which, had ABC Sports not prevailed, the fallout would have been disastrous for all of sports television, and particularly for events videotaped for delayed airing. It happened at the 1981 World Figure-Skating Championships in Hartford, Connecticut, and the issue was whether the local CBS station, WFSB-TV, had the right to air an event ABC had purchased for national telecasting. Originally, we told the station it could not use any coverage until we were off the air after "Wide World of Sports" the following weekend; then we modified our position to allow WFSB, or anyone else, to use footage from preliminaries in news programs but none from the finals. Still, the CBS station filed suit in federal court, claiming the championships constituted a local news event that it should be allowed to cover as an obligation to its local viewers. Despite a snowstorm, I flew in a chartered aircraft with our lead attorney, Phil Forlenza, and his associate from La Guardia Airport to the Hartford-Brainard Airport on the outskirts of Hartford. We arrived near midnight, and I testified the next morning that "exclusivity is at the heart of our business and we had paid for exclusive rights to these championships."

The judge ruled in our favor. He determined that to permit local television coverage would be a violation of the rights that ABC Sports had bargained for in good faith, and thus would negatively affect the ABC Sports program that was to follow. The ruling was extremely important in that it maintained the integrity of exclusive rights. If we had lost, what would have prevented local stations in Chicago, or Los Angeles, or anywhere else, from doing the same thing with other events to which the networks had purchased rights? The answer is, nothing could have prevented it, so it really was a landmark decision. Had the judge ruled the other way, it is doubtful that the "Wide World of Sports" type of program could have maintained its stature for very long.

If that had happened, the world undoubtedly would have forgotten by now the ski-flyer who comes crashing into your living room each weekend on the opening montage of "Wide World of Sports." He's been doing it for years now, he's a

Yugoslav, and his name is Vinko Bogataj (pronounced Bo-gah-tie). His terrible fall took place during a ski-flying competition produced by Doug Wilson and directed by Lou Volpicelli, at Oberstdorf, West Germany, in 1970, but he wasn't badly hurt and, as a matter of fact, telephoned the site of the competition from his hospital bed to assure everyone he was all right. Years later, we sent a crew from "Wide World of Sports" to visit him at his home in Yugoslavia and were glad to find him still fit. In 1981, Vinko was a "surprise" guest at the twentieth-anniversary celebration of "Wide World of Sports." He received a standing ovation from the hundreds of invited guests at the Waldorf-Astoria in New York. Perhaps then he appreciated the tremendous fame he had achieved in a land far across the sea.

A few years ago, I thought maybe we'd sufficiently exposed the "spill," and seriously considered removing Bogataj from the "Wide World" opening. I was talked out of making that change. Hopefully, my idea will never be rekindled. Vinko has become a well-loved part of the "Wide World of Sports" family—indeed a part of American television sports.

22

CRITICS AND ETHICS

*Some Reflections on the
Print/Electronic Media Wars*

What a blessed thing it is that
nature, when she invented,
manufactured and patented her
authors, contrived to make critics
out of the chips that were left!

OLIVER WENDELL HOLMES

There is an adversarial relationship between the print media ("critics") and the electronic media, and it is an understandable one. The newspapers and magazines had the mass communications market to themselves for generations, then along came television and grabbed off the lion's share of the attention and the money and the glamour, and it was inevitable there would be trouble.

Los Angeles writer Bill Shirley capsulized the problems nicely in a 1985 piece entitled "Television New Ruler of Sports," about ABC's preparations for coverage of that year's Super Bowl:

"ABC swept into town with tons of equipment, an army of employees, several miles of cable and a lineup of celebrity announcers, then invited reporters in to hear how it would televise the game. Remarkably, about 200 sports writers showed up. This was further proof of the clout TV has in sports today. When it covers an event, it often becomes news. Nobody seems to care much how a newspaper does its job. Newspapers and TV have never been the best of friends. Some of the enmity probably stems from professional jealousy. Television pays better and seems to get preferential treatment from teams and promoters, but many sportswriters are offended by TV coverage of sports for stronger reasons. Most of the medium's reporting is shallow and much of it is more show business than journalism. In sports, as in other news, pictures can distort a story when they are not accompanied by adequate commentary. Once, when television had less impact on our lives than it has today, many newspapers virtually ignored it. Sportswriters particularly viewed their new competition with scorn. As TV cameras and microphones intruded on interviews and press conferences, some sportswriters fought back. They spoiled TV reporters' tapes with profanity. They demanded the interlopers be banished to a separate press room. As television grew more dominant, sportswriters' resentment increased in direct proportion to the medium's intrusion into events. Television bought exclusive rights to games and often dictated their dates and starting times to willing promoters. Games began to be played at odd hours. Access to the principals usually went to television first and newspaper reporters worried about deadlines. Television, in fact, drastically altered the character of sports events and reporting of them in newspapers. . . . The irony was that sportswriting and sports sections became better because of television."

I am essentially in accord with Shirley's essay, but disagree with the part about television dictating to sports organizers. I've said for years that if television negatively affects the integrity of a contest then television should be tossed out of the ball park. But anyone who thinks that television is not going to try to ensure that its economic investment pays off, and pays off handsomely, is being naive, and that's really the bottom line. In light of the huge amounts of rights money paid for events, generally nowadays in response to the demands of organizers, it is incumbent on television networks, as businesses first and foremost, to make certain those investments pay off.

Today the print-TV adversarial relationship is not quite so pronounced, the rivalries not as bitter, as they have been in the past. That's because many of today's writers are what might be called children of the television age. Having grown up with the tube, they do not consider it a natural enemy. They are more accepting of the role television now plays overall in our society, and even of the prominence and earnings of its performers compared to the stars of their own industry.

Here's what Howard Rosenberg, the Pulitzer Prize–winning television critic for the *Los Angeles Times*, and himself a regular featured performer on national television, has to say on the subject:

"When I first started in the newspaper business, a television critic was somebody about eighty-five years old whom you put over in a corner where you let him rewrite network press releases until he calcified at his desk. Everyone saw television as a competitor. The newspapers didn't want to give television any publicity because, as they saw it, that meant promoting a competitor. There was considerable resentment of television when I started my newspaper career in Louisville, and even today there are people here at the *Los Angeles Times* who have an orgasm when I kick hell out of television. But there came a time when it had to be realized that television was there to stay. It was like a tidal wave, and you just had to accept it."

When the television critic was an old gentleman rewriting network press releases, there was not much real criticism of what we put on the air, and we tended to ignore what little there was. However, as the industry grew too big for newspapers to ignore, formal criticism of the medium also grew. As that has grown, so has the notice taken of it by broadcasters, to the point today where the entire industry is very sensitive to all criticism, whether from the print media or via letters and telephone calls from viewers.

I've always been concerned about the motivation for television criticism, but the longer I've been in the industry, the more I've been able to accept the necessity for it and the positive impact it can have. These days I think the print media, with its probing and picking, serves a useful function in many areas, not least in keeping the electronic media on its toes. On the other hand, there are instances where the criticism is out of line, and especially in the tendency to prejudge, to go into a story with the presumption that television is automatically guilty just because it is television.

The most frequent example of this kind of criticism, as far as televised sports is concerned, is that broadcasters control athletic contests, or at least that they exert undue influence over them. I'm not talking here about events that are specially created for television, such as "The Superstars" competition, but about the established sports events that have been with us for years.

For example, it has frequently been written that television dictates time-outs during football games, to the point of interrupting the normal flow of the action. I would not dispute that this has happened in the past, but it's a rare occurrence today—and when it does happen, it's invariably the fault of the organizer, not the broadcaster. Most of the stoppages in football occur during natural breaks in the play. Clearly, the airing of blocks of commercials during time-outs happens because of television commitments, but every effort is made to ensure that they do not interfere with the flow of the game.

The colleges assign liaison officials to work with the television production people, and in theory at least they do not permit commercial time-outs when they would affect the conduct of the game. When a broadcaster falls behind in airing its commercials because there are no natural time-outs, the catching up is usually done in a subsequent quarter. There are no liaison officials at NFL games, but NFL referees are supposed to be sufficiently experienced in working with television to be able to accommodate its needs without disrupting the flow of the action. In fact, the NFL allows commercial breaks following fumbles, which I think is wrong. The team that recovers the ball is on a natural high, with a lot of new energy, and I believe the practice of permitting a commercial time-out in that spot should be revoked. Starting in 1985, the NFL increased the length of time allowed for individual commercial breaks during play from one to two minutes in order to accommodate more commercial time during each stoppage and in turn reduced the total number of commercial interruptions during the four quarters of play from twenty-two to sixteen. These changes have resulted in better-paced NFL games.

As I've said, the larger issue in all of this is that the networks have poured so much money into the NFL and its teams, via enormous rights fees, that they must be permitted to recoup and capitalize on that investment. Time-outs called for television commercials, in my opinion, are a small price to pay for the many hours of otherwise free entertainment provided the viewer.

Another favorite of the critics is changing the starting times of games. This happens in every sport, and in most cases there is, in my view, nothing wrong with it. The networks have contractual obligations with the suppliers of sports that sometimes compel them to insist on schedule changes. For example, ABC has had obligations to televise a certain number of college football games each season. To live with some of the specifications imposed on that coverage by the NCAA or CFA or Pacific 10/Big Ten, it has been necessary to ask schools to change starting times, or even to switch dates. That's a most sensitive issue, and we always gave schools plenty of advance notice when we came to them with such a request. Also, the schools always had the right to say no. But I don't think it is in any way onerous to ask a school to move a kickoff by a couple of hours, especially when one considers the heavy financial commitment invariably made by the asker.

Asking a major-league baseball team to move a starting time from, say, 7:35 P.M. to 8:05 P.M. shouldn't pose any great difficulties for anyone. Exceptions involve West Coast telecasts and a request to the Dodgers, say, to move from 7:35 P.M. to a 5:00 P.M. start to accommodate prime time in the East. Then you are asking a lot of both the Dodger organization and the Los Angeles fans, if only because of the traffic tie-ups on the Los Angeles freeways at that hour.

I'll never forget Graig Nettles, of the New York Yankees, during the World Series some years ago waiting in the on-deck circle, bundled up like he was about to embark on a sled-dog race while trying to warm his hands with a hot-water bottle. I believe this is a problem that will get worse instead of better, ultimately forcing baseball to really face the issues involved and come to a long-term policy decision. Unfortunately, doing that will require more courage and common sense than baseball's hierarchy has demonstrated to date.

Baseball is a summer game, a warm-weather game. The extension of the season to the time it now concludes is plainly an absurdity, since playing games outdoors at night in mid to late October clearly affects the integrity of the game. Unless Major League Baseball is willing to shorten its regular season to allow for postseason play to conclude earlier, the commonsense change would be for it to accept fewer dollars for the televising of the League Championship Series and World Series entirely in the daytime. For once, the verities of the game should come before the money that can be made from it. I am not, however, holding my breath for that to happen.

I once shared a plane ride with the late celebrated writer Red Smith, and he was adamant that baseball was being "used" by the television networks, who, he believed, were calling all the shots. I tried for the duration of the trip to explain to him that television was not baseball's master, and that all baseball had to do in order to have all the World Series games played in the daytime was to decide and state that that was the way it would be. However, I'm certain Red went to his grave totally convinced that the broadcasters are the black hats.

In earlier contracts between the networks and baseball, it was specified that weekday World Series games would be played at night, and that weekend games would be played in the daytime. But money has become so important to baseball that in the current agreements, in exchange for enormous rights fees, it has handed the networks the right to determine when the games should be played. Now the best way for ABC and NBC to maximize their revenues to cover those vast rights payments is to have all the games played in prime time, where the largest audiences are available. The potential of World Series games on seven nights versus the five in the old contract does not represent a very substantial difference and doesn't warrant the criticism it has generated. As Eddie Einhorn of the Chicago White Sox said during the negotiations for that contract, "Give us the money and we'll play the games whenever you want." Well, the present schedule is not necessarily what television wants, but rather what baseball has forced it to favor by wanting cash more than anything else.

The noted baseball writer and historian, Charles Einstein, came up with the following proposal, which he believed would solve the problem. After the World Series contenders are determined through the established playoff system, let them take an entire week off to overcome any minor aches and pains, and to permit the type of promotional hype that nowadays seems indispensable to the pre–Super Bowl week. Then play all the games in the Series in Hawaii at two in the afternoon. With the time difference between Hawaii and much of the continental United States, the telecasts would begin in prime time for most viewers.

Purists will argue that this would rob hometown fans of an opportunity to see their local heroes in their own ball parks. To me, having the games played under ideal conditions more than offsets that argument. Also, there is the factor that, for the most part, corporations have a stranglehold on World Series tickets.

An area where the networks have been unfairly criticized involves the Chicago Cubs and night baseball at Wrigley Field. For many years, the Cubs have been reluctant to install lights and have been faced with a local ordinance which prohibited them from doing so. The "Citizens United for Baseball in the Sunshine"—CUBS—have also provided strong opposition to any move toward night games at Wrigley Field. However, ABC and NBC, you will remember, according to their current baseball contracts, can require that the All-Star Game, League Championship Series and World Series be played at night. In February of 1988, the Chicago City Council passed a new ordinance which permitted the Cubs to play a limited number of regular season games plus baseball's "jewels" at night at Wrigley Field. This measure enables the now-not-so-reluctant Cubs to have games televised in prime time by superstation WGN. If the Cubs had chosen to preserve their unique tradition, a solution would have been for major-league baseball to reduce the rights payments from the networks and thereby allow the Cubs to play in the daytime.

A few years ago, when the American and National leagues fixed their playoff schedules, there was considerable criticism of ABC Sports because the Dodgers and Phillies played one day in Los Angeles, then flew across the country to play the next day in Philadelphia. Syndicated columnist Dick Young said ABC "required" the teams to do that. That's ludicrous. If the National

League and the commissioner's office thought it was wrong to make up a schedule like that, all they had to do was give the teams a day off. In rebuttal to Young, we stated on the air that we had no involvement in the League Championship Series scheduling.

Another time, Yankee owner George Steinbrenner did a tap dance on ABC Sports because his team had to play a Monday night game on national television, which led to a tight travel schedule for the Yankees that week. He was quoted on how terribly wrong he thought it was for ABC Sports to cause that sort of thing. As soon as I read the quotes in the newspaper, I called George and told him ABC was getting a bum rap. He knew we had nothing to do with the scheduling. At least, he knew it after we talked.

"Jim, I'm sorry," he said. "ABC Sports is a good friend of baseball and a great friend of the New York Yankees. You know what I think about you guys. I think there's a misunderstanding about what I said."

George Steinbrenner showed class on that occasion, by going back to the man who had written the story and explaining that he, Steinbrenner, had unfairly criticized ABC Sports.

Another favorite of the television critics is the use of replays to check official calls on the field. The system has been used by the National Football League for a few seasons now, and while it has positive aspects, I'm opposed to it in principle and for practical consider- ations, if for no other reason than the unequal number of cameras utilized to televise NFL games, thereby creating an unfair situation where one telecast has more replay angles than another. If an erroneous call can be corrected, that's positive and good for the game, but philosophically, I think it's wrong for any sports orga- nizer—in this case the NFL—to involve an outside agency like a broadcaster in decisions regarding the conduct of the game. From a legal point of view, the networks cannot prohibit the NFL from using the pictures transmitted over the air. What's happening is that by using the network replays—even though they are monitored and in effect controlled by league officials—the broadcaster is being involuntarily involved in the conduct of the game, which is wrong.

The NFL should operate its own replay system without any

broadcaster ties whatever. As things now stand, the NFL officials sitting in their booth atop the stadium use their own video recording and playback system, but, by taking a line feed, can see *only* what the network airs to the viewer at home. The weakness of this system was illustrated in the 1987 Super Bowl game between Denver and the New York Giants, where there was clearly an incorrect call, but no network replay was available until it was too late to make a change. The way to avoid this is for the NFL to employ cameras and videotape machines of its own, and operate them independently, costly as that would be.

Critics long have complained about broadcasters leaving game action for "cutaways," pictures of the crowd or some other background scene, and I happen to think they are right on this score. When the game is on, that's what people want to look at, period.

Broadcasters leaving events before their conclusion is a major complaint of many critics, and it's one of mine, too. There is almost no excuse for it. CBS and NBC have done it frequently, ABC almost never. The network rationale is that viewers, advertisers, and affiliates are scheduled to receive a program at a particular time, and that to delay the start of it, or join it in progress, are disruptions that potentially lose both viewers and commercial revenue.

One year, televising the Hawaiian Open, we hoped to get off the air by 7 P.M. Eastern Time, but the golf tournament ran late. Our policy was that we should carry all events to conclusion. Fred Pierce was the sole decision-maker here, however, and in this case the tournament was to be followed by a special commemorating the twenty-fifth anniversary of ABC. Pierce prevailed, and we signed off from Hawaii by saying we were sorry and that we'd cut in later with the final results. It's still my belief that we were wrong.

CBS and NBC have improved in recent years, partly in response to media and viewer uproar, but for a long time CBS almost habitually aborted coverage of golf tournaments for the "60 Minutes" show. Well, it is a certainty many more viewers want to watch that outstanding program than a golf tournament, but that's not the issue. The issue is the commitment you made to provide live television coverage of a particular event. The viewers of that event are loyal to you, too, and you're cheating them by leaving it before it is concluded.

No one in broadcasting will ever forget the incident of November 17, 1968, in which NBC left live coverage of a New York Jets/Oakland Raiders game in order to start its "Heidi" program on time at 7 P.M. Eastern Time. I was told later that NBC Sports chief Carl Lindemann was trying to telephone to give instructions to stay with the football game, but could not get through in time. The bottom line was that the Raiders came back to score twice in the last forty-two seconds and win the game 43–32. Quite properly, NBC has never been allowed to forget that blunder.

It's always been my strong feeling that sports-event organizers should never have the right of approval of television announcers, and I was proud when we stood up to baseball and insisted that Howard Cosell be on the Monday night broadcast team. Such differentiation between the organizer and the broadcaster is essential to ensure the integrity of the commentary.

So how come ABC would use Frank Broyles, the athletic director at Arkansas, for NCAA football, and Tim McCarver, the New York Mets' broadcaster, on "Monday Night Baseball"? The answer is that whenever we televised a game involving Arkansas, we made certain Broyles was not assigned to the broadcast, and the same with McCarver—he did not work when we televised a Mets game. However, before I left ABC, everyone came to feel that McCarver was such a unique talent, and had become such an integral part of the broadcast team, that we should make an exception in his case.

Don Drysdale was particularly sensitive about this point when he worked on ABC's baseball telecasts. He had done California Angels and Chicago White Sox telecasts on a local basis, and we, consequently, held him out of our lineup when we televised their games nationally, and he wasn't at all happy about it. "I understand your principle," he told me, "but I criticize the local team when I'm doing their games, and no one can accuse me of bias in favor of them."

I explained to Don that there was a perception involved, even though we knew he wasn't a "homer." We didn't want to put him in a position of being subjected to criticism simply because he was associated with one of the competing teams. He never bought the argument, and, eventually, in light of the McCarver decision, ABC did let him broadcast White Sox games.

The whole matter of journalism versus the relationship with organizers is and will always remain a sticky one. Organizers want their events presented in the best possible light by broadcasters with whom they have entered into contracts, and in almost every case that desire provides fertile ground for problems. The NFL, for example, is not fond of television pictures showing fights between players; basketball would prefer the networks to ignore, or skip lightly over, cases of players being banned for drug use; golf isn't thrilled when a camera lingers on a controversial player who has been critical of the establishment. The NCAA, as we noted in an earlier chapter, was strongly opposed to ABC plugging "Monday Night Football" games during college football telecasts. Happily, most of the time, such issues get resolved with little or no bloodshed, thanks to reason and compromise on both sides.

The classic example of this type of confrontation came some years back when Jack Whitaker, then working the Masters golf tournament for CBS, referred to the crowd as a "mob." The late Clifford Roberts was so incensed that he ordered CBS not to assign Whitaker to the Masters, and for a long time he was persona non grata at Augusta National. Roberts was an absolute dictator as far as the tournament and the club went, and an extremely tough-minded one. Since it was his policy to sign only one-year contracts for the Masters television rights, CBS bowed to his demands. I'd like to be able to say that ABC Sports would never have given in to that kind of pressure, but I'll settle for saying I'm glad the problem never arose for us.

Promoters of boxing championships for years dealt with two sanctioning bodies, but today there are three: the World Boxing Council, the World Boxing Association, and the International Boxing Federation. The print media has constantly insisted that television wanted multiple champions so it could air more big fights. I can assure you that ABC Sports felt that there should be just one champion in each weight class, and I'm sure CBS and NBC feel that way as well, if only because a single titleholder means more significant fights and fewer mismatches.

Television didn't create those boxing organizations, and it has no part in their operations. But because initials like WBC, WBA, and IBF seemed to give more credibility to what we covered in the sport, we used them, and sometimes we were at fault in leaning too heavily on their vanities and sanctions. When an event has the term "championship" attached to it, it automatically acquires greater potential appeal for both advertisers and viewers.

CBS for a long time had a boxing consultant named Mort Sharnik, in effect a matchmaker, who spent a lot of time in gyms and got very involved with certain boxers. Then, after a CBS-televised fight, you'd see Sharnik in the ring hugging the winner. Clearly, there should be an arm's-length relationship between a broadcaster and the events it televises. Sharnik's conduct was definitely out of order.

It also surfaced that Gil Clancy, who provides solid fight commentary for CBS, was financially involved with boxing promoter Bob Arum in the purchase of racehorses. While I would never suggest there was anything evil or sinister about that, it is to me without question a conflict of interest. You simply cannot have someone who is doing television boxing analysis for a network being in any shape or form the business partner of a man who's promoting fights televised by that network. When CBS and the press became aware of the Clancy-Arum association, there was a quick meeting at the network and their horse-racing partnership was dissolved.

Ferdie Pacheco ("the Fight Doctor") once did boxing commentary for NBC on matches he had put together for the network. I believed that was a terrible conflict of interest and said so publicly. To Ferdie's credit, his role has changed to analysis, at which he is one of the best in the business. But I found it intolerable when he commented on fights for which he had been, in effect, the matchmaker.

Certain writers are convinced that the television networks conspired to invent golf's system of sudden-death playoffs, because of the added drama and excitement they bring to the game, and even to have had a hand in two of the "majors"—the Masters and PGA—changing to sudden-death. Both as a golfer and a television executive, I'd prefer an eighteen-hole playoff any time, even though extending a championship for another day presents difficult and costly problems for a broadcaster (and a lot of other people, too). The British Open used to have a next-day eighteen-hole playoff, but has now changed to a five-hole same-day format that seems fairer than a sudden-death shootout. Only the U.S. Open among the majors has stayed with the eighteen-hole, next-day playoff format, and personally I hope it always does.

What television did invent was "trash sports," to use a phrase coined by Bill Leggett of *Sports Illustrated* that frankly is not one of my favorites. The epitome of these competitions was the "Superstars" program. We aired a pilot for a potential "Superstars" series in 1973, the last season of ABC's NBA coverage before the package moved to CBS, then knocked the socks off CBS in the ratings when we put a full "Superstars" series and Sunday "Wide World of Sports" on the air in 1974.

I confess I was clearly opposed to the program when it was first proposed, believing it to be hokey and contrived, but I was wrong. "Superstars" turned out to be wholesome and enjoyable entertainment, and it endured for over a decade on ABC before moving to NBC in 1985. At least in American commercial television, the ultimate test is what the public thinks, and the public liked "Superstars" very much indeed. Early on, it was heavily criticized, but as the viewers warmed to the program, the attacks by writers waned. The flip side of "Superstars" was the "World's Strongest Man" program on CBS. To me, men carrying refrigerators on their backs is contrived, degrading, and embarrassing, and has no place on network television.

Critics have long gotten hot and bothered about both the amount and tone of ABC's on-air promotional plugs for upcoming events, and there's no question that the network has at times gone overboard in this area. On the other hand, promotion is the lifeblood of television sports, and it played a vital role in ABC becoming the industry leader. The point here is that television sports, while in the information business, is primarily motivated by ratings and profits; thus, it is necessary to promote one's programming.

I draw a more distinct line when it comes to imparting gambling information on television. There was a time you didn't see any of that kind of material on the screen or in the newspapers, but nowadays almost every major metropolitan newspaper prints the daily point spreads in major sports activities. My personal feeling—and ABC's policy through the years—was to avoid programming or commentary that might have the effect of promoting gambling. We certainly never gave point spreads on the air, and I've never liked seeing Jimmy "the Greek" Snyder on CBS, or Pete Axthelm or Paul Maguire on NBC, providing television fans with their game selections. Axthelm, the *Newsweek* columnist who did NBC's pro football show for some time, actually told viewers which teams he bet, which to me is very wrong indeed.

I believe that it is wrong, too, for sports announcers to appear in television commercials, and our policy was to oppose the practice, to the point of having the standard ABC talent contract forbid it. Our rationale was that it distracted from an announcer's credibility; that it was not proper for a commentator to be peddling a product on the one hand and delivering objective commentary on the other.

However, when Frank Gifford joined ABC Sports, he already had a handsome deal to do commercials for Westinghouse. We swallowed it as part of the price for getting him to jump from CBS to ABC, then later also permitted him to do ads for a brand of sherry. After that, we could hardly say no to others who were in demand, like Howard Cosell, Jim McKay, and Keith Jackson. Thus, McKay did spots for Timex watches, while Cosell did one showing him hanging over a cliff, interviewing some guy for Fruit of the Loom underwear, which I thought was particularly degrading for both Howard and ABC Sports.

I'm sorry we were not stronger in our opposition to these practices, but at least we resisted them as and when we could.

One of the reasons announcers' salaries escalated the way they did was due to our compensating them for the money they might otherwise have been making by appearing in commercials.

I don't know a single television executive or television performer who is totally insensitive to criticism, but it certainly bothers some more than others. For example, I think media criticism altered the career of Chris Schenkel; I believe that what newspaper people said about Howard Cosell had a significant effect on his professional life; and I believe that Al Michaels' extreme sensitivity to media criticism could short-circuit his considerable talents.

Jim McKay is an announcer who has accumulated a ton of honors and awards, along with, inevitably, some criticism. Here are his thoughts on the subject:

"I've never felt a tremendous adversarial relationship with newspapermen. Some of them naturally have a resentment against people in television because they make so much more money than newspapermen do. But I've always tried to get along with the newspaper guys, and I have a lot of friends among them. If you just started out in television and got some criticism you might think, 'Who the hell do those guys think they are and why aren't they saying nice things about me?' But that isn't their job."

Just what *is* their job?

Television critic Howard Rosenberg: "My job is not to tell people what to watch. *You* have to decide whether you should watch something. It would be arrogant on my part to say that you are not to watch because I don't like something. I see my primary goal as getting people to *think* about what they watch. There are times when you come home and you sit down and use television as an escape, but television is too powerful, too important, to be used that way all the time. Television is a very powerful social force. We should use it that way, as a way to change society, and change it for the better. So, as a critic, I see myself as both a reporter and a social commentator."

Rudy Martzke has become the media "darling" of the networks, in part because his column appears in a national newspaper on a regular basis. Television sports columnist for *USA Today* since 1983, Martzke acknowledges that an adversarial relationship exists between television and the print media in a general sense, but that because most television columnists really do understand the role of television, they are not usually adversarial to the medium. According to Martzke, television columnists "write the way they see it, try to bring balance to their stories, educate the reader as to why things are done in the industry, and provide information on trends and announcers."

Keith Jackson has rarely responded to things said or written about him, although like everyone else in the business, he's had his share of both praise and criticism:

"The press and I don't always get along. Over the years, I'm sure people wrote to the network and complained about me, but I have to say that, for the most part, the American public has been very kind to me. Certainly kinder than the media. You have to understand that critics are hired to criticize, and they embrace that assignment with great zest.

"Some years ago, I was with the late Bear Bryant on a Sigma Delta Chi program down in Birmingham, Alabama, and I opened it by saying that I had once met two newspapermen I had liked, and that both of them were now dead. Bear muttered to me, 'Well, you've screwed this one up, Jackson.' But I'm not working for the television critics nor the sportswriters. My loyalty isn't to them. The only loyalty you have in this business is to the guy who works his ass off eight, ten, or more hours a day, five or six days a week, and spends eight hundred bucks for a color television set that amounts to maybe half his entertainment—that's the guy you owe your allegiance to, and I ain't gonna change."

While Keith Jackson has largely shunned the press, director Andy Sidaris—the only director still at ABC Sports who was there at the very beginning—has assiduously courted the print media throughout his career, and has been prepared to accept both the praise and criticism he has thereby invited. Andy is the director who became well known among the critics for what the industry calls "T and A shots," the initials standing for certain parts of the female anatomy:

"I'd rather see a great-looking body than a touchdown any-time. You can see thousands of touchdowns every weekend, but a great-looking woman is something to behold. A classic moment with a beautiful woman comes just once in a while. We may as well enjoy it.

"When we did the old American Football League games, let's face it, we had no crowds—three hundred people was a throng. So we had to go in close to get what we called a crowd shot. We focused on people, and that's what the ABC philosophy always had been from the outset—concentrating on people rather than on events. Then I did a Texas-Arkansas football game in Austin with those powerhouse rivals going head-to-head, coached by two good friends, and great adversaries, Darrell Royal and Frank Broyles. Texas pushed Arkansas all over the field, yet couldn't deliver the knockout punch, and on the last play of the game Arkansas kicked a field goal and won. We went away for a commercial or two, and the stadium emptied like there had been a bomb threat. When we came back, I spotted Coach Royal's wife sitting in the stands with her children. She was crestfallen. She seemed almost frozen. I had a camera zoom in on her as she and her family sat there, practically alone in that great stadium. You could see a tear trickling down her face.

"Ever since then, I've been on the lookout for great shots in the stands. And if the pictures happen to be of beautiful women, that's a real bonus. They're a lot more fun than football, anytime."

Like Andy, ABC at times almost went out of its way to invite criticism.

One year when Kansas City and the New York Yankees were involved in the League Championship Series, we assigned Keith Jackson to a Friday afternoon baseball game in New York, then put him on a chartered jet to do play-by-play the following afternoon for the Texas-Oklahoma football game in Dallas, then got him on that same airplane to make a quick return trip to New York to handle a Yankee-Royals broadcast from Yankee Stadium that Saturday night. We simply should not have spread Keith that thinly, for, as capable as he is, he could not do complete justice to either of the last two telecasts.

We also pulled a boner in delivering Jackson to Yankee Stadium the way we did. A young production assistant was under orders to get Keith from La Guardia Airport to the ballpark in the shortest possible time. The ingenious—and ingenuous—young woman arranged to have an ambulance standing by, the driver of which then raced from Queens to the Bronx with lights flashing and sirens wailing full tilt, getting Keith there with a few moments to spare.

The incident would likely have gone unnoticed had Howard Cosell not made reference on the telecast that night to the splendid work the emergency ambulance crew had done in transporting his colleague from airport to ballpark in record time. New York Mayor Ed Koch was particularly upset, and, as is his style, made no secret of his displeasure.

To compound our corporate embarrassment, I would learn later that on the previous day, on its way to Dallas with Jackson, our chartered jet had run into unexpected headwinds, forcing an unscheduled refueling stop in Nashville, Tennessee. There the pilot had wheeled boldly in ahead of another aircraft waiting for the gasoline refueling truck, inside of which sat former President Gerald Ford.

At a World Series game in Baltimore, we learned late in the afternoon that President Reagan would attend, and that he would consent to being interviewed. For a time, the president sat in the private box of the Orioles' owner, Edward Bennett Williams, after which he came over to the ABC broadcast booth to be interviewed between innings by Howard Cosell. The president and Cosell began chatting while I observed nearby, and they continued to chat, and chat, and then chat some more. I was getting nervous, the umpires were holding up the game, and the fans were beginning to boo, although I'm certain 99 percent of them had no clue why there was such a long interruption in play.

At long last, Cosell concluded the interview and the game resumed. When I shook hands with the president, he smiled and remarked, "You know, I could tell baseball stories all night." I thought, "Mr. President, thank God you didn't!"

Although I communicated frequently with the press during my years at ABC Sports, once Roone Arledge made the switch to news, the responsibility of responding to inquiries from the print media fell mainly on me, and I think my relationship with its members was on the whole a good one.

The day after I left ABC, Jack Craig, the television sports critic for the *Boston Globe,* wrote an article about me that characterized my relationship with the written media, and included the following:

"[Spence has] a reputation for integrity and work ethic honed over two decades. He never dropped a line to the press designed to denigrate others while elevating himself. In a trade where truth is elusive and ethics situational, he never lied. Often there would be no story from Spence, but never a wrong story."

Although my relationship with the written media was not always pleasant and positive, I readily accept Jack Craig's comments.

23

MONEY AND
THE STARS

The Age of the
$2-million-a-year Sportscaster

Was Howard Cosell worth $1 million a year? Are Al Michaels
and Frank Gifford each worth more than a million dollars a year?
Is Dick Enberg worth $1.25 million, John Madden $1.5 million?
Can anyone justify signing Brent Musburger to a contract that
will pay him *$2 million* a year for television and radio work for
CBS before the end of this decade?

There's an old story about the Las Vegas entertainer who was
asked incredulously by a blunt-speaking newsman if he really
believed in his heart that he was worth the hundred thousand
dollars a week he was being paid by one of the major casinos. The
entertainer replied, just as bluntly, "Yes, if I can find one fool who
is willing to pay that kind of money."

When you have a sports broadcaster making ten times the
salary of the president of the United States, it's difficult to argue
against the contention that the tail is wagging the dog, and that's
exactly what has happened in network television.

Like all else in this business, the sums paid for rights fees, the
rates charged for advertising—for example, the 1988 Super Bowl
price per minute was listed at $1.3 million—the salaries of top
"talent" have simply gotten out of kilter. During the time Cosell,
Gifford, and Meredith were the "Monday Night Football" triumvirate, their combined salaries approximated $2.5 million a

year—or the equivalent of the gross national product of some of the emerging nations of the world! Why, you ask, did ABC pay these enormous amounts? It was strictly a matter of paying what was necessary by present market standards to get the talent you thought you had to have.

In 1987, ABC Sports had approximately $3 million a year in salaries in the "Monday Night Football" booth. The network paid Dan Dierdorf $600,000 a year to get him to leave CBS, joining Michaels and Gifford to shore up the announce booth. Insanity? When you compare such numbers to what people like teachers and nurses make in this country, the answer obviously is yes. But if you compare them to the going rates for top entertainers in other fields—a Cosby, a Hope, or a Sinatra, for example—the answer is no. In the final analysis, sports television, just like all other television, is show business, and the numbers in show business simply have no relation to the "real" world that most of us choose or are forced to live in.

As salaries escalated, so did the jealousies. One of the consuming pastimes in all of television is trying to find out how much the other guy is making. With the advent of players' associations and their growth in strength, plus the forcing of the owners to open their books, there now are few secrets about the incomes of professional athletes, but sports announcers still try to guard their salaries more closely than they would the family heirlooms. Unfortunately for them, it's so common for one agent to represent a number of talents that with a little effort anyone in the business can find out what anyone else is making.

Twenty years ago that wasn't true. During an AFTRA (American Federation of Television and Radio Artists) strike in the 1960s, some of the ABC broadcasters were fined by their union for crossing picket lines, the amounts of the fines being based on what they were making at the time. Chris Schenkel was fined $25,000, Bud Palmer $18,000, and Howard Cosell $16,500. Cosell was livid because, through the fines being published, it was exposed that both Schenkel and Palmer were higher paid than he was.

More recently, when one of the top announcers at ABC Sports signed a new multiyear contract, the wife of one of his colleagues went to great lengths to learn the exact figures involved, even to calling the announcer's agent. He didn't tell her a thing, but I'm happy to let her know that the deal her husband signed brought him close to parity with the guy she was worried about.

Brent Musburger is the highest-paid sports announcer in the country. He has sound journalistic credentials, having come through the newspaper ranks in Chicago, and he does a terrific job of quarterbacking in the studio, which is more challenging than the layman can comprehend. The one problem I have with him is that sometimes he is just too "up," too enthusiastic, to the point on occasion of appearing to be shilling for whatever he's talking about. But apart from that, Musburger is the consummate professional—which, to my mind, still doesn't make him worth $2 million a year, or anywhere near it. But don't fault Brent. He has become, like a number of others, a genuine media celebrity; the "image," if you will, of CBS Sports. And when you are the image of a network sports department, and remain exceptionally good at what you do, you have reached a point where you can command enormous compensation for your services.

Before Musburger signed his last contract with CBS, he and his brother Todd, who represents him, met with a number of us at ABC Sports to explore the "chemistry," so to speak. Our thinking was to involve Musburger in both "Monday Night Football" and "Monday Night Baseball," and without question he would also have been a major player in our coverage of the Olympic Games. We ended up making him what we thought was a very attractive offer, but he chose to remain with CBS. His flirtation with ABC made good copy in the television columns around the nation, and I came away from the experience feeling that we had been somewhat used by the Musburgers as a means of improving Brent's deal with CBS.

This actually was the second time over the years we had talked with Musburger about the possibility of his joining ABC Sports; he said he could accept our offer of $950,000 a year, but was concerned about what he'd be doing the first quarter of the year. CBS then offered him the play-by-play role for its telecasts of the NCAA Basketball Championship "Final Four," plus a lot more money. (When Al Michaels became aware that we were thinking of hiring Musburger, he—through Barry Frank, his agent at the time—asked ABC Sports for a role in determining what Brent's baseball assignment would be. Had we signed him, no such privilege would have been granted.)

Pat Summerall is one of those former athletes who has become a most competent performer on television, a very likable person usually laid back to the point of being a little bland. He has always enjoyed good print reviews, although for me he doesn't add much to most telecasts, chiefly because of his disinclination to say anything very provocative.

John Madden is an interesting guy, a self-made "colorful character," likable and enthusiastic, but I suspect some viewers may be getting a little OD'd on all the "whams" and "pows" and "kabooms" and "kaplooeys," etc. John simply talks too much, and often at too high a decibel level, and I for one don't think his content includes as much substance as the critics claim it does. Listen carefully and see how many real insights you pick up. John's great energy is good for the industry and the game, but there is some good substantive information and personal stories about players and coaches out there that a guy like Madden could search out and pass along to the viewers. Perhaps a contributing factor is that Madden is doing so many things in the commercial field and other areas that he's spreading himself too thin to really work at football anymore. Maybe he ought to get back to basics before he gets swallowed up by the character he's created.

Terry O'Neil, who put Madden and Summerall together for CBS in 1981, realized Summerall was so laid back and unselfish that teaming him with Madden would give the "coach" the time and room needed to really do his act. I'm certain it doesn't bother Pat that Madden has become the star of the show, just so long as they don't forget to send the checks.

Dick Enberg has the warmth Al Michaels lacks, plus Musburger's enthusiasm but with less hype, which makes Enberg very good at any event he undertakes. Dick comes in well prepared, is polished in both manner and content, is not verbose, and is sure of himself without coming off as arrogant or all-knowing. A genuinely nice man, Enberg wears well and will last as long as he wants to in the medium.

Dick's partner on NBC's telecasts of NFL games, Merlin Olsen, is competent but bland, somehow lacking the fire he showed as a defensive lineman for the Los Angeles Rams. I think he would add a lot more to the telecasts if he could resurrect some of it.

Jimmy "the Greek" Snyder, affable off-the-air, is another professional "character" who has built a reputation on CBS as a sports guru. His nickname was probably intended to persuade people he was the same kind of guy as the legendary Nick the Greek, who gained an international reputation as a two-fisted gambler during the early days of Las Vegas. To me, Jimmy the Greek often lacks credibility, which he compounds at times with a somewhat unpleasant air of superiority. As the late comedian Jack E. Leonard was fond of saying, the man has a world of confidence, but for the life of me I don't know why. (These comments about Jimmy were written before his dismissal on January 16, 1988 by CBS Sports for racial remarks he had made the day before in Washington, D.C.)

Bob Costas is one of the brighter young performers in the industry, well-trained, capable, versatile, and enthusiastic, if sometimes a little too wise for his years. Certainly, he is one of NBC's future stars.

Joe Garagiola made himself into a media darling, playing sportswriters and television critics like a piccolo, but in recent times he's begun to collect some hard knocks from the writers. All those stories about Yogi Berra and "the hill" in St. Louis have worn thin; his humor has become a little shopworn. Joe should dump the cornball material in favor of fresh journalistic insights.

Joe's partner on NBC's baseball telecasts, Vin Scully, looks good, sounds good, has cultivated an extensive vocabulary, expresses himself extremely well, and overall is a man of style and versatility. Sometimes, though, he gets a little heavy for his audience; in fact, I sometimes wonder if he has sat up half the night in his hotel room memorizing chunks from *Bartlett's Familiar Quotations*. A little bit of Keats, Shelley, and Shakespeare goes a very long way on American sports television, where most fans would probably think of such guys as some old, long-forgotten double-play combination.

Jim Lampley came to ABC Sports in 1974 as a college-age reporter, via a search committee we had formed to look for bright young talent for our college football telecasts. Lampley did a piece on George Mira, the quarterback at the University of Miami and a good friend of Jim's from high-school days, which allowed him to get "inside" his subject and turn out an extraordinarily good audition tape.

Lampley has an outstanding mind and solid journalistic instincts, but also the same stumbling block as Bob Costas: He looks awfully young (isn't it terrible that in television sometimes looking very young is a handicap?). Also, he sometimes comes across as either cold or a little bit cocky, or both. I sat with Jim on more than one occasion and urged him to try to become warmer, more engaging, on the air, but it's obviously a difficult thing for him to do.

Lampley left ABC in the summer of 1987, which was not a total surprise to me in that his departure was preceded by a personality conflict with ABC Sports president Dennis Swanson. Jim walked out on a $700,000-a-year contract, blaming the uncertainty over the role he would play in the Calgary Olympic Games telecasts. He would be paid for the remainder of his contract, but I was surprised no compromise was worked out to keep him at ABC, because there remains a need to bring along young talent like him to eventually replace star announcers who are reaching the twilight of their careers. While at ABC, it was my thinking that Al Michaels would be our play-by-play star of the future, with Lampley topping the bill in the studio. Shortly after leaving ABC, Jim joined CBS Sports.

The business could use a lot more Curt Gowdys. Capable, prepared, considerate, knowledgeable, versatile, confident, warm—you name it and Gowdy has it, which is why I hate to see him doing the less important shows he's now doing much of the time. Curt is a legend, and legends shouldn't be covering minor events. (Curt Gowdy, Jr., is a prominent producer at ABC Sports and coordinating producer of "Wide World of Sports.")

NBC also has perhaps the most versatile of sports broadcasters in Marv Albert, although his delivery is a bit rigid at times for my taste. Overall, though, Marv is one of network television's most competent performers.

It appears that ABC intends to build Al Trautwig into a star. Al came over from the USA Cable Network, bringing good basic skills plus a strong journalistic sense, but some of the pieces he does include forced humor, and, invariably, when an announcer tries to be a comedian on television, the result is strained and sometimes even degrading to both him and his employer.

Combine Dick Button on figure-skating with Tim McCarver on baseball and Billy Packer on college basketball, and you're looking at the triple-A group among expert sports commentators.

Off-camera, Dick Button has been controversial, and he may be the worst interviewer I've ever seen, but when it comes to setting up events and predicting how competitors will perform, assessing what their performances will mean in the final standings, and providing insightful comments during competitions, no one was ever of more service to the viewer. I was very much in favor of hiring McCarver, and although Roone Arledge was lukewarm about him, we eventually added Tim to our baseball announcer lineup. McCarver is definitely not a part of the jockocracy. Unlike most "jocks," Tim has made a smooth transition from the playing field to the broadcast booth, is intelligent, articulate, and introspective in providing the viewer with much more information than he can see, which is the very essence of expert television sports commentating. Billy Packer provides some of the most incisive commentary on network television. He displays an intimate knowledge of basketball and is able to communicate it very effectively to viewers.

Dave Marr and Lee Trevino on golf, bowling's Nelson Burton, Jr., and Marty Liquori on track are among the elite of expert commentators on network television. Al McGuire remains as colorful as ever on college basketball, and Dan Dierdorf has a chance to become a major star on NFL football. However, if I had to select one individual to single-handedly capture the mood and the essence of an event, it would be Jim McKay. Over the span of years, there simply has been no one more believable in all of television sports.

24

GOOD-BYE SUITES AND LIMOS

Crystal-Balling an Industry

The American people don't watch network television sports as much as they once did. There was a time, not so long ago, when they had only three primary sources for sports coverage—ABC, CBS, or NBC. Today many people have three or four, or even five or six, more choices than that.

Combine basic cable and pay cable with superstations like TBS in Atlanta, add regional syndication, independent stations, then consider the growth of home video systems, and you have a lot of reasons why viewers no longer sit glued to the three commercial networks.

Just at the time I was leaving ABC Sports, William Taaffe wrote in a cover article for *Sports Illustrated*:

"There's a dagger aimed at the hearts of the NFL, Major League Baseball, the Sugar Bowl, the Kentucky Derby and other sports leagues and events we've come to know and love. The dagger isn't drugs or alcohol or under-the-table payments to college athletes. It is the financial problems besetting network television, the sugar daddy that has allowed owners, promoters and athletes to reap fortunes that 20 years ago would have seemed unfathomable. All of a sudden, things are changing.

"After years of paying ever-increasing millions for the rights to broadcast sports events, the networks now say that the gravy train has ground to a halt. The party's over. Some sports will have to live with less or take a walk, a situation fraught with peril for owners, athletes and fans, who may be asked to pay more for tickets if the TV spigot taps out. . . . Network sports programming has become less profitable, largely because demand among advertisers for commercial time on those telecasts has slackened considerably. With so many advertising options available, the networks often fail to sell their commercial spots—or they are forced to sell at prices that are lower than those on their rate-cards. The networks foresaw little of this and paid too much for the rights to sports events. Now they have to pay the price."

Taaffe is 99 percent right in what he says, but his last point needs amplification.

It would have been great if someone had been able to peer into a crystal ball and foresee what would take place. However, you can hardly blame the people running network sports television for not doing so when many top economists fail to guess right about our nation's economy (how many "experts" predicted the record stock market plunge in October of 1987?). What happened is that, starting in the latter part of 1984, the sports marketplace simply fell apart. Essentially, it was the slowing of inflation that put the networks' backs to the wall. Unable to raise prices to consumers who were no longer getting handsome inflationary wage increases, advertisers simply had no option but to cut off or at least sharply decelerate their flow of dollars into sports television. While the marketplace may fluctuate over the years, I believe the days of exorbitant spending by advertisers in sports are gone forever, along with their willingness to blithely accept constant increases in the cost of commercials on sports television.

Recently, I came across something Theodore Roosevelt said back in the 1920s that I think nicely applies to this situation:

"It is not the critic who counts, nor the man who points out how the strong man stumbled, or where the doer of deeds could have done better. The credit belongs to the man who is actually in the arena . . . who, at best, knows in the end the triumph of high achievement; and who, at the worst, if he fails, at least fails while daring greatly . . . so that his place shall never be with those cold and timid souls who know neither defeat nor victory."

While we were rarely timid souls, I can't recall a single time in my quarter century at ABC when we ventured into a project without full regard for the consequences, financial and otherwise. There was no disregard for any of the circumstances that, so far as we could tell, would affect either our programming or our bottom line.

ABC's March 1983 deal for baseball, for instance, projected a network profit of $71 million over its six-year term. The five-year NFL deal that expired after the 1986 season had a projected profit for ABC of $45 million. We thought our maximum offer for Calgary should be $275 million, but even when we went to $309 million, we still forecast a net profit of between $15 million and $23 million. Was it all just wishful thinking?

Year after year after year, ABC Sports had made handsome profits: some $300 million between 1975 and 1984, with the latter our best year ever. However, everyone recognized that 1984 would have been a losing year except for the Sarajevo and Los Angeles Olympics, so, following them, we began to make cuts all across the board in both facilities and personnel. In other words, there were circumstances that we failed to foresee—along with CBS and NBC—but we were far from irresponsible in the way we ran the store. Our mistakes were ones that largely occurred despite research and careful planning.

Where we were most at fault was in believing that the service we were selling was so powerful and so indispensable that the advertising community would never pull the plug on the flow of dollars. There is some validity to the accusation that we operated on a "can't-lose" philosophy, especially when it came to frontline sports events. If the cost of the rights goes up, fine: We'll increase not only the number of commercials per hour, but the hours of coverage as well; and on top of that, we'll jack up the price of all those commercials. If a failure to anticipate when this formula wouldn't work anymore was due to overconfidence—or as many critics averred, to a degree of arrogance—then we would have to plead guilty.

In that light, let's take a hard look at the 1984–89 baseball package that proved onerous for both NBC and ABC, but particularly for ABC.

Baseball had formed a three-man negotiating committee, made up of the then commissioner, Bowie Kuhn, Eddie Einhorn of the Chicago White Sox, and Bill Giles of the Philadelphia Phillies. This committee called itself by the acronym KEG, and it was obvious from the start that KEG wanted two things: First, for one of the networks to "make a market" (in other words, come forth with a beginning figure as a basis for negotiations); and, second, to ensure that baseball would be televised by two networks in the final deal. KEG felt that two networks competing against each other would ensure the quality of coverage and guarantee heavy on-air and print promotion for the game.

I argued with Einhorn that baseball should make the market— "After all," I told him, "you're the seller"—but KEG refused. When ABC still declined to name a figure, NBC did so: $500 million for a five-year split contract, or $1 billion for *all* of network-televised baseball. The suggested deal was so structured that if a second network didn't involve itself, NBC would benefit from a secret $100 million reduction in this payment, but Commissioner Kuhn's conscience got to him concerning the arrangement, which he disclosed to us several days after KEG had insisted that NBC was firmly committed to the full billion dollars for the entire package.

The NBC proposition meant that ABC's half of the deal would have cost $500 million. We turned it down, partly because of that number, but also because of a concern that a five-year deal would give NBC three World Series to two for us.

KEG then offered the same deal to CBS, who, as we expected, passed. That left KEG with two options: Take the $900 million package from NBC alone, or come back to ABC and drop the price.

NBC at that time was in a serious bind. It was running a poor third in prime-time programming; it had hired Vin Scully for a lot of money and his long suit was baseball; and it had been burned by losing the NCAA Basketball Championship to CBS. Nevertheless, to this day it is incomprehensible to me why NBC went with so huge a figure. It had "made a market," but that market was way too high.

Baseball was hell-bent on squeezing out every last dime it could, and in the face of that pressure it is my belief that NBC simply overreacted. The network had had major-league baseball since the days of Mordecai (Three Finger) Brown and Dizzy Dean, and it wasn't about to lose it, whatever the cost. I have a great respect for the many good things NBC has done in sports over the years, but in this case the network played right into baseball's hands. Indeed, Eddie Einhorn told me later, "Frankly, Jim, we picked on the weak sister."

So when the baseball folks came back to us, it was with a price of $450 million. But that still left us with two World Series to NBC's three, so we counterproposed a six-year contract, for 1984 through 1989, with NBC paying $550 million for Saturday afternoon telecasts plus the World Series, the League Championship Series, and the All-Star Game in alternate years, and ABC laying out $575 million for the rights to televise 120 games in prime time, plus Sunday afternoon games and the "jewels" in alternate years. This was the deal that stuck. Not long afterward, a major advertising executive whose group represented Anheuser-Busch, a top sponsor of baseball, told me that, in his opinion, both networks had paid as much as $150 million more than they should have.

Later, at an industry seminar, I cornered Arthur Watson, the president of NBC Sports, and asked him why his network had "made the market" so high. After all, we both had first-refusal clauses, which meant that baseball could not drop its price without first coming back to each of us, giving us another shot. We both also knew CBS was not a serious player. Arthur tried to justify the deal, but really didn't have much of an answer for me.

Why was ABC so bullish on baseball? Very simply, we thought that if a broadcaster was going to be the leader in sports television, the game generally regarded as the national pastime should be part of its inventory. We also wanted very much to continue our presentation of baseball's "crown jewels."

Within weeks of the deal being struck, Bill Temple, a vice president involved with long-range planning at ABC, suggested in a memo after analyzing it that the best way for ABC to proceed, in terms of the bottom line alone, would be to not televise *any* prime-time games during the regular season, and to air entertainment programming in the time periods set aside for them. I immediately phoned Temple's boss, Al Rubin, and suggested that he be the one to call Commissioner Kuhn and pass the idea on to him. There was no way I was going to be the purveyor of this embarrassing concept, which was never executed.

Our original plan was to televise 108 of the 120 prime-time games we purchased at the rate of 20 games per season, except for the Olympic year of 1984, when we'd do eight only. In addition to the difficult marketplace, one of the reasons Major League Baseball is such an albatross for ABC Sports is that it is airing fewer than half of the prime-time games to which it purchased rights. Instead of televising baseball in prime time, ABC is airing movies and other entertainment programming, which creates a very negative financial situation for the sports department while making things look healthier from an overall network standpoint. Essentially, ABC airs rerun programming during most of the originally planned baseball time periods, which produce higher revenues and ratings than baseball would generate.

It is clear that ABC will not conclude a similar arrangement with major-league baseball in the future, but if they do make a new deal, unlike their current relationship, I trust they will be fully committed to making it successful.

The NFL deal that expired in 1986 was a very unhealthy one for ABC, causing losses at the multimillion-dollar level over the term of the agreement. In consequence, the deal ABC concluded with the NFL for 1987–89 involved dropping five non–Monday night games that had not performed well in the ratings. Some critics interpreted this as a financial coup for the network, but, in reality, while ABC got rid of those troublesome games, they are now paying more—$7.5 million per game over three years—than they did under the 1982–86 contract. This means that ABC's rights payments have not been reduced on a *per-game* basis from the level that previously incurred those huge losses. (Capital Cities/ABC was able simultaneously to work out a deal for ESPN that should prove lucrative for the cable network, which is 80 percent owned by ABC.) The ABC, CBS, NBC, and ESPN deals running through 1989 represented overall a 3.3 percent *decrease* in rights monies, both historic and significant in light of the NFL's television history with the three networks.

As we detailed earlier, CBS took a large leap in dollar outlay for NBA rights, and also for the NCAA Basketball Championship. The latter went from a $95 million to a $166 million contract for three years running through 1990 that also includes some other collegiate events—the women's basketball final, gymnastics, outdoor track and field, and volleyball, plus the College Baseball World Series. Despite the extras, an escalation of that size flies right in the face of what CBS Sports president Neal Pilson said in a speech in 1984 about the problems of vastly increased rights fees, but Pilson claims the NCAA Basketball Championship is worth what CBS is paying because of the exclusivity factor, and contends that CBS will make money on the package. I hope he is right.

Financial sanity in college football telecasts was forced on everyone by the U.S. Supreme Court decision wiping out exclusivity. ABC had the College Football Association package for three years, from 1984 through 1986, and CBS had the Pacific 10/Big Ten package. In 1987, the two switched, the CFA going to CBS for four years for $60 million, and the Pac 10/Big Ten package to ABC via a four-year deal for $52 million. ESPN, because it's televising more CFA games than CBS, is shelling out about $70 million for its rights.

Despite three-network gross sports advertising sales revenues of over $2.3 billion in 1988, including approximately $950 million for the Calgary and Seoul Olympics, the answer to all of this is, quite obviously, fewer dollars for everyone—owners, promoters, organizers, athletes, and everyone else making money from sports, as well as the broadcasters. However, that is only going to happen in painful response to overpowering market forces, never voluntarily among any of the participants, so the ride is likely to be rocky for however long it takes for the industry to shake out and settle down. As Michael Goodwin wrote in the *New York Times Magazine* in January 1986:

> There are some who say that this new profit problem in televised sports will result in only a temporary, and minor, market adjustment. But others predict that it will soon mean less money for the teams, less money for players, higher ticket prices for the fans and fewer sports events on the three major commercial networks, with many events showing up elsewhere on the dial, particularly on cable.

I'm with the "others," and the only question in my mind is how long it will take.

There was a time when advertisers virtually lined up to buy time on hot sports events, and a few of the "classics" still pretty much sell themselves, but the bonanza days are long gone. Today the advertiser is looking harder and harder for ways to receive special benefits, particularly clear and frequent on-air identification; and the television management and sales people, pressed above all else in the final analysis to sustain and increase profits, are trying equally hard to find ways to accommodate them.

Thus, one thing we will definitely see more and more of is "entitlement," or inclusion of sponsor names in the titles of televised sports events, plus sponsor identification at event sites. Over the years, I resisted this trend, believing that to call an event the Bing Crosby National Pro-Am or the Bob Hope Desert Classic was one thing, but to televise, say, a Budweiser Rose Bowl totally another. But facts have to be faced and the economic facts today are cold and hard, and unlikely to get any warmer or softer over the long haul. The truth is that we will see a lot more of this kind of thing down the road—perhaps one day even an "entitled" Super Bowl or World Series.

Although rights acquisition accounts for about 75 to 80 percent of sports broadcasting costs at the network level, another change under way is a significant reduction by ABC, CBS, and NBC in the actual production of telecasts, work that is more and more being contracted out to independent production companies.

Not long ago, it would have bordered on the unthinkable for ABC to have a sports show put together outside the company, but that now happens quite frequently and is becoming increasingly common at all three networks, if only because of their union situations. The bald fact is that production work done outside union jurisdiction is considerably less expensive, to the point where the broadcast unions may eventually have no option but to soften their traditionally iron-clad negotiating stances. ABC and NBC have contracts with the National Association of Broadcast Employees and Technicians (NABET), while CBS is contracted with the International Brotherhood of Electrical Workers (IBEW). NABET, in particular, is strongly fighting the move to nonunion personnel doing work that has been mostly theirs.

A few years ago, I would also have argued that you could not get network-standard production quality in a telecast of a top sports event from any cable broadcaster, be it basic, pay cable, or pay-per-view, but that's not true today. In addition to people they have developed, the cable folks have picked up talented personnel from those let go by the economizing at the networks in the last few years to equal, and sometimes even surpass, network production standards, given only the necessary budgets.

Pay-per-view is going to become a major player in sports television in the years ahead. American homes wired for pay-per-view will number approximately 15 million in 1990, with the projection that 35 million homes will have the facility by 1995. By the turn of the century, I believe we will be watching many of the major sports events on a pay-per-view basis rather than on network television, since by then almost 50 million homes will be technically capable of receiving pay-per-view programming.

Taking an event that has been on free television forever and switching it to pay-per-view is a sticky proposition in some ways, not least of which is that there is no way for organizers to enjoy the same size audiences. However, pay-cable entities like Home

Box Office and Showtime are already making themselves felt in sports television.

A number of years ago I asked a maitre d' if his restaurant had HBO. "No, sir," he said stiffly. "We just have fish and chops." Now everyone, including the entire sports industry, is familiar with those initials.

The influence of pay-cable was brought home most vividly in 1986 when ABC made multifight deals for future heavyweight champion Mike Tyson and the 1984 U.S. Olympic boxers. In each instance, ABC had to permit a pay-cable arrangement concurrent with the network deals, thereby setting an industry precedent.

It should never be forgotten that most sports organizers are, first and last, businessmen, and thus much more concerned with profit than any ideals inherent in what they are creating.

Another growing concern in this area is the packaging of major events such as the Super Bowl and World Series with regular-season activity. One day soon, organizers are going to have to make a hard judgment about potentially reduced revenues from network television versus the money available from pay-per-view, in light of the fact that the networks will no longer have the climactic season-ending games, which will reduce the value of regular-season packages.

Where all the parties may have some problems is with Congress. The moment the NFL put part of its package on ESPN in 1987, the politicians began protesting about the American television viewer being robbed of what he has come to consider as one of his inalienable rights. There is no doubt that this issue will sooner or later have to be fully addressed and resolved by organizers, broadcasters, and elected officials working together.

In our free-enterprise system, money drives the buggy, thus, in the end, money alone will dictate that many of the major events we now watch for free will go to pay-per-view television. Indeed, I believe that in my lifetime the Kentucky Derby, the Preakness, and the Belmont Stakes, the Indy 500, the U.S. Open Golf Championship, the NBA finals, even the Olympics, in part, the World Series and, despite NFL equivocation, the Super Bowl, will wind up on the home television screen only if the owner of the set is willing to pay directly for the privilege of watching.

Between now and then, the television networks more and more are going to be looking for sure and proper returns on their investments in sports, because the risk/reward factor has now become truly critical for them. Mae West was quoted as saying that "too much of a good thing is wonderful." For a long time, that was certainly true of sports television, but increasingly today "more" is the way to lose money and "less" the way to stay in the black—even if not as solidly as in former days.

ABC Sports acted on this premise in 1984 when it made unilateral cuts for 1985 in almost every program. As examples, we took a camera and a tape machine away from "Monday Night Football," while similarly trimming on programs like the "Pro Bowlers Tour," CFA college football, the Kentucky Derby, the Indianapolis 500, and our golf shows.

Network shows with less powerful audience appeal became victims of the changing economic conditions. At ABC, the beautifully produced award-winning program "The American Sportsman" was discontinued after twenty years on the air.

Previously, we had pulled in our horns on some rights fees, too, topping our bidding for the 1987 World Track and Field Championships in Rome at approximately $3 million and letting NBC finally buy the package for $5.2 million.

We had paid $600,000 for World Cup soccer from Spain in 1982, and offered between $2 million and $3 million for the 1986 event. I decided we wouldn't go higher, and Roone Arledge later expressed disappointment about that decision, telling me that ABC president Fred Pierce was upset that we were not more aggressive. As it turned out, NBC paid more than $6.5 million for the rights, had to guarantee thirty hours of coverage, and ended up with a financial disaster.

We bowed out of the bidding on the Breeders' Cup horse-racing package, partly because we did not feel it would be a successful television event over a protracted period of time, and partly because we'd have had a conflict with our college football coverage, but mostly because the dollars were out of line.

Without question then, ABC and the other networks will continue to pay big dollars for top events and top value. But the key word today is "value," and that isn't likely to change in the foreseeable future. More than ever, the profit motive will drive the industry.

As we said many pages back, easy street stopped with that $309 million for the Calgary Olympics. Good-bye suites and limos.

AN AFTERWORD

When my collaborator was about to interview the late Woody Hayes for the first time, after a 1951 football game at Ohio Stadium, his mentor, the venerable Associated Press sportswriter Fritz Howell gave him some sage advice: "This is a stadium, not a cathedral. This is a Saturday, not a holy day. Football is just a game, not a way of life. And Woody Hayes is just a football coach, not a god."

Sports television is just that: televised sports. These are the *games* that people play, and television is but a chronicler of the fleeting dramas involved, the successes and the failures. What they do on the fields and in the arenas is not Armageddon, and what we do in the production trucks is not brain surgery. And, yes, we do it in the final analysis for money, whatever ideals we choose to protect and promote along the way.

But we are supposed to inform and to entertain, and all of it is supposed to be fun. And it surely has been great fun for me. I confess to still being a fan, and an unabashed one at that. I also regard myself as one of the luckiest people on the face of the earth, to have been part of a great organization that helped to change the face of television for the better, and to have been able to make a living in a world that provided me with more thrills each year than most people experience in a lifetime.

For instance, I'll never forget game seven of the 1970 NBA Championship, when Willis Reed, who had been hurt in game five and did not play in game six, made his late and dramatic entrance into Madison Square Garden, hobbled onto the court, hit his first two field-goal attempts, and gave the New York Knicks the inspiration to defeat the Los Angeles Lakers for New York's first world championship.

Then there was my first trip to St. Andrews in Scotland, in 1978. My wife Lynn and I walked over to say hello to Chuck Howard, who was producing ABC's telecast, to wish him and the crew well. Chuck had some extra armbands and asked if we'd like to wear them, so we could see the action from inside the ropes. It was a tremendous thrill to follow Jack Nicklaus for eighteen holes, at the birthplace of golf, and watch him—up close and personal—win his third British Open. A close second to that in golf thrills was watching the same man complete the back nine at Augusta National in thirty strokes to capture his sixth Masters in 1986, capped by a lovely, warm embrace with his son, Jackie, who had caddied for him.

Game six of the 1986 World Series at Shea Stadium was an extremely exciting and memorable event for me. The Mets were behind by two runs with two out in the bottom of the tenth inning, then scored three times and won the game—and the Series the day after—when Bill Buckner of the Boston Red Sox let a ground ball slither through his legs.

Right alongside that, I'd rate the 1977 World Series game in which Reggie Jackson hit home runs in three consecutive at-bats in Yankee Stadium against the Los Angeles Dodgers.

Another unforgettable moment was the great Pelés exhortation—"love," "love," "love"—to the thousands gathered at Giant Stadium in New Jersey as he bade farewell to soccer during an emotional ceremony in 1977.

Is there anyone who was not moved by the U.S. Olympic hockey team's stupendous triumph in the 1980 Olympic Games at Lake Placid? I was seated next to Lynn Swann, a man who played for the Steelers in four Super Bowl games, and he was like any other fan, overcome with excitement. When the U.S. team captain, Mike Eruzione, scored the winning goal in the 4–3 victory over the USSR, the emotions I experienced were completely overpowering and forever indelible.

I saw the end of Franz Klammer's run in the downhill in the 1976 Olympic Games at Innsbruck, and watched Notre Dame's 24–23 victory over Alabama in the 1973 Sugar Bowl, with legendary coaches Bear Bryant and Ara Parseghian going all out at each other for the national championship. I cannot recall a single event that had more buildup, and lived up to it better, than the Muhammad Ali/Joe Frazier fight at Madison Square Garden in 1971. Their other battles were great, too—the second one in 1974, and the one they called "the Thrilla in Manila" in 1975, with Ali winning both of them. But their first fight was unforgettable. Ali had been stripped of his title and was trying to get it back from Frazier, but Joe knocked Ali down late in the fight and won the decision.

By the very nature of the fury that was packed into such a short span of time, I'd rate the Marvin Hagler/Thomas Hearns fight in Las Vegas in 1985 as the most electrifying I've ever witnessed. And then I saw, too, that phenomenal fifteenth round of the Larry Holmes/Ken Norton duel in 1978, one of the greatest rounds in heavyweight history, as the two giants stood toe-to-toe, inflicting incredible punishment on each other as they battled for boxing's greatest prize.

Perhaps in part because I'm a long-time New York Jets fan, I rate the Jets' 16–7 victory over the Baltimore Colts in the 1969 Super Bowl among my all-time thrills. There was the usual extraordinary buildup for that game, but unlike most Super Bowl contests, it actually lived up to all the ballyhoo.

At the 1972 Olympic Games in Munich, after I learned of the tragedy that was unfolding, I went to the ABC Broadcast Center, which was adjacent to the Olympic Village where the athletes were housed. Walking toward the entrance to our headquarters, knowing there was very serious trouble, I suddenly heard people cheering in an arena next door. For reasons I cannot explain other than curiosity, I went into that arena and stood near the door for perhaps five minutes, watching an Olympic volleyball game. Moments later, as I walked into our control room, there on the screen was the riveting picture of an Arab terrorist with a mask over his face, and the beginning of the massacre of eleven members of the Israeli Olympic team. All I could think of was the indescribable contrast between the wanton killing for unspeakable reasons and the lofty ideals of the event that formed the backdrop to it.

Ten years earlier in Stanford Stadium in Palo Alto, California, something took place that still gives me chills whenever I think about it. The Cold War had everybody on edge, worrying about the future, as Kennedy and Khrushchev made ever-more-ominous gestures. ABC Sports was televising the U.S.-USSR track and field meet, and I had worked the competition part of the program as a production assistant. When it came time for the closing ceremonies, I was fortunate enough to find a spot from which to watch them in a corner of the announce booth.

There were more than eighty thousand people in the stands when the athletes from the two great nations began to parade, arm in arm, around the track. The young men and women—representative of the future of their countries—were waving and smiling to one another, and to the crowd. I was close enough to hear Jim McKay's commentary, and suddenly I found myself overwhelmed by it all. I stood there, tears streaming down my face, but entirely unashamed of my emotions, thinking about how wonderful this world could be if only the brotherhood of sports would somehow find its way into other elements of the human experience.

I wouldn't have missed that quarter of a century at ABC Sports for anything on earth.

INDEX

Jim Spence was born in Bronxville, New York, and raised in Westchester County. He graduated from Dartmouth College with a Bachelor of Arts degree in 1958. Mr. Spence joined ABC as a production assistant in 1960. He served as assistant to the executive producer of "ABC's Wide World of Sports," then as coordinating producer of that series for almost five years, during which time the series won four Emmy Awards for outstanding achievement in sports programming. He was named vice president, program planning, in 1970 and became senior vice president of ABC Sports in 1978, with day-to-day responsibility for supervision and coordination of all areas of what became the most successful television sports organization in history. Mr. Spence left ABC Sports in February of 1986 and is president of Sports Television International, Inc., a production, consultation, sales, and marketing company he formed in July of that year. Mr. Spence and his wife, Lynn, live in Manhattan and Rye, New York.

Dave Diles is a native of Middleport, Ohio, a graduate of Ohio University, and a recipient of that school's distinguished alumni award. He spent a dozen years as a newswriter, editor, and sports editor for The Associated Press before launching a career in television. He handled a variety of assignments for ABC Sports for twenty years and, for thirteen years, hosted the College Football Scoreboard show. The father of two children, Beverly Diles Fenton and David Lisle Diles, he now lives much of the time on his country retreat near Racine, Ohio. He has written five other books, *Duffy, Nobody's Perfect, Twelfth Man in the Huddle, Archie,* and *Terry Bradshaw: Man of Steel.*

. . . *and this one is for Bonnie*
Dave Diles